Righteous Violence

D1737297

ETHICS AND PUBLIC LIFE

This book is part of the series 'Ethics in Public Life' edited by Professor C. A. J. (Tony) Coady, Professorial Fellow in Applied Philosophy in the Centre for Applied Philosophy and Public Ethics at the University of Melbourne. The series aims to provide intellectually challenging treatments of the ethical dimensions of issues of public importance. The perspective is broadly philosophical, in that issues are examined with a view to their basic presuppositions and underlying fundamental values. But the series is geared to inter-disciplinary input and a concern for practical ramifications.

Other titles in the series are:

Terrorism and Justice: Moral Argument in a Dangerous World, edited by Tony Coady and Michael O'Keefe, 2002 (reprinted in 2003).

Violence and Police Culture, edited by Tony Coady, Steve James, Seumas Miller and Michael O'Keefe, 2000.

All Connected: Universal Service in Telecommunications, edited by Bruce Langtry, 1998.

Codes of Ethics and the Professions, edited by Margaret Coady and Sidney Bloch, 1996, (reprinted 2002).

ACKNOWLEDGEMENTS

The editors would like to acknowledge the support of the Australian Research Council Special Research Centre for Applied Philosophy and Public Ethics at the University of Melbourne and the school of Social Sciences at La Trobe University. The Centre sponsored the workshop from which this book grew. Our thanks to Irena Blonder for her help with the organisation of the workshop, and Andrew Schaap for providing research assistance on Tony Coady's chapter. Alanna Vivian also deserves thanks for assistance in compiling the index.

Righteous Violence

The Ethics and Politics of
Military Intervention

Edited by

Tony Coady and
Michael O'Keefe

MELBOURNE
UNIVERSITY
PRESS

MELBOURNE UNIVERSITY PRESS
an imprint of Melbourne University Publishing (MUP Ltd)
187 Grattan Street, Carlton, Victoria 3053, Australia
mup-info@unimelb.edu.au
www.mup.com.au

First published in 2005
Text in this collection © C.A.J. (Tony) Coady and Michael O'Keefe 2005
Copyright in the individual pieces remains with their respective authors.
Design and typography © Melbourne University Publishing (MUP Ltd)
Typeset by Syarikat Seng Teik Sdn. Bhd., Malaysia
Printed in Australia by McPherson's Printing Group

National Library of Australia Cataloguing-in-Publication entry

Righteous violence: the ethics and politics of military intervention.

Bibliography.
Includes index.
ISBN 0 522 85116 9.

1. Humanitarian intervention. 2. Intervention (International law)—Moral and
ethical aspects. I. Coady, C. A. J. II. O'Keefe, Michael.

341.584

CONTENTS

PREFACE

Almost nightly we are presented with graphic images of the latest humanitarian catastrophe unfolding across the globe. Ordinary citizens, the politicians who represent them, and the practitioners that implement their policies are forced to make value judgements about the justifiability of military intervention in faraway places to seek remedies for these disasters. Increasingly, too, there are demands for armed intervention that address not humanitarian crises but perceived political threats, such as that of terrorism. Beyond the directly moral and legal considerations these value judgements raise are a range of partly practical partly moral questions, not the least of which is whether we have the capability to intervene, and could we cause more harm than good? The existence of state breakdown, 'rogue' states, fragile states and humanitarian crises pose acute dilemmas about the efficacy and moral suitability of military solutions.

So it is not surprising that armed intervention against states that are not engaged in aggression is now on the international agenda in a new way that represents a striking shift in attitude amongst thinkers and activists of very different political persuasions. From the end of World War II until the mid-1990s, military intervention was largely rejected on moral, political and legal grounds. The reasons for this are complex, but many of them concern reactions to the cataclysm of World War II. That terrible conflict changed many things but one of its most significant effects was to concentrate thinking about the morality and politics of war in a particular direction. For the Allies, the war was primarily one of defence against egregiously aggressive and militaristic powers. In their different ways, Nazi Germany and Imperial Japan were bent upon expansion by violent conquest and they glorified war-making as a political tool. Their militaristic policies had the further edge that they served ideologies advocating racial superiority.

Against this background, it was hard not to see the Allied cause as a just one, in spite of the often doubtful means used to wage the war, such as targeting civilian populations with area bombardments, culminating in the atomic bombings of Hiroshima and Nagasaki. It is true that the Axis powers were not the first in history to wage aggressive, racist wars, but they did so on a scale and to a degree that made a defensive, military response seem a paradigm case of a just resort to war. Just or not, however, World War II caused massive casualties and destruction and it seemed essential that the new world arising from its ruins should disown resort to war for any purpose other than self-defence and purposes closely related to it. Hence, there was a heavy emphasis in the UN Charter and in subsequent international law on the evils of aggressive military force and on the right of self-defence against it. Other threats to peace were to be dealt with through the United Nations itself. This involved a repudiation of the doctrine of Clausewitz that war was a mere instrument of politics like any other: 'a continuation of political activity by other means'.[1] It also involved both a revival and a reformation of the ancient moral tradition of the just war. This tradition had always been at heart restrictive, seeking to put some constraints on the resort to war and on the way it was fought. It had nonetheless also envisaged more just causes for war than self-defence, though that had been the central legitimating cause. The postwar consensus about aggression tended to make self-defence, and some natural extensions of it, such as aiding others in self-defence, the sole legitimate reason for resort to armed force.

It was a consequence of these developments that armed intervention by one state in the affairs of another state was effectively ruled out both morally and legally. This trend was reinforced by two central features of the post–World War II political climate: the demise of colonialism and the emergence of the Cold War. The first stressed the right of self-determination and the associated significance of national sovereignty, and the second produced an emphatic endorsement of the need for stability in the face of nuclear catastrophe.

These factors diminished in influence as the twentieth century entered its last decade. Overt colonialism was a fading memory and there were question marks over the sovereignty and genuine self-determination of many of the new nations that had emerged from colonial rule. The Cold War had ended in the collapse of one of the superpowers and thereby the demise of a bi-polar world order. This left the United States in a position of unchallenged military superiority and with many of its influential political figures anxious to use that military power to advance its economic, political and even moral policies. At the same time, the much-heralded 'new world order' was beginning to resemble a new world disorder, as the disintegration of the Soviet empire produced destabilisation in the former Yugoslavia and in parts of the former Soviet Union. This was accompanied by the outbreak (or continuation) of violent ethnic or tribal conflicts in Africa, continued violence in parts of Central and South America, and escalating warfare between Palestinians and Israel. Added to this was the rise of fundamentalist Islamic terrorism as embodied in al-Qaeda and associated groups. These trends motivated the construction of new normative models for armed conflict that are much more sympathetic to armed intervention. These models differ according to the causes they consider as legitimating intervention and the authority they envisage as required for it. Some urge intervention only for humanitarian causes, others for preventing the development of threatening situations, others for combating terrorism. Some think intervention should only occur when authorised by the United Nations or other multilateral bodies, others are more expansive about the authority required.

Clearly there are important political, military, legal and ethical concerns raised by this turn of events and this book draws together a number of perspectives on the problem. The contributions are drawn from the disciplines of philosophy, strategic studies, political science, and legal theory. The contributors have interestingly different national and professional backgrounds: one was a serving military officer in the Australian forces in Iraq and elsewhere, another is an

American Jesuit philosopher, another is a German sociologist and strategic analyst from a Berlin think-tank, and another is the former director of an independent strategic policy institute advising the Australian government. The collection arose from a project funded by the Australian Research Council and a workshop held at the University of Melbourne. There has been no attempt to impose a unity of perspective upon the contributors and, indeed, the book benefits from having a variety of outlooks on a topic that is bound to stimulate such variety. In this, it offers something quite different from single-authored works such as, for example, the Anglican Bishop Tom Frame's recent book on humanitarian intervention that explicitly aims to provide a Christian moral perspective. It is also different from works produced by non-government organisations in the field that understandably focus on the horrors unfolding in front of them. *Righteous Violence* places international crises in a context that can assist in making informed decisions about the morality of deploying military force in the name of humanitarianism.

Righteous Violence is divided into two parts. The first focuses on the philosophical and political problems that arise when deciding whether to intervene for humanitarian reasons. The second focuses on the practical dilemmas raised by using force in the name of humanitarianism.

The book begins with a discussion of the ethics and international politics of rescue by John Langan. Langan aims to elaborate a coherent approach to decisions about military intervention for humanitarian purposes by policy makers. He examines and contrasts the forces required to undertake peacekeeping and humanitarian interventions, and the motives of states, particularly the US, that have the capability to quickly and effectively intervene in crises.

Tony Coady urges a degree of scepticism about the moral value of armed intervention, including humanitarian intervention. He argues that 'political realism' is best understood as providing a caution against moralism rather than morality proper. Coady argues that an ideal of peace should be an important ingredient in the discussion of armed intervention of any sort. As such, it can serve to heighten awareness of the moral and prudential dangers that beset humanitarian intervention.

Hugh White explores the moral and political justifications for the US invasion of Iraq. He applies the principles of just war to that invasion by critically appraising the justifications used by US and Australian decision makers to resort to war, and finds them lacking. His critique is particularly significant in that he makes clear his admiration for many of the positive outcomes that he discerns in US foreign policy over the years.

Seumas Miller examines the notion of collective moral responsibility and armed humanitarian intervention in international affairs. He offers an individualist account of collective moral responsibility, according to which it is a species of joint moral responsibility. This argument has serious implications for decision makers contemplating intervention and for those who seek to avoid participation in armed interventions.

Turning to the practical problems that occur when states deploy military force in an attempt to resolve humanitarian crises, Michael O'Keefe concentrates on Australia's recent intervention in its neighbourhood, and the intriguing rhetoric that has accompanied it. He disaggregates the national, regional and alliance interests and responsibilities, and humanitarianism used to justify intervention. A convincing explanation for the current policy is found in the enduring aspect of Australia's strategic culture that seeks to exclude states or groups from exercising influence in the region—Australia is acting as the self appointed regional 'Sheriff'.

Paul Muggleton analyses the legal aspects of the doctrine of humanitarian intervention when applied to the NATO air strikes against the Federal Republic of Yugoslavia. The primary issue addressed is whether NATO's use of force was consistent with contemporary public international law. He finds that the air strikes were not a case of self-defence and did not have the express authorisation of the UN Security Council and as such were a breach of contemporary public international law.

A solution to the political deadlock or apathy that often hampers the provision of effective humanitarian intervention is provided by Lutz Unterseher. He outlines a blueprint for constructing a permanent UN legion that could immediately respond to humanitarian crises. Unterseher details how to establish such a force, what resources would be required and how it would overcome the problems besetting UN peacekeeping operations.

Moya Collett's chapter reviews the tenuous agreement to bring an end to the conflict in Côte d'Ivoire and the legitimacy of the forces that have attempted to keep the peace. The declaration of peace has been implemented by relying on peacekeeping forces co-ordinated separately by France, the Economic Community of West African States and the UN. The effectiveness of foreign involvement needs to be questioned, with legitimacy determined by both ideological and practical considerations.

In the final chapter, William Maley tackles the pressing issues associated with the role of the United Nations in humanitarian intervention. Maley provides a succinct overview of the challenges associated with planning, approving and undertaking UN humanitarian operations in the post–Cold War era. He surveys the successes and failures of the UN in this area and examines recent proposals for reforming the organisation in ways that might equip it better to meet the intricate political and moral problems posed by humanitarian crises.

The combined impact of the essays presented in this volume is to challenge complacency about simple solutions, especially military solutions, for the complex disasters and threats to peace that now loom so large in our consciousness. Faced with violent injustice at home or abroad it is natural to confront it with righteous violence. None of the contributors denies that there may sometimes be a legitimate role for military responses to massacres, violent persecution, or terrorist campaigns, but they point to a variety of practical and moral difficulties that bedevil the resort to armed intervention. These difficulties highlight the need for caution in the resort to military force, the value of alternative approaches, the significance of prudent planning, and the dangers of viewing the international scene as a stark battleground of good versus evil.

Noble intentions are not enough. Resort to righteous violence must have a firm ethical basis and must heed the lessons of past conflicts. The costs of failure are great, and they are costs we can ill afford.

Tony Coady and Michael O'Keefe

CONTRIBUTORS

C. A. J. (Tony) Coady is Professorial Fellow in Applied Philosophy in the Centre for Applied Philosophy and Public Ethics at the University of Melbourne where he was formerly Boyce Gibson Professor of Philosophy. He has published extensively in both academic and more general venues and is a frequent commentator on public issues in the media. His book, *Testimony: A Philosophical Inquiry* (Oxford, 1992), was widely and enthusiastically reviewed internationally. He has a particular concern with issues to do with war and terrorism and has published widely on these topics. He was a Senior Fellow at the United States Institute of Peace in 1999–2000, researching issues concerned with humanitarian intervention. In 2002, he published *The Ethics of Armed Humanitarian Intervention* as a Peaceworks booklet from the USIP.

Moya COLLETT is presently researching state failure in the Côte d'Ivoire at the London School of Economics. She is on leave from the University of New South Wales where she is a PhD candidate studying peacekeeping in West Africa. She has also published on ethnicity and nationalism in the region, with particular focus on Côte d'Ivoire and the effects of French colonialism and neo-colonialism. She has undertaken voluntary work for Amnesty International and the International Youth Parliament.

John LANGAN, SJ is the Joseph Cardinal Bernardin Professor of Catholic Social Thought at Georgetown University. He is a senior research scholar in the Kennedy Institute of Ethics and Walsh School of Foreign Service, Georgetown University. He teaches courses on ethical theory, ethics and international affairs, human rights, just war theory, and capitalism and morality. He holds a PhD in philosophy from the University of Michigan. He has edited or co-edited six books, among which are *Human Rights in the Americas: The Struggle for Consensus* (Georgetown University Press, 1982), *The Nuclear Dilemma and the Just War Tradition* (Lexington Books, 1986), *The American Search for Peace: Moral Reasoning, National Security, and Religious Hope* (Georgetown University Press, 1991) and *Catholic Universities in Church and Society* (Georgetown University Press, 1993). He has recently edited *A Moral Vision for America*, a collection of the addresses of Joseph Cardinal Bernardin on ethics and public life in the United States.

William MALEY is Professor and Director of the Asia–Pacific College of Diplomacy at the Australian National University, and has served as a Visiting Professor at the Russian Diplomatic Academy, a Visiting Fellow at the Centre for the Study of Public Policy at the University of Strathclyde, and a Visiting Research Fellow in the Refugee Studies Programme at Oxford University. He is author of *The Afghanistan Wars* (New York: Palgrave Macmillan, 2002); edited *Fundamentalism Reborn? Afghanistan and the Taliban* (New York: New York University Press, 1998, 2001); and co-edited *From Civil Strife to Civil Society: Civil and Military Responsibilities in Disrupted States* (Tokyo: United Nations University Press, 2003).

Seumas MILLER is Professor of Philosophy at Charles Sturt University and the Australian National University (joint position) and Director of the Centre for Applied Philosophy and Public Ethics (an Australian Research Council funded Special Research Centre). He is also a Professorial Fellow at the University of Melbourne. He is the author or co-author of over 100 academic articles and ten books, including *Social Action* (Cambridge University Press, 2001), *Corruption and Anti-Corruption* (Prentice-Hall, 2004) and *Ethical Issues in Policing* (Ashgate, 2004).

Lieutenant Colonel Paul MUGGLETON (retd) graduated from the Royal Military College, Duntroon, in 1976 and served as an officer in the Australian Army until 1995. During his career he served as a Liaison Officer with the Multinational Force and Observers in Egypt (Sinai) and Israel as the Chief Legal Officer for Western Australia. After leaving the Army in 1995 he was appointed as a Delegate to the Armed and Security Forces for the International Committee of the Red Cross. Between 1995 and 1998 he conducted international humanitarian law activities in Poland, the Czech Republic, Slovakia, Hungary, Slovenia, Croatia, Bosnia and Herzegovina, the Former Yugoslav Republic of Macedonia, the Federal Republic of Yugoslavia, Bulgaria, Albania and Romania. Since mid-2001 he has been an Associate Director of the Asia Pacific Centre for Military Law and has held the position of Acting Director of the Australian Defence Force's Military Law Centre. In 2003 and 2004 he returned to the Army and was deployed to Iraq to work with the Office of General Counsel within the Coalition Provisional Authority. He holds a Bachelor of Arts (Hons) and Bachelor of Laws from the Australian National University.

Dr Michael O'KEEFE teaches and researches US politics and international relations in the Politics Program at La Trobe University. He is also an Honorary Fellow at the Centre for Applied Philosophy and Public Ethics at the University of Melbourne. He is particularly interested in Australia's security policy, alliance politics, the ethics of armed intervention and war, terrorism, and AIDS as a security threat, particularly in the South Pacific. He has edited two books in the Ethics in Public Life series—*Terrorism and Justice: Moral Argument in a Dangerous World*, co-edited with Tony Coady (MUP, 2002) and *Violence and Police Culture*, co-edited with Tony Coady, Steve James and Seumas Miller (MUP, 2000).

Dr Lutz UNTERSEHER, sociologist and political scientist, is chairman of the international Study group on Alternative Security policy (SAS), headquartered in Berlin, and co-director of the private social research institute UP/TEAM, based in Düsseldorf. In addition to conducting research on intra-organisational communication and the military as a man–machine mix, he has been acting as an adviser on military reform to the Slovene Ministry of Defence, three social democratic parties in Europe, and the Budget Committee of the German Bundestag. He is a senior lecturer on defence planning and security policy at the universities of Münster and Osnabrück.

Hugh WHITE is Professor of Strategic Studies at the Australian National University. He was the founding Director of the Australian Strategic Policy Institute, a non-partisan centre established by the Australian government to provide independent advice about Australia's strategic and defence policy choices. He has worked in strategic policy and related fields for two decades. He has served as an intelligence analyst with the Office of National Assessments, as a journalist with the *Sydney Morning Herald*, and as a senior adviser on the staffs of Defence Minister Kim Beazley and Prime Minister Bob Hawke. He was a senior official in the Department of Defence, where from 1995 to 2000 he was Deputy Secretary for Strategy and Intelligence. In an earlier life he studied philosophy at the University of Melbourne and Oxford.

PART I

The Philosophical

Problems

1 ETHICS AND THE INTERNATIONAL POLITICS OF RESCUE: GETTING BEYOND AN AMERICAN SOLUTION FOR AN INTERNATIONAL PROBLEM

JOHN LANGAN, SJ

The American viewpoint for considering humanitarian intervention, while crucially important for pragmatic reasons, is at the same time limiting. It is limiting both in the de facto primacy which it accords to American interests and perceptions and in the way it fails to challenge what seem to be truisms when stated in Washington but which, when stated in Canberra or Paris or Moscow or Belgrade, turn out to invite scepticism and even outright rejection.

These remarks would hold for almost any issue connected with humanitarian intervention, but they are particularly relevant for questions about right authority, about the making of judgements of proportionality, and about last resort. These are questions which form an essential part of thinking about justifications for the use of force in just war theory. Even when theoretical affiliations and traditional commitments are set aside, they are also questions which reasonable persons are going to want to answer when they contemplate something so risky and so potentially costly as sending armed forces into unfamiliar and unstable areas where sovereignty is disputed or only loosely established. Intervention for humanitarian purposes is, of course, not to be equated with war; but the questions which the resort to force raises run parallel in the two types of cases.

The fundamental question about right authority is who, in the midst of a humanitarian emergency occurring within the territory of a sovereign state, has the right or the duty to intervene by using force. This is a question which I intend to raise as a moral question, which I take to be prior to and not reducible to the legal question about who is authorised to intervene in the present order of international law. I take the answer to the moral question to be the basis for normative criticism of the existing state of law. Aggression by one state against another does not raise this problem. The state which is attacked has both the moral and the legal right to defend itself, and the duly constituted and recognised government of that state has the relevant authority. It may ask for help from other states in virtue of established alliances or on an ad hoc basis. But it is clear that the state suffering aggression is the proper authority to decide on the use of force, even if it decides that it cannot effectively defend its people and its territory and so must surrender and yield to superior force. The state which is the victim of aggression has the right to wage war in self-defence. It has both proper authority and just cause when it does so.

In the standard case of a humanitarian emergency, however, the victim of the attack is a group, most often an ethnic group, which is not likely to have a significant current share in political power and which may well have been denied access to most forms of political participation for a long time. The group will not then have a generally recognised authority to use force to defend itself, its members, and its interests, even though its members will continue to have rights to self-defence as individuals. Its calls for help, even when transmitted and amplified by the international media, do not in themselves resolve the question about what authority can justify the use of force. Unlike a state, such a group does not have an already recognised authority to use force which it can in effect extend to legitimate the actions of allies and rescuers.

The question then becomes: who among outsiders has the authority to use force in order to rescue those imperilled by prospective or incipient genocide or some other humanitarian emergency? More specifically, does the authority to rescue by force rest with one state, with a group of neighbouring or affected states in the region, with a broad coalition of states, with previously established regional organisations such as the North Atlantic Treaty Organization (NATO) or the African Union (AU), or with the United Nations (UN)? What are the morally appropriate structures which can undertake the task of using force to rescue groups in peril within the boundaries of another state, even if that state is a failed or non-functioning state?

Here it is helpful to recognise a certain moral claim which outsiders have when they provide resources for rescue without deploying force. If humanitarian organisations arrive at the boundary of a country offering to provide goods and services such as medicines, food, clothing, temporary shelter for those whose lives are in danger, our common judgement is that their help ought to be welcomed unless the state can provide adequate resources on its own. The reason for this is that there is an obligation on public authorities to allow others to help when national resources are insufficient or are unavailable to satisfy pressing human needs and rights. We commonly think that it is outrageous and inhumane for a government to refuse food and medical care offered to its citizens when it is unable or unwilling to provide these necessities of life itself. It may, however, be a reasonable exercise of governmental authority to establish tests of competence for humanitarian organisations and to monitor or restrict some of their activities.

But when providing help and protection for those in peril involves the use of force, then we do not think that there is a similar prima facie obligation to accept help or to permit others to provide it. Affirming an obligation for a state to accept the presence and activity of forces under foreign control on its territory is a serious reduction of that state's sovereignty and requires correspondingly serious justifying reasons. Unfortunately, in most of the scenarios in which military action for humanitarian purposes is a plausible solution, the state within whose territory intervention is to take place is not merely concerned for its sovereignty and territorial integrity, but is an active threat to the human rights and to the survival of many of the citizens over whom it claims jurisdiction. This situation makes it much easier to meet the burden of justification, but also makes the prospect of resistance, casualties, and higher costs in the operation much more likely.

In the ordinary course of events, intervention is not to be considered, much less attempted, in a state which is meeting its obligations to its neighbours and its citizens. Once a state has become an active threat to the lives of large numbers of people, however, it calls in question its place in a peaceful society of states. It is committing something akin to aggression against a body of its own citizens. This point should not be interpreted in such a way as to prejudge the moral assessment of the parties in a civil war or to deny that the state may legitimately use force to defend itself and its citizens against internal threats as well as external threats. The dynamic of situations of this type, for instance in the 1999 crisis in Kosovo, is closer to the commencement of a war than it is to the provision of humanitarian relief.

The absence of a state capable of exercising its sovereignty in an effective and credible way, as in Somalia in the early 1990s, can plausibly be regarded as reducing the burden of justification, but it does not always produce a corresponding reduction in the practical difficulties of intervention. For instance, resistance to the intervention can be provided by loosely organised groups which may be incapable of meeting the tasks of a full-fledged state but which can engage in violent resistance over extensive territories for an indefinite period of time. Somalia with its numerous warlords and tribal divisions is an obvious case in point.

WHO SHOULD INTERVENE?

After affirming the moral barriers to intervention and acknowledging the often considerable practical difficulties which intervention is likely to encounter, we need to come back to the question of what,

The Philosophical Problem *John Langan*

if any, moral difference it makes who does the intervening and who has the authority to intervene. It is clear that any intervening power will need to have sufficiently strong reasons to be able to surmount the moral barrier which sovereignty constitutes. The strength of the reasons will usually correspond to the gravity of the human rights violations and crimes against humanity which are occurring within the country which is the proposed locus or object of intervention or which are reasonably judged to be likely to occur. If this is true, then the strength of the reasons for intervention will not generally be agent-relative. The reasons for intervening in Bosnia or Rwanda are a function of the crimes and atrocities committed there rather than of the interests and projects of the intervening parties. This would lead us to expect that all nations would have equally strong or weak reasons for intervening in a humanitarian crisis. This would, of course, be a misleading simplification of the way states and their policy makers think about these matters; proximity, ethnic and religious solidarity, economic and financial connections, all provide more specific reasons for or against actually deciding to intervene (even if in some cases they ought not to play that part). But the point still seems to me to be an important one, even if it is not easily integrated into a realist understanding of international politics.

The humanitarian crisis can be compared to a hospital which is on fire and in which a large number of patients and staff are likely to perish. We think that the important thing is that anyone in a position to bring help in such a situation should do so, without anyone's being very much concerned about credentials and official authorisations. One will want to ensure priority for fire-fighters and medical personnel; but, especially at the beginning, one will not be overly concerned by worries about just who shows up in a bucket brigade or who offers to lead people to safety. An emergency situation calls forth improvised responses and for many purposes does not require much differentiation among those who are ready and willing to help. Our attention is rightly directed in the first instance to the victims, actual or potential; and our first question about the rescuers is not about their authority, but about their likely effectiveness.

In considering interventions across international boundaries to rescue communities and groups which are at risk, matters are inevitably more complex. An important part of our concern has to be with the effects of such interventions on the future order and stability of the region, since we are not looking at victims and rescuers who are in a temporary and accidental relationship (in this analogy, for instance, someone who is driving along the highway and happens to see the fire in its early stages), but we are dealing with groups and communities which have been involved with each other for long periods of time and which may well have an important, even if problematic, future together, for instance, Serbs and Kosovars or Hutus and Tutsis.

Furthermore, once intervention begins to involve the use of force across national boundaries, we are dealing with behaviour which can look and sound very much like warfare, even though it originates in a quite different set of intentions. It is then more likely to be seen as a set of moves in regional and even global politics and to be interpreted and criticised in ways which are customary for the understanding and assessment of actions by states and other players in the international arena. The questions and the reactions which arise in such situations are quite different from those which arise when we think about non-governmental organisations (NGOs) and the provision of international emergency relief. This shift brings with it a significant tendency to reduce the importance of moral and humanitarian considerations in assessing the behaviour of states and to interpret humanitarian interventions as efforts to project power or to resolve problems affecting the national interest of the intervening parties. To put the shift succinctly, the moral enterprise of humanitarian intervention is seen through lenses provided by realist theories of international relations. This is not simply a matter of interpretive moves made by analysts and observers, but is also a matter of responses by other players in the international system. The debunking questions of realism are more likely to be raised when people notice that some powers are interested in intervening in some areas but not in others where there are rather similar problems and similar needs for rescue and protection.

In reaction to this shift, one can attempt to present intervention as something more in the nature of a judicial response to a breakdown in order. In this effort it is important to present the interveners in a positive way. They are not motivated by considerations of national interest; they are aiming to use force solely to meet the moral demands of the emergency situation. They are not carrying on discredited patterns of imperial conquest and paternalistic domination; they are not attempting to take advantage of the state where they are intervening; they are not attempting to advance their own ideological, ethnic, or religious causes. This, I should remind you, is an idealised type, not the portrait of an actual intervention. It should be apparent that this approach addresses a different set of concerns about intervention than an approach which stresses the importance of effectiveness in establishing control over the territory and which sees in such effectiveness the most reliable means of protecting lives and communities at risk. If intervention can be presented as something undertaken by parties who are themselves disinterested, not directly affected by the outcome of local conflicts, neutral between the contending parties in the local conflict, and not driven by religious or ideological considerations, then it seems likely that the intervention will more readily meet the moral requirement of justification and that justice will be seen to be done in this particular emergency situation. Thinking along this line leads to a preference for multilateral over unilateral action in intervention, for actors drawn from a distance rather than from the neighbourhood or the region, for parties which lack broadly recognised affinities with the contending parties over parties which might be suspected of partiality. Composing an intervening force in this way seems to be a promising way of shielding the force and its activity from being criticised for partisanship or for being an instrument for promoting the interests or designs of outside powers.

This concern for neutrality and for the appearance of neutrality grows readily out of the experience of peacekeeping, in which a force (usually a multilateral force) is interposed between the contending parties with their consent. A continuing perception of the neutrality of the intervening force is necessary for its credibility and often for the continuation and renewal of its mandate. The participation of military units from nations which are distant and which do not have a high profile in the area is commonly thought to be desirable.

This sort of situation brings with it some mutual recognition by the contending parties and is more likely to occur as a way of winding down hostilities from a previous peak, in which the opposing sides had tested each other and discovered that the other side was not so easily removed or pacified as it had earlier thought or hoped.

Peacekeeping is different from many of the situations in which emergency rescue measures are called for, since these often occur within a state which denies recognition to its internal opponents, which is ready to threaten and even to resist an intervening force, which is likely to perceive the intervening force as facilitating the progress of its opponents to their goals, and which resents the opening of its territory and the scrutiny of its activities by outside investigators and journalists. In this sort of situation, a force which can be quick and flexible in response to threats to the people and groups whom it is commissioned to protect; which can be firm in opposing threats and manoeuvres by regimes which are willing to resort to terror, massacre, and perversion of the police and criminal justice systems; and which depends for the continuance of its mandate on players in the international system who are genuinely concerned for populations at risk is more appropriate than a force designed to meet quasi-judicial expectations and ideals.

If one accepts this contrast between forces appropriate for peacekeeping and forces appropriate for humanitarian intervention intended to rescue a population at risk, then it follows that effectiveness in carrying out the mission should be a more important consideration than achieving the appearance or even the reality of impartiality. This will have significant implications for the questions raised earlier about authority to carry out humanitarian interventions. If effectiveness is the primary consideration, that is, the ability to carry out the task of rescue despite the possibility of serious resistance, then it is necessary to turn to states which have the logistical capability to intervene and to support an interventionary force over time, which have the intelligence capability to estimate and track threats in the area, and which have the overall military capability to deter the state which is suffering intervention or its potential allies from violently resisting intervening forces or attacking internal groups which it might attempt to treat as hostages. A clear and over-whelming preponderance of military capability makes it much more likely that the intervention can be conducted in a way which in practice keeps it quite distinct from warfare waged by one state against another or from protracted civil war.

Focusing on these elements of effectiveness directs our attention to the one country which has these capabilities and can deploy them to most areas of the globe, namely, the United States. This does not mean that the US is the only effective intervener. Depending on the magnitude of the problem and the resources available to those who would resist intervention, it will often be possible for a regional power or a regional coalition or an ad hoc clustering of concerned states to intervene effectively. For instance, Australia has clearly demonstrated this capability in East Timor and in the small states of Oceania, when the need arises. But it does mean that ambitious or extended exercises in humanitarian intervention will usually need to be able to draw on the resources of the surviving superpower or on some form of co-operation with it; this can range from tacit consent and permission to active involvement in the planning and execution of the intervention.

On the other hand, effectiveness is not reducible to these three forms of capability. A steadfast political will in the intervening state, resolute political leadership, perceptive understanding of local conditions and cultures, flexible and imaginative diplomacy are also elements in effective humanitarian intervention. They are not in such reliable supply in the US as the first group of elements. At the same time, one need not be an American chauvinist to doubt whether these important and desirable qualities are usually present in greater strength in the UN.

It may seem that in stressing effectiveness so much, I am confusing the distinction between authority and power, that I am restricting and distorting the sense of a moral obligation, and perhaps that I am helping to implement some American hegemonic scheme. In responding to these charges, let me make two preliminary observations. The first is that if there is a right or duty to intervene in another country in order to rescue populations threatened with genocide, it is the sort of right which in a special way needs to be exercised well. Often enough when we think about rights, we think about them as giving us justification for doing a certain activity, even if we are going to do it poorly in various ways. The right of free speech does not require that, if we are to exercise it, we must speak distinctly or loudly or even truthfully. The right of self-defence does not require that we be good marksmen or powerful athletes. But I would argue that in most situations where it is plausible to think that states have a right or duty to intervene, the stakes are going to be so high that it is very important that the intervention be carried out well. Botched interventions are likely to result in increased casualties all round, to provoke oppressive governments to intensify their repressive measures, to put hostages in heightened jeopardy, and to tempt the oppressed to do rash and vengeful things because of a mistaken belief that their hour of deliverance is indeed at hand. Intervention on humanitarian grounds is, as we have seen, justifiable precisely as an effort to save lives and to protect communities. A poorly conceived and executed humanitarian intervention is likely to cost more lives and thus to fail to meet reasonable tests of proportionality in the use of force.

Second, initiating an ineffective humanitarian intervention may well convert the operation into warfare, in which, instead of the intervening force establishing control of the area in which people are at risk and moving swiftly to protect them, the strength of resistance is sufficiently great that the intervening force has to engage in extensive hostilities with the forces of the state which is suffering the intervention. During this time, the protection of the people at risk is likely to be no more than partial. (Of course, it is possible for events to go in the opposite direction, that is, for war to create a new political situation in which the hold of central authority is loosened and groups become politically restive and are at risk of serious retaliation from the central government. This is illustrated by the necessity for military activity in order to protect the Kurds of northern Iraq from potentially genocidal treatment by the government of Saddam Hussein after the defeat of the Iraqi forces in the Gulf War of 1991.) War will generally be marked by an escalation of objectives and legitimate means, even while the original objective of humanitarian intervention becomes less obtainable. This is not a transformation which proponents of humanitarian intervention should welcome.

CONCLUSION

While I am strongly convinced of the importance of designing humanitarian interventions with effectiveness as a primary criterion, I do not want to dismiss all the considerations offered by the proponents of impartiality as the primary criterion to be used in shaping our views about the choice of intervening powers. Multilateral approaches do show the existence of a consensus about the gravity of a situation, and they prevent single powers from acting out their own moral and not so moral preferences. Avoiding intervention by neighbouring powers, which may have scores of their own to settle, and by former imperial powers are both important as ways of preserving the moral integrity of a project of intervention. The UN provides an important legal framework for justifying and limiting intervention.

My concern is that considerations of this type should not be taken as determinative in themselves and that considerations of effectiveness should not be relegated to an appraisal of instruments and techniques after the main moral issues are presumably settled. It is likely that approaching the task of humanitarian intervention as I envisage it would produce a larger place for politics and political consideration in the discussion of what is to be done and how and when it is to be done; but this would not, in my view, be a bad thing. The interventionist impulse, while highly moral and altruistic in its origins and many of its formulations, stands to gain in credibility and motivational power if it is conjoined with careful and disciplined thinking about strategies for using force and with a realistic sense of the constraints which international and internal politics put on the efforts of democracies and their citizens to do good and to resist evil.

2 INTERVENTION, POLITICAL REALISM AND THE IDEAL OF PEACE

C. A. J. (Tony) Coady

The debate about the ethics of armed intervention has taken a notable shift in the last five or six years. Or perhaps it would be more accurate to say several shifts and stumbles amounting almost to a shuffle. Although there were plenty of armed interventions in the post–World War II period, there was a fairly widespread consensus that, if a moral position on such matters was at all permissible, then there was a strong moral presumption against armed intervention. This moral presumption was embodied in most versions of modern just war theory, and was echoed in international law as it developed after World War II. It is this presumption, or its strength, that is now under challenge.

The prohibition on intervention was variously defended, and allowed of certain exceptions. In Michael Walzer's version of just war theory, for instance, an exemption was allowed for a small number of exigencies, most notably, and most plausibly, for interventions to prevent genocide.[1] Yet the bias against intervention was still very strong. In practical terms, this was no doubt influenced by the persistence of the Cold War and the fear that interventions could escalate to global disaster, though, in one of the many paradoxes of that frigid conflict, the nuclear might of the superpowers allowed for many interventions within their own secure spheres of influence, since conspicuous counter-interventions by the other side ran more risks than they were prepared usually to take. Indirect support to 'balance' intervention was, of course, another matter, and the consequences of much of this are still with us, as the dismal case of Afghanistan continues to remind us.

In theoretical terms, the bias or (almost) ban was often defended in terms of the importance of the integrity of states within the world order. In Walzer's writings, there was appeal to a domestic analogy whereby the states of the world were entitled to autonomy in getting on with the job of governing their population without interference from other states no matter (within limits) how bad a job they were doing. For Walzer, this policy of restraint was supported by recourse to the value of the self-determination of peoples; others treated the value of the existence of sovereign states and their independence more pragmatically. They respected them as the bedrock upon which international stability should rest, unless it could be shown that the stability itself required relaxing the policy of restraint. Walzer's position is important and merits a separate discussion. It raises difficult questions about the sort of 'self' and the sort of 'determination' involved but we cannot explore such questions here. Instead, I shall be concerned with the second response, often associated with the polyglot theory of 'realism'. A discussion of realism will help to open up some themes for later development.

By 'military intervention' I shall mean one power singly, or several powers jointly, acting without the express consent or invitation of the state invaded. Some would object that 'intervention' should have a wider meaning since outsiders should be taken to intervene even when the target country has agreed to their military presence. There is some linguistic justification for this proposal, especially where the consent is reluctant or pressured, but the more interesting moral issues arise when there is lack of consent, so I shall keep to the narrower interpretation. Hence, the Australian military response in East Timor does not count as intervention, for me, because Indonesia agreed to the Australian presence. This agreement may have been unpopular in many Indonesian circles, but it meant that the 'intervention' was in a quite different moral and political category from an Australian invasion that had no consent from the Indonesian government.[2] An adequate definition along these lines should probably include armed support for subversion as well as direct intervention.

The shift that I mentioned at the beginning occurred in the 1990s as an increased concern for what is often called 'humanitarian intervention'. This has its own definitional problems but I shall have principally in mind substantial armed military activity to protect people against severe violation of basic human rights. This motive has to be primary for an intervention to count as humanitarian, though it may coexist with other motives. It is tempting to hold that an intervention is not humanitarian if the humane motive would not have sufficed to produce intervention. Some would consider this condition too strong, but the motive must be at least necessary and prominent.[3] The Australian government's attempt to present the Iraq invasion as humanitarian when other motivations were shown to have been ill-based fails badly since John Howard made it clear before the invasion that the removal of the tyrant Hussein would not have provided sufficient reason for military intervention. An intervention cannot be humanitarian by afterthought. With the advent of the new millennium and the Bush regime in the United States, a further cause for intervention arose with the doctrine of preventive war. Here the idea was that a state could intervene with military power in another state when it believed that the other state might come to constitute a serious threat to its security, or the security of an ally.[4] In what follows, I shall be principally concerned with the case for humanitarian intervention, though I shall make passing reference to the preventive issue.

THE INTERPRETATION OF REALISM

Realism is the name for an elusive set of theories that have in common a suspicion of the role of morality in foreign affairs, and an addiction to the overwhelming importance of the concept of the

The Philosophical Problem *Tony Coady*

'national interest'. This leads many realists to be very respectful of state sovereignty, at least as a governing concept, and generally to be hostile to military interventions, especially where their grounds are moral or humanitarian. There is, of course, no direct logical entailment between such respect and blanket opposition to intervention. Many wars and military adventures have been justified on grounds of national interest, but, as a matter of fact, many realists nowadays often treat the national interest as involving an interest in world stability, and thereby the maintenance of the status quo in existing states, and the ban on intervention is often vindicated in this way. The more specific objection to altruistic or, as it is usually called today, 'humanitarian' intervention partakes of the same motivation, but is more directly supported by the suspicion of the employment of moral categories in international affairs. Realists also tend to be suspicious of preventive intervention on grounds of its likely negative consequences for world stability.

We need to get a little clearer about what this suspicion involves. Some versions of realism deny that morality is applicable at all to the international order. The toughest versions do seem to want to exclude morality totally (as is indicated in the title of an influential paper by Arthur Schlesinger Jnr called 'The Necessary Amorality of Foreign Affairs'), others that it is applicable but ineffective, others that it is applicable and effective, but dangerous and damaging.[5] Sometimes realists are better construed as making the point that the morality of international relations (or perhaps of politics generally) is different in kind from that of 'ordinary' or 'private' morality, and that one or other of the three points made above pertain to the application of private morality to public activities; this construe connects with the debate about 'dirty hands' in politics and with the influence of Machiavelli upon discussions of statecraft. Whether all these moral ships should sail under the one flag is a question for another occasion; for now, I want to make just three points. First, that the outright denial of moral applicability is confused, and usually inconsistent with the other things that the theorists want to say; second, that the ineffectiveness thesis makes an empirical claim that is pretty certainly false; third, that the most interesting allegation is that of damage. My first two comments will have to remain largely at the level of assertion, but I will amplify the assertion a little. The denial of moral applicability usually stems from some version of the anarchy thesis about the international order, coupled with an appeal to what is said to be Thomas Hobbes' view of morality as requiring both self-interested contract and supreme enforcer. For familiar reasons, I think the anarchy view overstated and, moreover, I think that the account of Hobbes' moral theory rests on misinterpretation.[6]

Furthermore, even if it were an accurate interpretation, the theory offers an unbalanced account of the moral life as both philosophical criticism and historical experience together testify. The philosophical objection simply challenges the plausibility of the idea that all of morality is based on convention. As to the historical experience, there is particular significance in the survival of moral virtue, understandably modified in various ways, even amongst many of the victims in the Nazi death camps, a fascinating account of which is given by Tzvetan Todorov.[7] If ever there were a situation of moral anarchy or state of nature, it was surely that of the death camps (at least for the prisoners) and yet forms of moral virtue and behaviour survived even there.

As for the denial of effectiveness, there is I think little doubt that morality has had some impact on the conduct of foreign affairs amongst at least some of the players involved. The efforts made on behalf of disaster relief by governments in contexts where their own national interests are at best minimal provide just one example, and there are sometimes efforts made to comply with what are basically moral demands in the conduct of war even where this is against obvious interest. It is always open to realists to dispute these cases on the grounds that they are not really morally motivated, and I can only say here that such efforts strike me as very implausible. They share something of the flavour of those adherents of psychological egoism who relentlessly show that all altruistic behaviour is *really* selfish, but succeed in doing so only by emptying the concept of selfishness, or self-interestedness, of any substantive content. When confronted by palpable counter-examples of unselfish behaviour, such as the mother who devotes herself to her handicapped infant child at considerable cost to her various enjoyments and interests or the fireman who risks life and limb to save victims in burning houses, the egoist insists that they wouldn't do these things unless they wanted to. Hey presto, they are acting from self-interest. But if we allow such paradigm acts of unselfishness to count as self-interest, then the egoist thesis merely amounts to the very unexciting truism that people act from desires or reasons that are *theirs*. Psychological egoism has shifted from a shocking empirical thesis about the contents of people's desires and reasons for action to a boring tautology. National interest egoism has a tendency to the same outcome.

Which brings me to the idea that the introduction of moral considerations into foreign policy is actually damaging and dangerous. This is the sort of thing often mentioned by realist critics of American foreign policy, especially in its Wilsonian flavours, when they object to the way that moral rhetoric and sometimes practice has bad outcomes. There is, of course, an appearance of paradox about this objection since the reference to bad outcomes seems to import the very moral element complained of. Realists usually try to avoid this paradox (when they are aware of it) by contrasting morality and rationality. The form of this response tends to vary with the realist making it, but the basic idea is that statecraft in the international domain, to be rational, must be governed by pursuit of the national interest. Morality either always or sometimes (depending on the theorist) gets in the way of such rationality and must be overruled.

One way in which a moral emphasis in foreign affairs may be irrational and damaging is when it insists on the impossible. In a revolutionary situation where negotiations are desperately needed, it may be sheer folly to rule out morally distasteful negotiations with anyone who has blood on their hands, since none of those that it is feasible to negotiate with will be blameless of killing. If spying is a legitimate activity, especially in wartime, then an absolute moral prohibition on lies and deceptions cannot be accepted. Some have thought that the same applies to diplomacy in general: Sir Henry Wotton famously remarked in the sixteenth century that 'an ambassador is an honest man, sent to lie abroad for the good of his country'.[8] It is, of course, dangerous to treat 'bon mots', no matter how apt, as premises for moral and political argument, and, in this instance, we would need more discrimination between concepts such as discretion, reticence, confidentiality, ambiguity, misleading behaviour, deception and lying, before we could assess the descriptive accuracy of Wotton's witticism. But the point remains that, with some qualifications to be made later, it can be no part of morality to enjoin what is impossible, at least not as specific imperatives here and now. Indeed, the issuing of moral injunctions that ignore relevant facts and circumstances that bear on the implementation of moral injunctions will generally indicate not morality at work, but moralism, and my suggestion is that realism retains considerable appeal, despite its many confusions and implausibilities, precisely because it offers a salutary warning against moralism.

I want to suggest that this idea offers a way out of the usual impasse of realism versus morality in discussions of international affairs, and I want to explore the relation of this way out to the role of ideals in moral thinking, and particularly to the ideal of peace in relation to armed interventions. But what is moralism? This topic is radically under-explored in moral philosophy, and I can do no more than gesture in the direction of an adequate account here, but I hope that it will be helpful in the discussion of intervention. Elsewhere I have discussed the issue of moralism in more philosophical detail.[9]

THE VICE OF MORALISM

Moralism is a kind of vice involved in certain ways of practising morality or exercising moral judgement, or thinking that you are doing so. The vice often involves an inappropriate set of emotions or attitudes in acting upon moral judgements, or judging others in the light of moral considerations. The moraliser is typically thought to lack a certain self-awareness, a breadth of understanding of others, and is deemed to be subject to an often delusional sense of moral superiority over those coming under judgement. Though these character traits are often associated with moralism, the vice needs to be specified in terms of its characteristic ways of working and so needs to be distinguished, for instance, from the often associated vice of hypocrisy. Nonetheless, it seems unlikely that moralism will take one simple form.

One form of moralism involves seeing things as moral issues that aren't, and thereby over-moralising the universe. There are moral dimensions to all human activities, but these dimensions will often be rightly muted because they are obvious or marginally important or already correctly agreed. Some issues are then best treated as simply questions of efficiency but the moraliser is likely to insist on dragging in moral concerns where they have little or no place. To take a simple illustration: it usually won't matter whether a pie has been exactly divided amongst the six people at the picnic as long as everyone gets enough to eat and the portions are roughly equal. Appealing to justice as an objection here would usually be moralistic.

Another way in which moralism can distort practical thinking is by treating complex matters of moral opinion as though they were matters of moral certainty. The moraliser tends to be overconfident in his or her moral judgements, and this can be particularly dangerous when it involves the imposition of those judgements on others. There are such things as the palpably good and the evidently evil, but a great deal of adult moral life consists in recognising that good, reasonable people can legitimately disagree about many other things that raise moral questions. A state whose leaders are armed both with powerful weaponry and too many moral certainties is likely to do a great deal of harm in addition to displaying moral arrogance.

A third form of moralism, particularly pertinent to the intervention debate, is a blindness to the practical difficulties involved in implementing the moral imperatives or ideals they accept. Moral intensity can be the enemy of clear vision, and prudence is often a victim of the moralising attitude. This seems to me to be particularly illustrated by recent interventions that have been motivated in part by lofty moral concerns. In Afghanistan, the US-led attack was fuelled by the desire to bring retribution upon those who planned the attack of September 11, but it quickly turned into a moral crusade against the Taliban with no serious concern for the disruptive and destabilising effect of siding with the Northern Alliance in a civil war.[10] In Iraq, the moral awfulness of Saddam Hussein and the appeal of the moral ideal of democracy helped to blind the 'Coalition of the Willing' to the high probability of anarchy, disruption and continuing violence that the intervention would bring about. Those, like President Bush and his advisers, who live in the lofty realm of Good and Evil are often incapable of implementing the earthy, moral virtue of prudence.

So, in spite of their many confusions, realists are in my view right to warn against the excesses of moralism, even though wrong to think that it is morality itself that must be jettisoned. A proper concern for morality should protect against the vice of moralism. It remains to test this lesson on the problem of ideals.

Reliance upon ideals is often one of the principal targets of the realists and it can be seen as involving moralism in its lack of regard for the prudential constraints of what is achievable. The complaint against ideals is seldom spelled out in any detail, but the basic idea is that resort to thinking in terms of ideals in international affairs leads to disaster because of the impossibility inherent in the ideal. Ideals seem to be essentially unrealisable and a hard sense of what is feasible and possible is essential to politics, especially on the international stage. So it is thought that ideals of democracy, freedom and even justice are too remote and unrealisable in many of the circumstances of foreign affairs for them to function as part of the practical reasoning that should guide our dealings with other states.

Earlier I mentioned that the idea that morality must be attentive to possibility and feasibility needed some qualification. The qualification that I had in mind, and perhaps this is not the only one necessary, is that required by the role of ideals. Although ideals will invariably be in some tension with the demands of current reality, they also condition the way we can view our present world and its potentiality. Idealists have often changed what people previously thought was possible and have thereby helped to bring about deep changes in the world. Where the ideals have been worthy ones, this has been a great benefit to humanity and gives a richer sense to what is realistic. Democracy itself is inspired by ideals of equality that were derided by tough-minded realists in the past. A clear-headed resort to ideals need not be moralistic.

INTERVENTION AND THE IDEAL OF PEACE

In connection with the topic of intervention, the most relevant ideal is the ideal of peace, though certain ideals of justice and liberty are also relevant. Like other ideals, it initially stands in opposition to reality, but can have a crucial role in guiding behaviour and determining what is actually realistic. We must now see how this relates to the question of armed intervention, particularly in the context of humanitarian intervention. My reinterpretation of what is significant in realism allows a place for genuine morality, including both ideals and prudence. This might be thought to open the way to a more sympathetic attitude to intervention. In some respects this is so, but in other respects the argument will go against intervention since a good deal will turn upon whether interventional arguments are moralistic and also upon the ideals that are in play. What follows should make this clearer.

It should be stressed that much of the traditional opposition to armed intervention is based, not upon realist or other forms of respect for sovereignty, but upon revulsion against war and attachment to the ideal of peace. In spite of the pseudo-medical euphemisms of modern military jargon like 'surgical strikes', 'neutralising', and so on, armed interventions standardly involve a great deal of killing, maiming and severe suffering. Sometimes this is rained upon 'the guilty', though there are notorious difficulties in specifying the meaning of this 'guilt' in the case of teenage conscripts starved of serious information about why they are in the field, but often it is inflicted upon the relatively or absolutely innocent, either directly or as 'collateral damage' or as planned or unplanned long-term effects on economies and ecologies. It is hard to oppose plans for violent measures to rescue thousands of victims of ethnic cleansing or deliberate starvation. Nonetheless, those of us who are moved by the ideal of peace and revolted by the realities of war, even that rarity 'just war', should be nervous about any revival of enthusiasm for armed intervention.

Bryan Hehir and others have called attention to the way that medieval versions of just war theory had much more expansive attitudes to war-making and intervention, and Hehir, at any rate, recommends, with qualifications, something of a return to this spirit.[11] Hehir thinks the narrowing of just cause in the direction of self-defence only is largely a consequence of the peace of Westphalia and the rise of sovereign states and a concern for their prerogatives, but it should be emphasised that it is also connected for many people with an increased awareness of the horrors of war, and with the developing momentum from the late nineteenth century onwards of that loose confederation of impulses called 'the peace movement'.

Those who hold out an ideal of a peaceful world, at least in the sense of a world without war, come from the ranks of outright 'absolute' but secular pacifists, religious groups broad enough to include Quakers and the Vatican, and some 'just war' theorists who allow the possibility of justified resort to large-scale violence, but see this as an emergency resort *in extremis* and look to a world in which it will be largely unnecessary. The ideal of peace is more than a picture of a state of non-fighting, though that is an essential ingredient in it. The state of non-fighting has to have something robust about it; it has to be more like calm weather than a mere lull between storms. Hence, the ideal requires institutional support within states and in the international order, though this need not mean that a peaceful world is identified with a fully just or even democratic world. It may be that only advances towards the sorts of societies that genuine democracies can involve will be required to sustain peace, but that needs argument, some of which indeed Michael Doyle has famously (or notoriously) sought to provide.[12] There are, of course, many objections to any such vision of a peaceful world, and they come again from a sense of the supposed 'necessity' of war, but there used to be similar objections to the realisation of other remote ideals that have now been realised or at least closely approximated. I am thinking of the abolition of slavery, the emancipation of women, and the elimination of duelling as just three examples. I will not argue further for the ideal of peace here, though I will shortly say a little more about its content, but I want to make the point against what seems to be Hehir's position, and against others who seek to extend the scope for war by invoking arms on behalf of humanitarian intervention, that there is a serious danger to the ideal of peace in the enlarged resort to such intervention.

This danger has several faces.

THE DANGER OF SHORT-TERM REACTIONS

The first is a certain short-sightedness caused by the entirely understandable 'gut-reaction' to carnage. This carnage is present in the living rooms of advanced industrial states in a way never before possible and it evokes a natural desire to 'rescue'. But the idiom of 'rescue' (deliberately invoked by Walzer's phrase 'the politics of rescue') is often inappropriate to what can actually be achieved militarily. In many of the cases of tribal slaughter, ethnic cleansing and the rest, an armed intervention is an inappropriate instrument of rescue. The atrocities and tragedies are enmeshed in structures, histories and institutions that mean a temporary separation of warring factions with some accompanying loss of life all round is not guaranteed to stop the slaughter and may merely accelerate a rate of later reprisal.

Consider the parallel with domestic violence such as child abuse. An individual who simply went into a home where a baby is being beaten and forcibly separated the violent parent from the child has usually done little to 'rescue' the child. Such an individual will usually have produced a respite rather than a rescue. Sooner or later after the intervener departs, it will all start up again. This is why, in extreme cases, children have to be removed from parental miscare and cared for elsewhere, but it is hardly to be seriously proposed that some foreign state or alliance will do anything analogous to that. Of course, an alternative in the domestic situation would be for the intervener to move in and restructure the family relationship (if possible) or remove the abuser and substitute someone else in their place. Something like this is meant by the term 'nation-building' and Walzer has (very tentatively) proposed in this spirit a reconsideration of the old ideas of trusteeship and protectorates.[13] In a dramatically changed world, with a strengthened United Nations and other international humanitarian agencies, such options may have some plausibility and value, but in the present world, it is hard to see how they could be either plausible or desirable. They would inevitably be seen by the proposed trustees as both costly and risky, and by the proposed beneficiaries and by other underdeveloped states as a return to a colonial mind-set.

So intervention that is 'nation-building' seems mostly unfeasible and dangerous; intervention that just stops a slaughter and departs seems to make no contribution to real peace. This point applies more widely, of course, than in the case of humanitarian intervention, since the disruptive effects of any military intervention will commonly require an aftermath of reconstruction that is fraught with political and often military difficulties, as the intervention in Iraq is demonstrating daily in dramatic fashion.

THE DANGER OF CULTURAL INCOMPREHENSION

There are epistemic and cultural barriers to humanitarian armed intervention that it may in principle be possible to overcome, but which are in practice frequently insurmountable. The problems encountered by UN troops in Mogadishu seemed to fall into this category. I do not mean to endorse any form of cultural relativity about values, but the interpretation of even shared values in a foreign culture can be no easy thing to master, and an understanding of the complex politics, hostilities, loyalties, and sensitivities of people very remote from the intervening power's experience has commonly been conspicuously missing. Even where government leaders have some grasp of these problems, and that is rare enough, it is stretching credibility to think that front-line troops will have the same understanding. This is why it is usual for humanitarian interveners to be welcomed by the victims but, soon after, reviled by them. The recent American-led intervention in Iraq could hardly be called a humanitarian intervention, except by those desperate to find *some* justification for the invasion, but it had a similarly inadequate grasp of the Iraqi cultural, political and religious scene. There were some initial signs of welcome, but the invading forces were soon widely viewed as conquerors and are now fighting an insurgency that has broad, if not universal, popular support. Incidentally, it is hard enough for close neighbours to achieve the understanding in question; they are sometimes worse than distant foreigners for an intervention role because their understanding of their neighbours may be distorted by historic hatreds, and their motives distorted by dominational interests related to those enmities.

The problems that arise here for enthusiasts of intervention are often problems of moralism. There is the same lofty distance from the facts to which moral judgement needs to applied and there is sometimes the tendency to unacceptable imposition of contentious moral and political values. Distancing ourselves from present conflicts, we can now see this moralism clearly at work in previous interventions. Let me cite the rhetoric of two previous US presidents as they prepared for military intervention. The quotes also show a close link between moralising and religiosity. The first is from President Taft in 1912:

> We are not going to intervene in Mexico until no other course is possible, but I must protect our people in Mexico as far as possible, and their property, by having the Government in Mexico understand that there is a God in Israel and he is on duty. Otherwise they will utterly ignore our many great complaints and give no attention to needed protection which they can give.[14]

The second is from President McKinley facing the problem of annexation of the Philippines:

> It came to me one night that we could not turn the island over to France or Germany, our commercial rivals; that would be bad business and discreditable. We would not give them back to Spain; that would be cowardly and dishonorable. We could not leave them to themselves; they were unfit for self-government. There was therefore nothing left for us to do but to take care of them and educate them and Christianize them.[15]

Just as the first quotation shows the delusional estimate of one's own moral position so often embodied in moralism (and in religiosity), the second quotation shows the high-minded disregard for relevant facts that is a mark of certain forms of moralism—after all, the Filipinos had been Christians for four centuries at the time McKinley spoke, even if not Christians of his persuasion.

THE DANGER TO PEACE

There is also the damage done to strivings for a peaceful world that may be caused by the employment of humanitarian violence. As argued earlier, a typical distortion of moralism is heedlessness about the long-term consequences of taking a moral stance now. Where morality itself recommends a certain prudent concern for long-term consequences (which is not to say, with the consequentialists, that this is the whole of morality), the moraliser tends to be indifferent to them. This imprudence was a marked feature of the ill-starred American-led intervention in Iraq. Of course, the case of intervention on behalf of protecting very basic human rights, such as the right of the innocent not to be killed, is so very difficult partly because sensible advocates of intervention will argue that the long-term consequences of intervention support the ideal of peace. After all, peace is already violated and the interventional violence is aimed at restoring peace. There is undoubtedly something in this response, though it has the disadvantage of paralleling the claims about World War I being 'the war to end war'. Violence may sometimes be a necessary and morally appropriate resort, but it tends to generate more violence, and hence does not promise to lead us to a peaceful world.

Of course, the closer one can make the international order approximate the domestic order of states, so that intervention is done by an authorised and representative agent, the closer even violent intervention comes to a police action. This reflects the extension of Hobbes' argument for the necessity of internal domestic security provided by individual states to the international scene more generally and posits the necessity of some form of world authority to mount legitimate interventions. Personally, I support such an idea, and sympathise with Lutz Unterseher's advocacy of a UN intervention force or 'legion'.[16] It is most likely to deliver the sort of world required by an ideal of peace, but there are formidable intellectual and practical obstacles to its feasibility.

THE DANGER OF MORAL RHETORIC

The fourth face of danger is that of empty moral rhetoric. Talk, they say, is cheap, and moral talk is sometimes cheap and dangerous. Though it is closely related to hypocrisy, we might think of this as a form of moralism different from those outlined above; it is the moralism of words over deeds. What I mean is that grand moral talk is easily evoked by tragic moral events, but not only is it much harder to translate into significant action, but it can stimulate false hopes, encourage victims to rash acts in the (vain) hope of outside support for them, and subsequently create bitter reactions of cynicism and disillusion. There are too many examples to need detailed citation, though candidate Clinton's talk in the 1992 US presidential elections of how ethnic cleansing in the former Yugoslavia 'must not be allowed to stand' provides a classic instance. Sometimes, perhaps often, the rhetoric is sincere enough, and the problem lies in its disconnection from mechanisms that might translate words into appropriate deeds. Too often the rhetorical words produce rhetorical gestures—actions that speak more softly than the words and are ill-adapted to the realities.

Some of the UN's clumsier efforts in Bosnia illustrate this and generated the sort of cynicism expressed in the witticism attributed to a senior relief official in Sarajevo: 'If the UN had been around in 1939 we would all be speaking German'.[17] Thomas Weiss poses sharply the sort of choice that may often be required: 'The moral of international actions in the former Yugoslavia is that hollow gestures are not necessarily better than no action at all. Earlier and more robust military intervention should have been pursued, or the situation left to the warring parties to settle themselves.'[18] In this choice, for most situations, the first option is fraught with difficulty, even though the second is agonising. In retrospect, more timely interventions will commonly look a better option, but this is sometimes because events have taken a dire course that would earlier have often been difficult to foresee and presumptuous to act upon.

CONCLUSION

All these strictures against moralism are likely to be met by the cry that *something* has to be done in the face of slaughter. Maybe it's dangerous, moralistic, faulty, but *these* lives must be saved. I am not unmoved by this appeal, but it needs to be set in context, particularly the political context, and it needs to be balanced by the consideration that what one does *here* for *these* people has human costs for other people elsewhere. Responses that are dictated by media visibility (the CNN factor, as it is often called) are bound to be selective and can be distortional of priorities. There are massacres, plagues and disasters occurring regularly around the planet that are equally deserving of our compassion and about which we do nothing or very little.

Apart from arming Saddam Hussein, the compassionate advanced states did nothing about the slaughter of the Iran–Iraq war, and no 'rescue' programmes were mooted for the appalling devastation—including rape, pillage, starvation, murder and enslavement—that was regularly visited upon the Southern Sudanese by the Northern Sudanese for decades, and continues today. Until recently, this 'forgotten war' got almost no media coverage but it was estimated in 1999 that more than two million people had died in it by then, which is more than in any other conflict since World War II.[19] Now there are diplomatic pressures and threats of more, but apparently no serious pressure for military intervention, partly because of the mess in Iraq. When we widen the perspective to encompass disease, the ravages of AIDS in Africa can be seen as a monumental and continuing disaster that surely deserves to trigger our 'rescue' responses as much as, if not more than, the usual candidates. It has been estimated that 35 000 children worldwide perish *daily* from poverty and preventable disease, and it has been plausibly argued that the funds devoted to the humanitarian relief of the 'loud' crises created by wars could be ten to twenty times more effective against the 'silent' emergencies created by poverty.[20] None of this even mentions the deaths, pain and suffering cheerfully tolerated in our own backyards—a prime example being the effects of the absence of a serious health system in the USA.

One difference, of course, between some of these situations and the paradigms proposed for intervention is that between killings and more diffusely caused deaths. Brutal killings seem to evoke more in the way of a need to respond, partly through the desire to punish, and partly because there are specifiable agents whose acts of harm seem open to prevention. The means for delivering that punishment and prevention seem, moreover, decisive and peremptory, especially such military measures as bombing. But not only can this appearance be delusive because much more protracted military measures than bombing may be required for success, but it may also be that there are underlying structural causes of the conflicts that bombing will not address, and that may be just as, or more, costly and difficult to confront as the causes of the AIDS epidemic.

We are a long way from the peaceful world that so many yearn for. I have argued that the realist tradition, with all its faults, can provide a useful caution against the high-minded resort to violence. Suitably reinterpreted, realism provides a prudential reminder that a distorted appeal to morality produces a moralism that threatens the striving for a peaceful world.

3 THE ETHICS OF INVASION: *JUS AD BELLUM* AND IRAQ

Hugh White

The invasion and occupation of Iraq by the US and its allies in 2003 is the most ethically controversial military operation undertaken by a Western country since the Vietnam War. I want to focus here on the questions of *jus ad bellum* ('just grounds for going to war'). That focus does not imply that I think that other moral questions about the war are not important. But as always the questions of *jus ad bellum*, though they do not necessarily take logical or conceptual priority over questions of *jus in bello* ('just conduct in waging war') or *jus post bellum* ('just ways of concluding war and controlling its aftermath'), do retain a kind of psychological priority. And after nearly three years of intense public debate in many countries, before and after the invasion, the bases for a judgement about whether the US-led coalition was right to invade Iraq remain as contested and, indeed, confused as ever. The aim of this chapter is to contribute to clarifying the issues and questions, and to offer some tentative conclusions. Along the way I will touch on some broader questions about the circumstances in which resort to armed force is legitimate.

There are three reasons why the issues of *jus ad bellum* in relation to Iraq are so unclear. First, the principles themselves are in flux. Over the fifteen years since the end of the Cold War, many questions about the scope and limits to the legitimate use of force have been opened up by experiences in Kuwait, Somalia, Rwanda, the Balkans, East Timor and many other crisis spots around the world. In the resulting debates about humanitarian intervention, many of the accepted principles of *jus ad bellum* have been called into question. The sanctity of sovereignty has been downgraded and the scope for legitimate military intervention has expanded. But the limits to these changes are far from clear. And after the terrorist attacks of September 11 2001, many people believed that even these updated and expanded rules and principles no longer applied, and new principles needed to be formulated to handle unique new circumstances. Second, the reasons for the invasion have been confused. Coalition governments have produced a wide range of different arguments to justify their invasion of Iraq, and their explanations have changed as circumstances have changed. So it has been hard to know what has been the real basis for the decisions actually taken by policy makers. Third, the facts themselves have been, as always, obscured by the fog of war and the no less dense fog of politics.

In what follows, my focus will be on the primary US decision to invade and occupy Iraq in March 2003, but my comments are clearly relevant to the Australian decision to join with the British and Americans in this venture since the Australian justifications mirrored the US reasoning to a very large extent. From the accounts published so far, it is not clear that the key US decision makers ever self-consciously made that decision at an identifiable time and place.[1] But the decision was nonetheless made, and it remains the critical act of those responsible for launching the war. I should perhaps make it clear that, since the idea was first mooted in early 2002, I have regarded the Iraq invasion as a *policy* mistake for the US for the purely realist, national interest reason that the costs and risks of the operation were not justified by the benefits that could be expected of it. I have been less clear in my own mind whether it was a *moral* mistake as well. That is my prime focus here: whether that decision, at the time it was taken, was morally right or wrong.

My approach will be to examine in turn five alternative grounds that have been advanced or need to be considered as providing a moral basis for the decision to invade. They are: the utilitarianism implied in much of the public debate, an appeal to the authority of the UN, preventive war, humanitarian intervention, and what I shall call 'strategic intervention'.

IMPLIED UTILITARIANISM AND DUE DILIGENCE

It is best to start with the broad public debate. Throughout the public debate about invading Iraq, ethical judgements about the rightness and wrongness of the decision have been most influenced not by the arguments about weapons of mass destruction (WMD) or the evils of Saddam, but by practical judgements about the chances of success and failure. Before the invasion, opponents on moral grounds also argued that it would end in failure; those that supported it also expected it would be a pushover. And since the invasion, critics have been pessimistic, and supporters have been optimistic, about events on the ground.

Behind this thinking is an implicitly utilitarian model of *jus ad bellum*. Since early last century, there has been a strong presumption that resort to armed force can only be justified in order to prevent worse outcomes. This is an intuitively attractive principle. Its application is reflected in the actual judgements people make about the war in Iraq: those who oppose the invasion as immoral argue, at least in part, that it will make things worse, while those who support it argue that it will make things better. On this account, there is not much anyone can say now about the rights and wrongs of the decision to invade Iraq: we have to wait until we know whether it succeeds or not. Success today probably means establishing, within a year or two, a cohesive Iraq with a stable and enduring government that genuinely serves the interests of its citizens and lives at peace with its neighbours, and thereby helps to stabilise the Middle East and encourage political reform there. Success in these terms is not likely, but it is not yet impossible. If all this happens, I will have been proved wrong in my judgement that the Iraq invasion was a mistake of policy. But what about moral judgements? Must they also await the outcome of events?

This highlights the limitation of the implicit utilitarian model. It suffers from the problem that Kant identified in his original critique of utilitarianism: that it makes the morality of actions contingent on outcomes which are inherently unknowable at the time the action is taken. Moral action is reduced to a kind of gamble on the outcome of events. Of course, no one can know what will happen when a decision is taken. This uncertainty is, in most practical cases, not merely theoretical—a matter of epistemology, so to speak—but an issue of urgent practical reality, inherent in the nature of military operations. In retrospect, the actual outcomes of events acquire a patina of inevitability. But when decisions are made, uncertainty about their consequences is, and remains, very real. We can see that in Iraq today.

So the implicit utilitarian model of *jus ad bellum* seems to offer no alternative but to suspend moral judgement on a military operation like the invasion of Iraq until the result is clear. This is surely not good enough—not least for decision makers themselves, who need some ethical basis to guide their choices when they make them, and before they can be sure of their outcomes. Nonetheless, it does seem intuitively important to maintain a clear connection between the rightness of a decision and its consequences.

One way to address this problem might be to borrow a phrase from the world of business. A company director cannot be morally condemned for failing to predict a business problem, but he can be condemned for failing to exercise due diligence—that is, failing to take all due care to ensure that he or she has assembled the relevant facts and given them proper consideration. The same might be said of strategic policy makers. It is important that judgements about the cost, benefits and consequences of armed intervention are well based. They need to be carefully made on the basis of all the evidence, duly weighed with an open mind. The responsibility is particularly strong when the issue is as momentous as the use of armed force, especially on the scale envisaged in the invasion of Iraq.

Due diligence requires not just the assembly of facts, but also the exercise of imagination: to consider how things might develop, and what unexpected or unintended consequences might arise from different courses of action. John Kennedy's decision making in the Cuban missile crisis is an example of this kind of due diligence: not being willing to be swept along by the advice of his officials, Kennedy thought carefully about how things might go wrong, and what that might mean.[2] Of course, moral judgements about the exercise of due diligence must not take advantage of hindsight: decisions need to be evaluated in the light of evidence and conclusions that would have been available and reasonable at the time the decision was taken. That in turn requires some imagination, on the part of those who look back and judge past decisions, to grasp what wasn't, and couldn't, have been known at the time.

Due diligence in deciding to use force also requires the exercise of cautious prudence. It is like the practice of medicine: the seriousness of the decisions, the consequences of error and the uncertainty of outcomes mean that the burden of evidence lies with those who favour action. Hence the physician's Hippocratic Principle—first do no harm. This is a good guide for strategists as well. And it suggests a further principle: rash and ill-considered judgement on the use of force is morally wrong, and remains wrong even if the consequences turn out well. There is an analogy here with gambling: if it is wrong to gamble with other people's money, it remains wrong even if you win. Likewise, it is wrong to gamble with the lives of others, even if the gamble pays off.[3]

So we might ask whether the decision to invade Iraq met the test of due diligence. This is something the decision makers themselves know better than we. But from the published accounts of the process, the reports of the many official inquiries about the handling of intelligence, and above all the manifest fact that the problems of post-Saddam Iraq were very seriously underestimated, there are significant grounds for doubt.

UNITED NATIONS AUTHORITY

As the debate over the invasion of Iraq unfolded, a lot of attention was given by both advocates and opponents to the role of the UN in authorising military action. Supporters of Operation Iraqi Freedom argued that UN Security Council resolutions at least implicitly authorised the action, thus providing a sound legal and ethical basis for the decision to invade. Some cited UN Security Council Resolution 1441 of November 2002 as providing authority for the attack in March 2003, but that argument hardly survives serious scrutiny. Nothing in the explicit language of the resolution supports it, and it is clear from members' comments at the time and subsequent conduct that many of the Security Council did not interpret it in that way.[4]

Supporters of the invasion have more plausibly argued that the Security Council had given authority to use armed force against Iraq in Resolution 678 of November 1990, under which Operation Desert Storm was launched. The subsequent cease-fire was conditional on Saddam's compliance with UN requirements that he abandon his WMD programs. So, the argument runs, his (apparent) non-compliance with these cease-fire conditions reactivated the authority under Resolution 678. A number of legal counter-arguments have been advanced against this claim,[5] but to my mind the most powerful rebuttal relies more on common sense than legal reasoning.

The argument runs as follows: Resolution 678 authorised military action only to enforce the Security Council's earlier resolutions requiring Iraqi forces to withdraw from Kuwait. It was absolutely clear at the time that Resolution 678 did not authorise the use of force to invade Iraq and depose Saddam. So, while it can be argued that Saddam's non-compliance with the cease-fire resolutions reactivated Resolution 678's authorisation of some kind of military action against Iraq, it is hard to argue that it provides authority for an invasion which was unambiguously beyond the scope of the resolution as originally adopted. In other words, the old resolutions provided authority for some kinds of military action against Saddam in response to his non-compliance—action like the periodic air strikes launched in the no-fly zones under operations Northern and Southern Watch. But they could not provide authority for full-scale invasion and regime change.

So the argument that Operation Iraqi Freedom was authorised by the UN cannot be sustained. How serious is this to the ethical status of the decision to launch the operation? Some opponents of the invasion believe that it is decisive. On this view, any use of force not sanctioned by the UN is, by that fact alone, unethical. There are three variants of this position. The fundamentalist variant holds that the UN Charter sets out limits on the rights of nations to use force which are morally binding in their own right: to wage war without UN authority is morally wrong simply and directly because to do so defies UN authority. But the processes of the UN cannot support this kind of moral authority. UN decisions on these issues depend on votes of individual national governments. It is hard to argue that a war which would be right if one or other of the delegates on the Security Council votes one way becomes morally wrong if they vote the other way. A war which is morally right if Chad, or Venezuela, or Australia, votes for it does not become morally wrong if for some quite irrelevant reason—pressure, whim or national interest—that vote goes the other way.

The second basis for arguing that making war without UN authority is morally wrong is consequentialist: that it is wrong to wage war without UN authority because, even if the war is in other respects justified, defying the UN makes it more likely that others will launch unjust wars in future. This is quite a strong argument as far as it goes, but it is hard to argue that it provides a basis for an absolute moral prohibition on resort to force without UN authority. The harm done to the UN's authority needs to be balanced in each case against the harm done by not taking military action. If the reasons for military action were compelling in the first place, then consequentialist concerns, though significant, might not outweigh the other considerations in play.

The third basis for UN authority is prudential. The UN provides a forum for testing the quality of your reasoning and judgements in choosing to use armed force. Failure to win UN endorsement for a military operation should give any decision maker pause. But if, having with due diligence reviewed the pros and cons in the light of arguments put in New York, the use of force still looks the right course, then opposition from the UN cannot by itself make it wrong.

These limitations on the UN's moral authority were all demonstrated in 1999, when NATO launched operations against Serbia over Kosovo without UN authority, because Russia was opposed to it. Much might be said about the wisdom of the decision and the way it was taken, and about the way the war was conducted, but it is hard to claim that the operation as a whole was wrong because it had not been endorsed by the Security Council. None of these arguments deny that the UN has real and significant moral authority, and that there is a moral responsibility to engage with the UN seriously in considering the use of force. But they do suggest that going to war without explicit UN authority is not, on that basis alone, wrong.

So, the US had no moral authority from the UN to invade Iraq, but this is not decisive in deciding the legitimacy of the decision.

PREVENTIVE WAR

The main argument advanced by the US government to justify the decision to invade Iraq before the event was that Iraq's WMD posed a threat to world peace, and to the US specifically, that was so grave and so urgent that the US was justified in waging preventive war to forestall it.

Of course, as it has turned out, there were no WMD in Iraq. Nonetheless, it remains important in judging the moral status of the decision to invade Iraq to consider whether the invasion would have been justified if Iraq had possessed a militarily significant stock of WMD. The argument for war related to Iraq's WMD was based on the doctrine of pre-emption, which allows a state to take military action to forestall an evident and imminent military attack. But the doctrine has limits, classically set out by US Secretary of State Daniel Webster in 1842: pre-emptive military action is only justified where the threat is 'instant, overwhelming, leaving no choice of means and no moment for deliberation'.[6] Justifying the invasion of Iraq as pre-emption required that doctrine to be significantly extended to cover a threat which was not immediate and imminent, but only a reasonable future possibility—more a matter of prevention than pre-emption. Some opponents of the invasion have argued against this extension of pre-emption, on the grounds that it is too permissive and would be open to abuse by allowing governments to launch military attacks on mere suspicion.[7] Supporters of the invasion, including the Bush administration itself, have argued that in the unique and unprecedented threat posed by the combination of global terrorism and

WMD, preventive wars could be justified. This argument was set out in President Bush's speech at West Point in June 2002 and in more detail in the National Security Strategy in September 2002.[8]

In fact, the doctrine of preventive war has a long and respectable history. It is not the invention of the Bush administration and is not simply a response to the new strategic circumstances that have followed September 11. Michael Walzer devoted a chapter to the subject in *Just and Unjust Wars* in 1977. He argued that, while there are limits on the right to wage preventive war, Webster's limits are too restrictive. He concluded that nations had a right to strike first at what he called 'the point of sufficient threat'. 'Sufficient threat', he says, requires 'a manifest intent to injure, a degree of active preparation that makes that intent a positive danger, and a general situation in which waiting, or doing anything other than fighting, greatly magnifies the risk'.[9]

This formulation, as far as it goes, is compelling. And it seems to fit exactly what the Bush administration was claiming about Iraq before the invasion. So I do not think the problem lies in the doctrine of preventive war itself: we cannot condemn the invasion of Iraq simply on the grounds that it was a preventive war. But there are three other issues to be addressed. The first is the question of whether Iraq really posed a 'sufficient threat' to the US. This is hard to sustain. The strongest basis for thinking Iraq and its WMD might pose a threat to the US was the possibility that Iraqi WMD could be passed to terrorists. The evidence of links between Iraq and terrorist groups targeting the US was always very weak. There remains a question whether, for all Saddam's bluster, he had a manifest intent to attack the US directly. It would be easier to argue that he had a manifest intent to attack his neighbours, or Israel. That might justify a kind of extended justification of preventive war analogous to the right of co-operative self-defence under Article 51 of the UN Charter. But it is pulling the doctrine in new and problematic directions.[10]

Second, there is the test of necessity, implied in Walzer's third condition quoted above. Military action to prevent an attack can only be justified if it is the only way to deal with the threat. This is hard to argue in the case of Iraq. Saddam's military ambitions were effectively contained, his WMD programs were at least constrained by the UN inspections, and the threat of retaliation if he did use his WMD remained real and credible. The argument that deterrence is no longer effective, made in the National Security Strategy, may be true in relation to terrorist groups, but it is much harder to sustain in relation to states like Iraq. So it was hard for the Bush administration to argue that there were no other options to deal with the supposed threat other than military action.

Third, and I think most importantly, there is the question of proportionality. Walzer's earlier treatment of the question in *Just and Unjust Wars* omits this issue, but he touches on it in his more recent writing.[11] Any preventive military action will involve an element of judgement and uncertainty. The less immediate the threat, the less certain it is that the threat would in fact eventuate if it was not pre-empted. Most likely, also, less force would be required to forestall it, economy of effort and cost being part of the underlying rationale of prevention. It seems reasonable, therefore, to require that the amount of force used in preventive military operations should be proportionate to the scale, imminence and probability of the threat. This means a country may be justified in undertaking limited strikes to prevent a threat, but not justified in launching a full-scale invasion. Israel's 1981 strike against Iraq's Osirik nuclear reactor is a perfect example, cited by Walzer.[12] A single strike, causing little collateral damage and killing relatively few people, did much to reduce the long-term risk to Israel. The action, though widely criticised at the time, seems defensible despite the fact that the threat was not imminent, precisely because the military operation was itself so modest.

This point has been developed recently by David Luban, who distinguishes between preventive strikes and preventive war.[13] In the debates over Iraq, much of the focus has been on the rights and wrongs of military action per se, rather than of different types of military action. Of course, any resort to force is serious and takes us across an important threshold. But there are clear moral as well as strategic differences between a decision to launch a limited campaign of air strikes against military targets, and a decision to launch a full-scale invasion. I have no doubt that a campaign of precisely targeted strikes against Iraqi WMD, provided that they could have been hit without too much risk to civilians, would have been entirely legitimate in the circumstances of 2003. An invasion was quite another matter.

The idea of preventive war is not itself a problem, but even if Saddam had had the WMD that the coalition leaders believed him to have, the invasion of Iraq was not justified as a response. Lesser military actions may have been.

HUMANITARIAN INTERVENTION

Since it became apparent that Iraq did not have substantial WMD capabilities, the principal justification for the invasion advanced by the US has relied on a version of the emerging doctrine of humanitarian intervention. Over the past decade, the scope for legitimate military action within another state's territory to prevent violence against individuals has been greatly expanded. How far that expansion can prudently be allowed to go remains a subject of debate. A Canadian-sponsored international commission has recently suggested some tests that might be applied to individual cases.[14] These tests include the immediacy and the seriousness of the threat of violence, whether non-military means are available to address the threat, the proportionality of the military action required to counter the threat, the balance of consequences (whether on balance military intervention would do more harm than good), and right intention (whether our motives are indeed humanitarian).

Does the invasion of Iraq meet these tests? The first issue relates to the nature of the humanitarian problem in Iraq. The threat to individuals under Saddam's regime was serious and immediate, but it was also long-established. The doctrine of humanitarian intervention had been conceived from the need to provide for a response to sudden emergencies like Rwanda, East Timor and Kosovo. There are clear humanitarian grounds for extending the doctrine to cover the violence perpetrated year in year out by stable and enduring oppressive regimes. But to do so would constitute a very significant extension of the doctrine. Could such an extension be justified? Is there a morally significant distinction between the slow, steady oppression of a whole population by a brutal authoritarian regime, and the sudden collapse of order which threatens immediate death or suffering to an entire population? I think there is. We are impelled to action in the paradigmatic cases of humanitarian intervention by a sudden catastrophe that simultaneously and immediately threatens whole populations. Iraq in 2003 was suffering from something quite different; no worse for the individuals immediately targeted by the regime's violence, but less disruptive for the bulk of the population. It was bad enough being an Iraqi in 2002, but not as bad as being a Tutsi in Rwanda in 1994, or a Kosovo Albanian in 1999.

It is important to remember that humanitarian intervention is an *obligation*, not a *right*. So the question is not whether the US and its allies would have been *right* to have invaded Iraq to liberate its people from Saddam; the question is whether they would have been *wrong* not to, as many people think we were wrong not to intervene in Rwanda to stop the killing. I think that would be a very hard argument to sustain, especially when we consider the scale of the obligation the US and its allies have taken on. One might be morally obliged to rescue a drowning child if one can do so without endangering one's own life, but one is not in the same way obliged to bring up and educate a destitute child. In the first case, the danger is sudden and immediate, and the assistance required is equally short term. In the second case, the danger is enduring, and the assistance required is equally enduring, and the burden (for that reason) much greater.

This leads into the second question about whether Operation Iraqi Freedom could have been justified as humanitarian intervention: the issue of proportionality. The sheer scale of the project—invading and occupying a substantial country, destroying its system of government, and establishing in its place a quite new state structure—goes way beyond the kinds of operations that have previously been contemplated under humanitarian intervention, even in the Balkans. If Saddam's regime had been engaged in systematic mass murder of a large proportion of its population, as the Khmer Rouge did in Cambodia in the 1970s, this kind of action might have been proportionate to the emergency, and therefore legitimate. But appalling as Saddam's regime undoubtedly was, he did not pose an immediate threat to Iraq's people on that scale.

And finally, of course, there is the question of right intention. No matter what is said by governments now, the historical record will not sustain an argument that the invasion really was undertaken primarily for humanitarian purposes. So, a retrospective justification of the decision to invade on these grounds does nothing to establish humanitarian intervention as a moral ground for that decision.

STRATEGIC INTERVENTION

The strangest thing about the decision to invade Iraq is that the least discussed rationale for the decision is probably the most significant in our judgement of the moral standing of the decision. It has been evident since before the event that the successive reasons put forward for the invasion do not capture the real motivation of the key decision makers. There has been a lot of instant history written already trying to unravel the strands of thinking that led to Iraq.[15] These provide a complex and at times contradictory picture of the ideas behind the decision. It will be several years at least before we have a complete enough picture, and enough detachment, to form a definite view. But we know enough already to describe the key ideas which principally motivated those who decided to invade Iraq. We might label this set of ideas the doctrine of strategic intervention.

During the 1990s a number of those who later became influential office holders in the Bush administration had developed a view that the proper goal of US strategic policy in the new century was to use American power, including US military power, to shape the world in ways which suited American interests by perpetuating US pre-eminence. This included removing regimes which did not share US interests and values. They believed that this was not only in America's interests, but the world's.

They believed that, with the end of the Cold War, American military pre-eminence meant that the US could use force to promote this objective at low cost and low risk. They came to view armed force as a natural and appropriate policy instrument for America to use in achieving its long-term policy goals. In this they moved away from more restrictive attitudes towards the use of force that had developed in liberal Western societies over the twentieth century, but which they tended to believe were primarily a reaction—or overreaction —to the Vietnam War.

This group concluded, long before Bush was elected, that in pursuit of these objectives America should give high priority to removing Saddam, if need be by force. Saddam's supposed possession of WMD was part of the reason for this but not the key reason, though they undoubtedly believed he did have an active WMD programme. They apparently believed that once Saddam was removed Iraq would easily develop a democratic, pro-Western government that would support US interests, and in particular would serve as a catalyst for the emergence of similar regimes in neighbouring countries.

After September 11 this pre-existing policy was transformed from an ambitious programme to promote American interests and values, to a defensive response to what they saw as an unprecedented attack on those interests and values. It is too early to say whether they really believed that Iraq and its WMD was the biggest threat to the US and therefore the highest priority in the 'War on Terror', or whether they promoted this argument to gain support for a policy which they were convinced was in America's broader interests. Perhaps they were not sure themselves. But whether cynically or sincerely, the situation after September 11 was interpreted in ways that justified a policy whose real origins lay much further back.

This powerful but radical set of ideas met relatively weak resistance among other members of the Bush administration, the wider US policy community and public opinion. This reflected the political and personal drive of the proponents of the invasion. But it also reflected the fact that many in Washington and beyond shared or sympathised with some of the key underlying ideas. Many more agreed that September 11 justified and perhaps demanded some kind of exceptional response that went beyond the boundaries of orthodox policy—and there were no alternative radical ideas on offer. And most, as always, simply followed the loudest drum.[16]

These are the ideas which underpin the Bush administration's National Security Strategy. It has been described by many, with some justice, as an imperial concept. If it lasts, it would constitute the most radical reorientation of US national strategy since the doctrine of containment was adopted at the start of the Cold War. On practical policy grounds, I do not believe that it is a sustainable strategic posture for the US. But the question here is whether this set of policy ideas could constitute the basis for legitimate use of military force. Prima facie, the answer must be no. The guiding idea behind strategic intervention is that America can and will use armed force to shape the world to suit American interests. I am not necessarily uncomfortable with the objective: it is true that America's example has much to offer the world, and that a Middle East transformed into a peaceful community of liberal democracies would be a better place for everyone. The problem is the means: the use of force to achieve these goals.

This approach to the use of force seems to me to be entirely at odds with the ethical principles about resort to force in international relations that have evolved in Western liberal societies over the past two centuries, and which have been embodied in key international norms and institutions during the twentieth century. The key to those principles and norms is the rejection of force as an instrument of policy except in the immediate defence of lives, territory and a stable international order against violence by others. The idea behind strategic intervention is that America should use force to build a better world—and a better world for America. If everyone had that right, the result would be anarchy. So no one would propose that this is a doctrine that could be applied universally. Arguments in support of it must therefore rely on the concept of American exceptionalism.

Three arguments of this kind have been advanced in defence of this revolutionary policy. First, there is an argument that America can be trusted to use force more often, and to achieve wider objectives, than other countries because it is, morally, better than other countries.[17] To many Americans, apparently including President Bush, this proposition is almost literally self-evident. Even to more sceptical minds, this argument cannot be dismissed out of hand. For the last 100 years at least, the US has been overwhelmingly a force for good in the world, and much that is good in today's world is the product of the fortuitous combination of American power and American principles. We might wonder what the twentieth century would have looked like without them.

But what are the sources of this moral strength? American political rhetoric today would have us believe that it springs from the inherent goodness of the American people. America's founding fathers knew better: they distrusted individuals and put their faith in strong institutions. If there is a rational basis for thinking that America can be trusted to use power more wisely than other countries, it is that America's institutions can be trusted to ensure that US policies are more reliably sensible—and moral—than other powerful countries' policies have proven to be throughout history. The strength of American institutions is the intense contestability of policy within the government system. Ideas of all kinds are subject to relentless scrutiny and debate, and in the process most of the bad ones are thrown out, and what remains are generally pretty good.

But the system is not infallible, and Iraq demonstrates how failures can happen. I think history will judge that Washington's decision making on Iraq represented a failure of contestability. The fact that the real reasons for invading Iraq have not been properly presented and debated in America is itself a failure of the political processes on which the doctrine of strategic intervention relies. There are several reasons for that failure: the political and emotional impact of September 11, the personal and political strength of the advocates of the invasion, the relative weakness of other key players, and at the heart of the process a president who does not seem actively to shape decisions. That does not mean America will not get most things right in the future, as it has in the past. It does mean US policy processes are fallible, just like everyone else's. No grounds for exceptionalism here.

The second argument advanced, since September 11, to justify a policy of strategic intervention by the US is that America is uniquely threatened by global terrorism and therefore needs to be granted wider latitude than other countries in responding to that threat. This claim suffers from two weaknesses. First, the threat of terrorism, serious though it is, is not as serious as the threats America has faced before, and which were not thought at the time to justify revolutionary expansions of the right to use armed force. What is called the 'War on Terror' has been compared to, and even described as more serious than, World War II and the Cold War in the scale of threat it poses to the US and its society. That does not seem sustainable: even the very real risk of nuclear terrorism against American cities is not as bad as the threat of global nuclear war which America, and the rest of us, lived with for decades before 1989. How quickly we forget. In retrospect we may downplay the risk because in the end it didn't happen, but the risk was very real. Those who see the new terrorism as raising unprecedented dangers are suffering from what Owen Harries has called the 'parochialism of the present', the beguiling belief that what is happening to us is more important than anything that has ever happened before, and of unique historical significance.

The second weakness in the claim that terrorism justifies an expanded role for US military power is that there is no evidence that the extensive use of armed force will help to reduce the threat of terrorism to America. Sometimes it can: military operations in Afghanistan in 2001 helped to disrupt al-Qaeda and were justifiable on these grounds. But no compelling argument has been advanced that removing Saddam would directly damage al-Qaeda or its affiliates, or directly reduce the risk of terrorism to the US. The arguments that support the Iraq invasion as a way to tackle terrorism rely on the claim that a free and democratic Iraq would help to transform the Middle East in ways which would make terrorism less likely in future, or that a demonstration of US resolve would discourage America's enemies. Perhaps, but the arguments for the contrary positions are equally compelling. Either way, it is hard to support the claim that the US has a special right to use force to combat terrorism if the use of force is not effective in doing so.

Third, it can be argued that the US has a right to use force more broadly than others because it has the power to do so. A recent commentary, apparently without irony, compared America's military superiority over any possible adversary with those of Homeric gods over mortals.[18] At first blush, the suggestion that this power gives the US special rights sounds like an unadulterated assertion of the right of power, in the finest Athenian tradition. But, as always, more sophisticated arguments can be marshalled to support the assertion.[19] However, there is no need to go into those arguments in detail, because the claim fails the first test of factual accuracy. US military power is very substantial and, in some respects, unprecedented. But it is not overwhelming in every field of military operations. America's capacity to dominate the sea, to destroy targets from the air and to conduct land force operations against opposing conventional armed forces is indeed overwhelming. Its abilities to control territory and populations, to fight insurgent campaigns, and to locate and identify critical targets in other countries are modest.

These critical deficiencies are clearly demonstrated by the problems the US is experiencing in Iraq. There is a tendency to blame these problems on poor planning, too few troops, or to discrete and avoidable errors like failing to prevent the looting after Baghdad fell. That is a misunderstanding: America's problems in Iraq arise from the very nature of the enterprise. More troops and better plans would not have removed the basic sources of the insurgency, nor done much to improve America's ability to contain it. These deficiencies revealed in Iraq are inherent in the nature of US power. They critically limit America's capacity to achieve the kind of ambitious political objectives that the more expansive trend in US strategic thinking has set for its armed forces. Olympian military superiority is a myth. The claim to Olympian rights to use that power vanishes with it.

America is an exceptional country, but I do not think the case can be made for the kind of moral exceptionalism that would be required to sustain the doctrine of strategic intervention as a basis for just war. I think for this reason, and because it is based on unrealistic assessments of US military capability, global tolerance and domestic public support, the imperial phase of American policy will not outlast the harsh realities of Iraq. Indeed, I think it will be seen as an unfortunate aberration.

CONCLUSION

It will be evident that I do not believe there is a moral case to be made for the decision to invade Iraq. The decision was made on insufficient grounds and with insufficient care, and presented with less frankness than the weight of the issue required. But I do not think that makes America a bad country, or its rulers bad people. Nor do I think the Australian decision, with its parallel reasoning, should produce a similarly jaundiced total verdict on us. In 'The Sources of Soviet Conduct', George Kennan quoted Edward Gibbon as follows:

> From enthusiasm to imposture the step is perilous and slippery; the demon of Socrates affords a memorable instance how a wise man may deceive himself, a good man may deceive others, and the conscience may slumber in a mixed and muddled state between self illusion and voluntary fraud.[20]

4 COLLECTIVE RESPONSIBILITY AND ARMED HUMANITARIAN INTERVENTION

SEUMAS MILLER

In recent times there have been a number of armed humanitarian interventions by nation-states in conflicts taking place within the borders of other nation-states. Here one thinks of Bosnia, Kosovo, Somalia, Rwanda and East Timor. In some instances, such as Rwanda, armed intervention was evidently morally justified; however, the armed forces deployed were inadequate and/or arrived far too late. In other instances, such as Kosovo, armed intervention might have been justified and timely, but arguably the force deployed was excessive, or at least of the wrong form.[1]

The first general point to be made here is that at least *some* armed humanitarian interventions are morally justified. Consider the case of Rwanda. According to Fergal Keane, in Rwanda after the deaths in a plane crash of the Rwandan and Burundian presidents on 6 April 1994 an orchestrated programme of genocide took place: 'In the ensuing 100 days up to one million people were hacked, strangled, clubbed and burned to death'.[2] The genocide in Rwanda, and like cases, constitutes a decisive objection to the claim that armed humanitarian intervention is *never* morally justified. Moreover, cases such as

East Timor appear to demonstrate that armed humanitarian intervention can be successful. On the other hand, the experience of cases such as Bosnia shows that even if armed intervention is justified, the situation on the ground needs to be adequately understood if that intervention is to be successful. Evidently, the United Nations failed to understand that the war in Bosnia was in large part genocidal and directed at the civilian population. So interventionist methods aimed only at keeping groups of combatants from getting at one another were inadequate; such methods cannot and did not protect the civilian populations.[3]

The second general point concerns the nature of the justification. The fundamental justification for armed humanitarian intervention is that genocide, or other large-scale human rights violations, are taking place, and armed intervention is the only way to put an end to it. This is a moral justification. So also are the justifications offered by the United States and its allies in relation to the recent Iraqi invasion, namely the so-called 'Weapons of Mass Destruction' (WMD) and 'Regime Change' arguments. The prevention of the use of nuclear, chemical and biological weapons is self-evidently a moral imperative. And the 'Regime Change' argument was presented principally in terms of the cessation of Saddam Hussein's ongoing violation of the moral rights of the Iraqi people.

Perhaps there can be decisive political or military justifications for armed interventions. Moreover, such non-moral justifications are not necessarily inconsistent with moral justifications; in some cases, armed intervention might be politically expedient as well as being morally justified. Some have argued as much in relation to the recent invasion of Iraq and the overthrow of the Saddam Hussein regime.[4] In practice, armed interventions are likely to be motivated by a complex mix of moral, political, military, economic and other considerations. However, my point pertains to good and decisive justifications: I claim that the *fundamental* justification for armed humanitarian interventions is a moral justification. Note that military success (and ultimately some form of political success) is presupposed by such a moral justification.

Granted the existence of this general moral justification for armed humanitarian intervention, at least four further questions arise.

First, should the armed intervention be undertaken by any nation-state or states that happen to have the wherewithal to prosecute it successfully, or should it be undertaken only with the participation, or at least consent, of the international community? Second, should the notion of large-scale human rights violations be a very narrow notion and therefore restricted to, say, genocide, or should it be relatively wide and embrace, say, authoritarian rule? Third, should the intervention go only so far as to terminate the rights violations that triggered it; or should it involve taking preventive measures in relation to possible future rights violations by the perpetrators, or indeed by the erstwhile victims?[5] Fourth, what form should the armed intervention take? For example, should aerial bombing—as opposed to, say, the use of ground troops—be the principal tactic?

My own view in relation to the first question is as follows. The moral responsibility to intervene is a collective moral responsibility —it is the collective responsibility of members of the international community to combat large-scale human rights violations taking place inside states whose governments are unwilling or unable to terminate those rights violations. (Indeed, the internal government might be the one perpetrating the rights violations.) Moreover, broad-based, multilateral interventions are less likely to serve the interests of any one state, or small group of states, and are therefore more likely to be motivated by genuine humanitarian, rather than purely political, considerations. Nevertheless, since the moral priority is to bring about the cessation of the rights violations—rather than merely determine who ought to be the one or ones to terminate it—then unilateral intervention might be justified in cases in which the international community is unwilling to act. (Here I am setting aside the admittedly relevant issue of the legality of unilateral interventions; a central concern in relation to, for example, the 2003 invasion of Iraq by US-led forces.)

In relation to the second question, I hold that the understanding of large-scale human rights violations should be narrow in that it should involve only those violations of the most morally despicable kind. Here I distinguish, first, between rights violations and injustice. Injustice does not provide an adequate justification for armed intervention. Second, I distinguish—admittedly somewhat arbitrarily—

between violations of the right to life and the right to personal security, on the one hand, and violations of other rights, such as the right to political liberty, on the other hand. The former, but not the latter, justify armed intervention. So genocide, but not necessarily authoritarian governance, justifies armed intervention.

However, the appropriate notion of large-scale human rights violations is wide in the sense that it should not be restricted to violations of so-called negative rights, such as the right not to be killed, but also to some positive rights, such as the right to a basic subsistence. Consider the case of an autocrat who for political purposes was deliberately refraining from the provision of basic medicine and foodstuffs to some needy element in his state.[6] In such cases there might be an in-principle justification for armed intervention. Why armed intervention? Because the nation-state in question is refraining from providing for the subsistence rights of its citizens.

In relation to the third question, I hold that interventions where possible should be preventive and therefore should not necessarily be restricted to the termination of occurrent rights violations. I acknowledge the dangers attendant upon permitting intervention in relation to future, and therefore only potential, human rights violations. Perhaps the recent US-led invasion of Iraq will prove to be a telling example of such dangers. It now appears that Saddam Hussein did not have the arsenal of WMD that the US and UK leadership led the world to believe he had.

Nevertheless, where a process of large-scale human rights violations has commenced, then intervention seems to me to be justified, at least in principle. Moreover, where it is clear, post-intervention, that the process of rights violations would recommence were the intervening armed forces to retire, then the continued presence of the intervening armed forces—jointly acting with civilians engaged in a programme of reconciliation and reconstitution of civil society —might also be justified.

I cannot here give a definitive answer to the fourth question beyond endorsing in general terms the *jus in bello* principles of just war theory. These principles are to the effect that: the armed force used should be the minimum necessary force; it should be proportionate; and it should be effective.[7] It has been argued that if

NATO had used ground troops in Kosovo, then some of these ground troops would have been killed, but the extent of the death of civilians and the destruction of property would have been much less. If so, from the perspective of just war theory, NATO should have used ground troops—assuming armed intervention in some form was justified. For the lives of one's own soldiers do not have a greater moral value than the lives of the innocent people one's armed forces have been deployed to protect.[8]

At any rate, I want to explore the notion of collective moral responsibility as it pertains both to nation-states contemplating humanitarian armed intervention in a variety of settings involving states or groups perpetrating human rights violations. I do so on the assumption that such interventions are the collective moral responsibility of the community of nation-states. I will further assume that humanitarian armed intervention is cross border use of armed forces, or the threat of such use, by a state or states for the purpose (though not necessarily the sole purpose) of protecting basic rights. Such intervention can be with or without the consent of the government of the state whose border is to be crossed, and it can include direct attacks on the armed forces of that government, as well as the deployment of armed forces to protect safe havens, ensure that food or other aid is distributed properly, and so on.

COLLECTIVE MORAL RESPONSIBILITY

For my purposes here I need to clarify the key notion of collective moral responsibility.[9]

Collective moral responsibility for good or evil has two main forms. First, there is collective moral responsibility for *actions*. Second, there is collective moral responsibility for *omissions*. Both actions and omissions can constitute rights violations. Moreover, rights violations, if they are sufficiently serious and on a sufficiently large scale, can generate a moral responsibility on the part of third parties to intervene to prevent or contain such violations. Moreover, where such third parties can or must act collectively to successfully intervene, the moral responsibility to intervene might be a *collective* moral responsibility.

The notion of collective responsibility is often given a collectivist, as opposed to an individualist, rendering. There are a number of collectivist philosophical theories of collective responsibility. These include the theories of David Cooper and Peter French.[10] On these views, a collective entity can be morally responsible for some outcome, even though few, if any, of the individual members of the entity are individually morally responsible. In the light of this and related problems, I will defend an individualist account of collective moral responsibility.

My suggestion is that collective moral responsibility can be regarded as a species of joint responsibility, or at least one central kind of collective moral responsibility can be so regarded.

Here we need to distinguish four senses of collective responsibility. In the first instance I will do so in relation to joint actions. What is a joint action? Roughly speaking, two or more individuals perform a joint action if each of them intentionally performs an individual action, but does so in the true belief that in so doing they will jointly realise an end which each of them has. Having an end in this sense is a mental state for one or more individuals, but it is neither a desire nor an intention. However, it is an end that is not realised by one individual acting alone. So we have called such ends, collective ends.

Consider the murder of 8000 Muslim men by Serbian soldiers in the UN-designated 'safe area' of Srebrenica in Bosnia in July 1995. The Serbian forces bombed and then took the town of Srebrenica, after NATO had failed to support the UN force 'protecting' the town. The Serbian soldiers then hunted down and murdered any Muslim men that they could find. Here was planned and orchestrated ethnic cleansing and mass murder in the service of ethnically pure territorial units and Serbian nationalism. There was joint action at a number of levels, but let us consider the alleged actions of a group of soldiers on the ground who were purportedly dressed as UN peacekeepers and driving stolen white UN vehicles. These Serbian soldiers guaranteed the Muslims' safety. They would then shoot them.[11] This is joint action. Some soldiers are driving the vehicle, another is looking for Muslims, then some of the Serbian soldiers are talking to the Muslims to convince them that they are safe. Finally, some of the Serbian soldiers shoot the Muslims dead. The soldiers co-ordinated their individual actions in the service of a collective end. Each performed a contributory action, or actions, in the service of the collective end of bringing about the death of the Muslim men.

Agents who perform a joint action are responsible for that action in the first sense of collective responsibility. Accordingly, to say that they are collectively responsible for the action is just to say that they performed the joint action. That is, they each had a collective end, each intentionally performed their contributory action, and each did so because each believed the other would perform his contributory action, and that therefore the collective end would be realised.

Here it is important to note that each agent is individually (naturally) responsible for performing his contributory action, and responsible by virtue of the fact that he intentionally performed this action, and the action was not intentionally performed by anyone else. Of course, the other agents (or agent) *believe* that he is performing, or is going to perform, the contributory action in question. But mere possession of such a belief is not sufficient for the ascription of responsibility to *the believer* for performing the individual action in question. So what are the agents *collectively* (naturally) responsible for? The agents are collectively (naturally) responsible for the realisation of the (collective) *end* which results from their contributory actions.

Further, on my account to say that they are collectively (naturally) responsible for the realisation of the collective end of a joint action is to say that they are jointly responsible for the realisation of that end. They are jointly responsible because: (a) each relied on the other to bring about the state of affairs aimed at by both (the collective end); and (b) each performed their contributory action on condition, and only on condition, that the other(s) performed theirs. Here condition (b) expresses the *interdependence* involved in joint action.

Again, if the occupants of an institutional role (or roles) have an institutionally determined obligation to perform some joint action, then those individuals are collective responsible for its performance, in our second sense of collective responsibility. Here there is a *joint* institutional obligation to realise the collective end of the joint action in question. In addition, there is a set of derived *individual* obligations; each of the participating individuals has an individual obligation to perform his/her contributory action. (The derivation of these individual obligations relies on the fact that if each performs his/her contributory action, then it is probable that the collective end will be realised.)

The *joint* institutional obligation is a composite obligation consisting of the obligation each of us has to perform a certain specified action in order to realise that end. More precisely, one agent has the obligation to realise a collective end by means of doing some action, believing that another agent has performed some other action for that very same end. The point about joint obligations is that they are not discharged by one person acting alone.

Notice that typically agents involved in an institutional joint action will discharge their respective individual institutional obligations and their joint institutional obligations by the performance of one and the same set of individual actions. For example, if each of the members of a task force seeking out war criminals performs his individual duties having as an end the locating of a war criminal, then, given favourable conditions, the task force will locate the war criminal. But one can imagine an investigating agent who recognises his individual institutional obligation, but not his jointly held obligation to realise the collective end in question. This investigator might have an overriding individual end to get himself promoted; but the head of the task force might be ahead of him in the queue of those to be promoted. So the investigator does not have locating the war criminal as a collective end. Accordingly, while he ensures that he discharges his individual obligation to (say) interview a particular suspect, the investigator is less assiduous than he might otherwise be because he wants the task force to fail to locate the war criminal.

There is a third putative sense of collective responsibility. This third sense of individual responsibility concerns those in authority. Here we need to distinguish two kinds of case. If the occupant of an institutional role has an institutionally determined right or obligation to order other agents to perform certain actions, and the actions in question are joint actions, then the occupant of the role is *individually* (institutionally) responsible for those joint actions performed by those other agents. This is our first kind of case; but it should be set aside, since it is not an instance of *collective* responsibility.

In the second kind of case, it is of no consequence whether the actions performed by those under the direction of the person in authority were joint actions or not. Rather, the issue concerns the actions of those in authority. In what sense are they collective? Suppose the members of NATO collectively decide to exercise their institutionally determined right to direct NATO forces to bomb Kosovo and not to use ground troops. The British wanted to use ground troops, the Americans and others did not. The Greeks did not want the bombing of Serbian civilian targets. At any rate, 'there was a clear and powerful majority in favour of air strikes'.[12] Moreover, NATO ordered this action in the absence of a positive ruling from the UN Security Council. Accordingly, NATO forces bombed Kosovo. So the members of NATO are collectively responsible for the bombing of Kosovo. They are also collectively responsible for ignoring UN protocols.

There are a couple of things to keep in mind here. First, the notion of responsibility in question here is, at least in the first instance, institutional—as opposed to moral—responsibility.

Second, the 'decisions' of committees, as opposed to the individual decisions of the members of committees, need to be analysed in terms of the notion of a joint institutional mechanism. So the 'decision' of NATO can be analysed as follows. At one level, each member of NATO voted for or against the bombing of Kosovo; and let us assume some voted in the affirmative, and others in the negative. But, at another level, each member of NATO agreed to abide by the outcome of the vote; each voted having as a collective end that the outcome with a majority of the votes in its favour would be pursued. Accordingly, the members of NATO were jointly institutionally responsible for the decision to order the NATO forces to bomb Kosovo. So NATO was collectively institutionally responsible for bombing Kosovo; and the sense of collective responsibility in question is *joint* (institutional) responsibility.[13]

What of the fourth sense of collective responsibility: collective *moral* responsibility? Collective moral responsibility is a species of joint responsibility. Accordingly, each agent is individually morally responsible, but conditionally on the others being individually morally responsible; there is interdependence in respect of moral responsibility. This account of collective moral responsibility arises naturally out of the account of joint actions. It also parallels the account given of individual moral responsibility.

Thus we can make the following claim about moral responsibility. If agents are collectively responsible for the realisation of an outcome, in the first or second or third senses of collective responsibility, and if the outcome is morally significant then, other things being equal, the agents are collectively morally responsible for that outcome and can reasonably attract moral praise or blame, and (possibly) punishment or reward for bringing about the outcome.

Here we need to be more precise about what agents who perform morally significant joint actions are collectively morally responsible for. Other things being equal, each agent who intentionally performs a morally significant *individual* action has *individual* moral responsibility for the action. So, in the case of a morally significant joint action, each agent is *individually* morally responsible for performing *his contributory* action, and the other agents are not morally responsible for his individual contributory action. But, in addition, the contributing agents are *collectively* morally responsible for the outcome or *collective end* of their various contributory actions. To say that they are collectively morally responsible for bringing about this (collective) end is just to say that they are *jointly* morally responsible for it. So each agent is individually morally responsible for realising this (collective) end, but conditionally on the others being individually morally responsible for realising it as well. So, in the Srebrenica example, a number of male Muslim villagers were lined up and shot by a number of Serbian soldiers. So Serbian soldier A might be individually morally responsible for shooting Muslim villagers X, Y and Z, soldier B for shooting villagers X, Y and Z, and so on for soldiers C, D. Suppose that, while X, Y and Z were shot dead, no single soldier fired any shots which were sufficient to kill any villager. Nevertheless, A, B, C and D are jointly morally responsible for the murder of villagers X, Y and Z.

Moreover, whatever the reason why each came to have the collective end in question, once each had come to have that collective end then there was interdependence of action. That is, each played his role in the massacre only on condition the others played their role. So the full set of actions performed by the individual members of the murderous group of Serbian soldiers can be regarded as *the means* by which the collective end was realised; and each individual contributory action was a *part of* that means. Moreover, in virtue of interdependence, each individual action is an integral part of the means to the collective end. Accordingly, all of the members of the group of soldiers are jointly, and therefore collectively, morally responsible for the massacre. For each performed an action in the service of that (collective) end, and each of these actions was an integral part of the means to that end.

Note the following residual points. First, it is not definitive of joint action that each perform his/her contributory action on the condition, and only on the condition, that *all* of the rest of the others perform theirs. Rather, it is sufficient that each perform his/her contributory action on the condition, and only on the condition, that *most* of the others perform theirs. So the interdependence involved in joint action is not necessarily *complete* interdependence. Nevertheless, if the action of one agent (or more than one agent) is not interdependent with *any* of the actions of the other agents, then the action of that first agent (or agents) is not part of the joint action. So, if one (or more) of the members of the group of soldiers in fact performed his action independently of the rest, and if the rest performed their actions independently of that one agent, then the action of the latter would not be part of the joint action. The action of the latter agent would not be part of the means to the *collective* end, and the agent could not be said to have had the death of all of the male Muslim villagers as a *collective* end.

Second, if an action is a means to some end, and if the action is sufficient for the realisation of that end, then the agent who performed the action has (natural) responsibility for bringing about the end. So the fact that the outcome in question might be over-determined by virtue of the existence of some second action performed by some second agent does not remove the responsibility of the first agent for the outcome in question.

Likewise we can conceive of two joint actions, each of which is sufficient for the same outcome. Here there are two independent actions, albeit two joint actions, performed by the members of two separate groups, respectively; and each of these (joint) actions is sufficient for some outcome. Just as the two individuals are both morally responsible for the outcome of their individual actions, so are the members of both of the two groups morally responsible for the two envisaged joint actions. The only difference is that in the former case each of the individuals is *individually* responsible for the outcome, whereas in the latter case the members of the first of the two groups are *jointly* responsible for the outcome in question, as are the members of the second group.

Third, an agent has moral responsibility if his action was intentionally performed in order to realise a morally significant collective end, and the action causally contributed to the end. The action does not have to be a necessary condition, or even a necessary part of a sufficient condition, for the realisation of the end. Fourth, agents who intentionally make a causal contribution in order to realise a morally significant collective end are not necessarily fully morally responsible for the end realised.

The second problem in relation to collective moral responsibility for actions arises in the context of the actions of large groups and organisations.

At this point, the notion of a layered structure of joint actions needs to be introduced. Suppose a number of 'actions' are performed in order to realise some collective end. Call the resulting joint action a *level two* joint action. Suppose, in addition, that each of the component individual 'actions' of this level two joint 'action' is itself, at least in part, a joint action with a second set of component individual actions. And suppose the member actions of this second set have the performance of this level two 'action' as their collective end. Call the joint action composed of the members of this second set of actions a *level one* joint action. An illustration of the notion of a layered structure of joint actions is in fact an army fighting a battle. At level one we have a number of joint actions. Consider the Croat forces attacking the Serbs in Knin in Croatia in Operation Storm on 4 August 1995. This was the turning point in the Croat–Serbian confrontation.[14] The Croat forces included artillery as well as ground troops. However, they were supported by NATO forces that bombed

Serbian communications systems, thereby greatly facilitating the progress of the Croat ground forces. So there are two level one joint actions. Now, each of these two (level one) joint actions is itself describable as an *individual* action performed (respectively) by the different military groups, namely, the action of bombing the communication systems and the action of overrunning and occupying the town. However, each of these 'individual' actions is part of a larger joint action directed to the collective end of winning the battle against the Serbian force. Each of these individual attacks on the position is part of a larger plan co-ordinated by the NATO and Croat commands. So these 'individual' actions constitute a *level two* joint action directed to the collective end of winning the battle.

Accordingly, if all, or most, of the individual actions of the members of the NATO force and of the Croat army were performed in accordance with collective ends, and the performance of each of the resulting level one joint actions was itself performed in accordance with the collective end of winning the battle, then, at least in principle, we could ascribe joint moral responsibility for winning the battle to the individual pilots of the NATO air force and to the individual members of the Croat army.[15]

At any rate, the upshot of this discussion is that agents involved in complex co-operative enterprises can, *at least in principle*, be ascribed collective or *joint natural* responsibility for the outcomes aimed at by those enterprises; and, in cases of morally significant enterprises, they can be ascribed collective or *joint moral* responsibility for those outcomes. This conclusion depends on the possibility of analysing these enterprises in terms of layered structures of joint action.

COLLECTIVE MORAL RESPONSIBILITY TO INTERVENE

Let us now turn to collective moral responsibility to intervene, and specifically to intervene in cases of large-scale human rights violations. Henry Shue has argued for the existence of what he terms basic moral rights.[16] These include the right to security, and certain so-called positive rights, such as the right to subsistence. He argues that these basic rights generate rights to protection and assistance. I accept Shue's arguments.

With the establishment of the nation-state, and specifically of policing institutions, the responsibility for protecting and assisting those whose life or security is threatened from within a society has to a large extent devolved to the police. When these rights are externally threatened, it is the military institutions of the state that bear the responsibility. So the state has a special responsibility to protect and assist its own citizens when there are either internal or external threats to their basic rights. So far so good, but what are we to say about cases in which the state is no longer willing or able to protect the rights to security of its citizens? Indeed, in some of these cases, the state is itself the source of the threat. The Rwandan genocide is one such case.

Shue has persuasively argued that the state has obligations other than the obligation to promote the interests of its citizens.[17] Specifically, the state has an obligation not to unduly harm citizens of other states. Examples of such obligations include the obligation not to attack other states purely for economic gain, the obligation not to deplete the ozone layer by destroying forests, and so on. Here I want to go further and suggest that the state not only has moral obligations not to harm citizens of other states, it also has moral obligations to assist and protect the rights of citizens of other states. Specifically, it has these obligations when three general conditions are met: (1) the rights in question are basic moral rights, such as the right to security; (2) the state in which rights violations are occurring is not willing or able to protect these rights; and (3) another state is able to protect these rights, whether by unilateral intervention, or by collective intervention with other states and/or local or international non-government organisations.

So, under certain conditions, basic moral rights generate moral responsibilities on the part of nation-states to intervene in the affairs of other states. Earlier I suggested that such basic moral rights are not restricted to so-called negative rights; rather, they include some so-called positive rights, for example the right to subsistence. Accordingly, armed intervention might be justified in a case in which a state is refraining from providing for the basic material needs of its citizens, or more likely a section of its citizenry. Let us consider some simple examples to test our intuitions for this theoretical claim.

Consider a destitute African person who is dying of HIV/AIDS, and who goes to a pharmaceutical company demanding drugs to enable him to live. When he is refused, on the grounds that he must pay for the highly priced drugs, he threatens to kill one by one the company managers responsible for the high price. Assume further that it is common knowledge that the drug could be produced cheaply, but that the company wants to guarantee its high profits and is therefore refusing to allow cheap production of the drug.

Intuitively, the AIDS sufferer's action seems morally justified, given that this action was the only way to preserve his life and the bystander could have assisted at little or no cost to himself. For the sufferer had a positive right to be assisted, and the bystander was refraining from carrying out his duty to respect that right. So the case is analogous to those involving negative rights, such as the right not to be killed, or the right not to have one's freedom interfered with.

So deadly force can in principle be used to enforce some positive rights, including presumably rights to subsistence, as well as to enforce negative rights such as freedom or the right not to be killed. Here we are assuming the usual principles of proportionate and minimally necessary force; deadly force should be used only as a last resort and loss of life kept to a minimum. Moreover, as is the case with negative rights, third parties—at least in principle—have rights, and indeed duties, to use deadly force to ensure that positive rights such as subsistence rights are respected.

Consider a modified version of the above HIV/AIDS scenario. In this version, the AIDS sufferer is a young African boy dying in his bed, and it is his father who threatens the pharmaceutical managers with deadly force—indeed, kills one of the managers to get the drugs to save his son. So deadly force can in principle be used to enforce positive rights, including presumably rights to subsistence, as well as to enforce negative rights.

This point has implications for governments who intentionally refrain from respecting the positive rights, including subsistence rights, of their citizens. For governments have a clear institutional responsibility to provide for the wellbeing of their citizens. Accordingly, the moral responsibility based on need—and the fact that those in government could assist if they chose to—is buttressed by this institutional responsibility that they have voluntarily taken on.

Consider the example of blacks in apartheid South Africa who were forcibly removed into desolate 'homelands', such as Qua Qua, and once there found they could not provide themselves with a basic subsistence. Now suppose that South African politicians declare such 'homelands' to be independent nation-states (as in fact happened) and thereby try to absolve themselves and their administrators from their pre-existing institutional responsibility for the wellbeing of the 'citizens' of these alleged new states. Since the 'states' were not legitimate —and were not in fact internationally recognised as legitimate— these politicians and other officials did not succeed in absolving themselves from their institutional responsibility. Accordingly, the armed intervention on the part of the African National Congress (ANC), with or without the assistance of third parties such as surrounding African states, might well have been justified.

The justification for armed intervention in the South African case is of the same general type as that used in relation to armed intervention to prevent genocidal slaughter in, say, Rwanda. The justification is that such a government is engaged in large-scale human rights violations, and the rights in question are basic rights. The fact that in some cases the rights are negative, and in other cases positive, is not a consideration of sufficient moral weight that armed intervention is justified in the former case, but not the latter.

In the light of this discussion, let us assume that under certain conditions large-scale violations of basic rights, including violations of some so-called positive rights, generate a moral responsibility on the part of external states to intervene militarily to terminate those rights violations. Why is this moral responsibility a *collective* moral responsibility? It is a collective moral responsibility because the notion of a state in question, that is a state that *intervenes*, is the notion of a collective agent.

Moreover, in so far as a state contemplating armed intervention is a hierarchical complex comprising a government and a military force, then its real and putative 'actions' can be understood as a layered structure of actions (as discussed earlier). So in this sense the government and the military are collectively morally responsible for intervening or failing to intervene.

At this point, a further question arises. This is the question as to whether or not there is a collective responsibility to intervene in the sense that the community of nations has a collective moral responsibility to intervene. In the light of our above analysis of collective responsibility, this question amounts to asking whether or not each member of the community has an in-principle moral responsibility to intervene militarily in cases of large-scale human rights violations, and this responsibility is possessed jointly with the other nation-states.

Let us first take a closer look at the collective responsibility to intervene to terminate, reduce or prevent rights violations. The failure to discharge such a collective responsibility constitutes a morally culpable act of omission. This is because the following three conditions exist: (1) the wrong being done, or about to be done, is such that someone ought to intervene, and those on whom the collective responsibility to intervene falls are in a position to successfully intervene; (2) those who have the collective responsibility to intervene have that responsibility by virtue of the nature and extent of the wrongdoing as well as an institutional obligation that they have taken upon themselves; and (3) the cost to be incurred as a consequence of intervening is not prohibitively high.

Moreover, the persons whose rights are being violated have a right to the collective action which it is the collective responsibility of the putative interveners to perform. Not only is the failure to intervene a morally culpable omission, but those who need the intervention to take place have a moral right to intervention.

Here we need some theoretical account of culpable collective responsibility for omissions. I suggest that members of some group or community are collectively morally responsible for failing to intervene to halt or prevent some serious wrongdoing or wrongful state of affairs if: (1) the wrongdoing took place, or is taking place; (2) the members of the group intentionally refrained from intervening; (3) each or most of the members intervening, having as a (collective) end the prevention of the wrongdoing, probably would have prevented, or have a reasonable chance of halting, the wrongdoing, and the cost of so intervening would not have been prohibitively high; (4) each of the members of the group would have intentionally refrained from intervening—and intervening having as an end the prevention or termination of the wrongdoing—even if the others, or most of the others, had intervened with that end in mind; or (5) the members of the group had a collective institutional responsibility to intervene. Note that on this account, if an agent would have intervened, but done so only because the others did (i.e. not because he had as an end the prevention or termination of the wrong), then the agent would still be morally responsible, jointly with the others, for failing to intervene (given conditions 1–3).

The first thing to note in relation to this account of collective moral responsibility for omissions is that it presupposes a community or group that could act together, if they chose to do so, in order to realise a collective end. I take it that the international community is such a community for the following reasons (at least).

First, there is a high level of mutual awareness, including by way of the international mass media and through the work of international groups, such as Amnesty International, that monitor human rights violations, of large-scale human rights violations. So each nation-state is aware of any episode of such violations, and each is aware that everyone else is aware, and so on; there is mutual awareness.

Second, there is a high level of economic and political interdependence across nation-states. They constitute a community in the sense that the interests, and therefore political and economic policies, of any one nation-state are interdependent, and interdependent in the long term, with those of other nation-states. As such, they have a raft of common problems, including the strength of the global economy, the quality of the environment, the preservation of international security (especially in the context of weapons of mass destruction), the reduction of international crime, and so on. In the contemporary setting, national isolationism makes no sense.

Third, a set of international institutions has been developed in relation to the actions of nation-states. These include the UN, the World Trade Organisation (WTO) and various pieces of international legislation and associated international courts. Indeed, there are rules and international institutional mechanisms for armed intervention in relation to genocide.

So, in the contemporary world, there is a *community* of nation-states. The only question is what the moral standards governing the actions of that community ought to be. Is it to be a *moral* community? Protection of basic human rights constitutes the minimum moral standard for human interaction. No political community, international or otherwise, can tolerate large-scale human rights violations and intelligibly conceive of itself as a moral community. But this is just to say that members of any political community have a collective moral responsibility to terminate or prevent such violations if they possibly can and if the costs of so doing are not prohibitively high. It follows that the members of the international community have a collective moral responsibility to terminate or prevent such violations if they possibly can and the costs of so doing are not prohibitively high.

I take it to be self-evident that there are instances of large-scale human rights violations that the actions of the members of the international community could terminate or prevent at relatively small cost to themselves, if they acted together having as a (collective) end the termination or prevention of those rights violations. Therefore, there is a collective moral responsibility to do so.

Notice that the above account of collective moral responsibility does not presuppose that *any* individual nation-state acting on its own could successfully intervene in relation to large-scale human rights violations occurring in another nation-state. Perhaps most nation-states could not. On the other hand, it does not presuppose that *none* could successfully intervene on their own. Indeed, to do so would be clearly false. For example, France, the US and others could have successfully unilaterally intervened in Rwanda at minimal cost to themselves. Moreover, it may be the case that one nation-state is so powerful that even all of the others acting collectively could not successfully intervene—or could not intervene without suffering significant costs—in relation to massive human rights violations taking place in that very powerful nation-state. If so, there might not be a collective responsibility to intervene.

CONCLUSION

There are three final important points in relation to the above account. My account offers an elaboration and justification of the *collective* moral responsibility of nation-states in relation to armed intervention in states in which large-scale human rights violations are taking place. This account is consistent with two sorts of 'individual' moral responsibility.[18]

First, there is a prior moral responsibility on the part of the government and citizenry of the nation-state in which the human rights violations are taking place, or are about to take place, to terminate or prevent those human rights violations. It is only if the government (or its citizenry) is unwilling or unable to discharge this responsibility that external intervention should be contemplated. In the presence of an internal solution, there is no external collective responsibility to intervene (militarily or otherwise).

Second, the collective moral responsibility on the part of members of the international community to intervene in cases of large-scale human rights violations is consistent with an individual moral responsibility on the part of some nation-states which are able to do so. However, I have not sought to elaborate or justify this individual moral responsibility, and do not have the space to consider it here. However, I can say that individual moral responsibility would come into play in two sorts of cases: those in which the collective moral responsibility has not been discharged, and those in which the collective moral responsibility cannot be discharged. In the contemporary world there are few cases in which the collective moral responsibility *cannot* be discharged. There are quite a few cases in which the collective moral responsibility is not *in fact* discharged. But it is seldom a good idea to foist responsibilities on one individual or small group because another individual, or the community at large, has failed to discharge theirs in the first place. Moreover, given the costs of armed intervention to the party or parties intervening, broad-based, multilateral armed intervention is preferable to unilateral armed intervention. For one thing, the costs borne by a state intervening unilaterally are likely to be greater than if the burden is shared; so the individual state needs a greater incentive in terms of its self-interest than it might if it were part of a broad-based group engaged in multilateral intervention. For another thing, if a state intervenes unilaterally it might feel entitled, and have a greater capacity, to make peace more in conformity with its own interests, than the needs of the victims it has rescued. This is precisely the charge that is being laid against the US by its political enemies in relation to its invasion of Iraq. At any rate, broad-based, multilateral humanitarian interventions are more likely to be motivated by humanitarian, rather than purely political, considerations, if only because the self-interest of one state can often be kept in check by the self-interests of the others.

Finally, I have suggested that if a person or group has a basic right to assistance, then they may well have a right to enforce that right to assistance in relation to those directly responsible for the rights violation in question. However, from the fact that a group might have a collective moral responsibility to assist some needy community, it does not follow that the needy community has a right to use deadly force to ensure that that collective moral responsibility is discharged. Not all those who fail to discharge their collective moral responsibilities in relation to large-scale rights violations are themselves rights violators. This is especially the case in relation to third parties. It would not have been morally justified for the ANC to conduct its armed struggle against (say) the Reagan administration when the administration decided to pursue a policy of so-called 'constructive engagement' in relation to the apartheid government of the day. Similarly, it would not have been morally justified for Bosnian Muslims to use deadly force against UN personnel and/or officials of the European Community when the latter groups failed to discharge their collective moral responsibility to intervene and protect the Bosnian Muslims—indeed, arm them—in the face of the genocidal 'ethnic cleansing' operations being conducted by the Serbian forces.

PART II

The Practical

Dilemmas

5 AUSTRALIAN INTERVENTION IN ITS NEIGHBOURHOOD: SHERIFF AND HUMANITARIAN?

MICHAEL O'KEEFE

Since the end of the Cold War there has been an increase in armed intervention in the name of humanitarianism. With surprising regularity, governments have expended 'blood and treasure' ostensibly for non-citizens abroad. There have also been a number of spectacular failures to intervene, which have led to wholesale slaughter, starvation and destruction. Rwanda is a case in point, and Sudan has all the hallmarks of a humanitarian catastrophe.

One difficulty in assessing the so-called 'right of humanitarian intervention' is that the motives of the interveners are difficult to judge.[1] The orthodox view of this 'responsibility to protect' non-citizens is that it must be undertaken by disinterested parties out of benevolence. The problem is that this view presumes trust in the good nature of states—a presumption that is challenged by apparent dominance of Realpolitik and self-interest in international relations. Furthermore, since September 11, the 'War on Terror' has refocused attention on providing security to citizens at home, often by attacking terrorists abroad.[2]

States are preoccupied with the maintenance of international order. This concern is particularly evident in the behaviour of 'middle powers' such as Australia.[3] The end of the Cold War and the September 11 attacks on the US have acted to exaggerate this search for stability. Australian decision makers have attempted to shape the international and regional strategic environments in a number of ways. In the immediate post–Cold War era, the Keating government concentrated on the UN and multilateral regional institutions. The Howard doctrine focuses on bilateral relations with the US and multilateralism in the proximate region. Support for US actions in Afghanistan and Iraq and deployments to East Timor and the Solomons should be seen in this light. A major problem for decision makers has been how to justify these interventions to the international community and domestic constituencies, both of which are sceptical of the motives behind foreign policy. By its very nature, humanitarian intervention needs to be legitimated by the consent of the 'intervened', and in Australia's case the charge of neo-colonialism is never far from the surface of regional diplomacy.

Increased intervention is made more intriguing by the rhetoric that has accompanied it. Australian decision makers have not hesitated to emphasise the humanitarian motives behind deploying military forces to distant conflicts. The humanitarian implications of state failure and the 'War on Terror' have been strung together to justify intervention. The government treats the threat of terrorism from the region as a possible consequence of state failure.[4]

The government's justifications are muddled and far from convincing. For instance, in the White Paper on Terrorism, the link between failed states and terrorism is simply a one-sentence assertion: 'they may easily develop into safe havens for terrorists'.[5] One reason that these justifications are viewed with suspicion is that they are often used to gain international and domestic legitimacy after the intervention is already under way, such as in the case of Cambodia in the early 1990s and more recently Iraq. Another problem is that there are good reasons for believing that self-interest has played a significant part in decision making. In Australia's case, the persistent charge has been that reflexive support for US foreign policy interests undermines its humanitarian credentials.

Clearly, Australia's participation in the 'Coalition of the Willing' in Afghanistan and Iraq is a case of self-interest: it is deemed to be in Australia's interests to support the interests of its 'great and powerful friend'.[6] A post-hoc humanitarian justification does little to dissuade observers from this sceptical view. These observers have been quick to characterise Australia as a 'Deputy Sheriff' to the United States.[7] There is much confusion about this term. It was originally attributed to John Howard, a charge he has strenuously denied. When first used, it caused a furore amongst Australia's neighbours and amongst segments of the Australia's foreign policy establishment. However, it has now become entrenched as a description for Australia's reflexive support for US foreign policy actions.

Intervention in what the government terms the 'arc of instability' —the archipelago to the north and the South Pacific—does not necessarily conform to this generalisation.[8] Despite the many problems associated with state failure and the amorphous threat of terrorism, the case has not been made to explain why the Howard government shifted emphasis from Iraq to the South Pacific in 2003. The national and alliance interests and responsibilities, and the humanitarianism used to justify Australian intervention must be disaggregated.

This chapter will review the claim that Australia is acting as a 'Deputy Sheriff' in its proximate region, which weakens the government's humanitarian justification for intervention. Australia's unique strategic culture will be reviewed in an attempt to shed light on the motives for intervention. Weaknesses in an the descriptive value of strategic culture will lead to a reappraisal of the recent history of Australian intervention in its proximate region. Attention is focused on the veracity of the government's 'state failure' justification for action in the Solomon Islands. Finally, intervention in Papua New Guinea (PNG) is discussed to flesh out the implications of this argument.

THE ENDURING INFLUENCE OF
AUSTRALIA'S STRATEGIC CULTURE

'Strategic culture' is a valuable theoretical construct that can be used to deepen our understanding of the reasons behind Australia's overseas interventions. It has been defined as 'a distinctive and lasting set of beliefs, values and habits regarding the threat and use of force, which have their roots in such fundamental influences as geopolitical setting, history and political culture'.[9] The locus of these 'beliefs, values and habits' is the executive and foreign policy and defence establishments that formulate security strategy, but they are evidenced in broader political culture and are reflected in public opinion. Desmond Ball, Graeme Cheeseman and others have adapted this framework of analysis from the behaviour of the US and Soviet Union during the Cold War to Australia's foreign policy.[10] In Australia, these beliefs are expressed in the four dominant aspects of defence and foreign policies: armament, alignment, regionalism, and internationalism, which have been present in varying degrees since Federation.

The influence of strategic culture means that policy makers are often predisposed to view international affairs through a particular lens. The main implication of accepting the explanatory value of 'strategic culture' is that decision-making models based purely on rational appraisal of a decision maker's options at a given time must be tempered by the influence of distinct national cultures.[11]

Geography and history play a major role in Australian strategic culture. Cheeseman has convincingly argued that, in Australia, strategic culture has been based on 'Anglo-Saxon', 'Anglo-American' attitudes.[12] The alienation from, and fear of, Asia characteristic of the colonial era has been established as its centrepiece. Australia was viewed as a sparsely populated colonial outpost (later an independent state) adjacent to Asia that could not defend itself against the threat from culturally dissimilar and potentially threatening neighbours.[13] Almost paradoxically, strategic culture placed great stock in Australia's economic superiority over Asia, and the importance of trade with Europe and the US reinforced this sense of isolation.

The fear of Asia is so entrenched that it has continued to underpin strategic culture, despite the demographic shift from a relatively homogeneous population to a more diverse multicultural population and the transformation from trade primarily within the British Empire to close economic interaction with Asia. It is as if continuity and inertia could be added to the list of Australian strategic cultural traits.

For many Australian policy makers, fear of Asia has been inextricably linked to dependence on 'great and powerful friends' for protection. This dependence has focused on great powers with which Australia shares a cultural affinity, namely the UK and the US. The legacy of World War II and Vietnam for political leaders such as Howard, or for the planners in the Department of Defence, reaffirmed the need to keep a 'great and powerful friend' engaged in the region and, conversely, the consequences of failure to do so. It has also involved an exaggerated sense of Australia's importance to its ally, especially in relation to the significance of largely token military commitments to coalition operations. As there has been much debate about 'punching above our weight', I do not intend to develop the theme further.[14]

The rhetoric relating to the reliance on allies has become more nuanced over time, but many of the underlying assumptions have remained.[15] Decision and policy makers have become more aware of both the inaccurate view of Asia and the waining prospect of allied military support, but have done little to dissuade the public from maintaining these attitudes. It may be that a strong domestic constituency in support of intervention is required, and the basis for this support is less important to decision makers than the support itself.

This dependence has had its costs, notably involvement in distant conflicts linked to the national interests of Australia's allies. It is this aspect of strategic culture that informs criticisms of the reflexive support for US military operations. That is, Australian decision makers are charged with offering forces to participate in allied operations without weighing up the costs in terms of national interests, other than the national interest of maintaining a close alliance.[16]

The risk of isolation from 'great and powerful friends' has resulted in an orthodox response: a focus on armament and alliance rather than other alternatives. Armament and alignment can both be evidenced in recent defence purchases, such as attack helicopters and tanks, or efforts to increase interoperability with US forces, such as the creation of joint training establishments in northern Australia.

At this stage, a word of caution is warranted. The explanatory value of strategic culture should not be overestimated. It describes the context within which policy is developed and decisions made, but this does not mean that it determines decisions and outcomes. What is clear is that the 'statist military logic' that underpins the international system interacts with national strategic cultures to sustain a focus on armament and alliance.[17] Furthermore, the influence of strategic culture transcends the politicking of a particular government —governments come and go but the background influence of strategic culture is enduring.

From the standpoint of this chapter, an important weakness in strategic culture is that it is almost silent on relations with Australia's proximate region. Australian decision makers have consistently sought to exclude unwelcome states or groups from exercising influence in the region,[18] and confusion over Australia's motives in the proximate region could be reduced if strategic culture were broadened to include this enduring trend.

STRATEGIC CULTURE AND INTERVENTION IN THE PROXIMATE REGION

Much attention has gone into analysing Australia's involvement in Iraq. For some critics of Australia's security policy, Australia is viewed as a 'Deputy Sheriff' acting as part of the US posse in Iraq.[19] The nub of the argument is that Howard supported Bush in Afghanistan and Iraq to pay alliance dues, with the expectation that the 'investment' would be returned if need be. The implication is that Australia's sovereignty, security and interests in Asia have been undermined by reflexive support for the US. This perspective conforms neatly with several aspects of strategic culture, but also misses the mark in relation to the proximate region.

This critique is seemingly applicable to Australia's increased interventionism in its proximate region. The East Timor and Solomons interventions could be viewed as cases of 'Deputy-Sheriffing' in the region. However, this transference is problematic because a number of crucial distinctions can be drawn between the reasons for intervening in Iraq and intervening in the South Pacific.

By associating the Howard doctrine with the school of thought that supports armament and alignment, observers are quick to place these tendencies in opposition to regionalism and internationalism (which was aptly summarised by the Hawke–Keating foreign policy).[20] This generalisation does no justice to either government's foreign policy—neither Hawke's or Keating's emphasis on alliance and armament nor Howard's interventionism in the proximate region.

In the post–Cold War era, Australian foreign policy has championed preventive diplomacy in the region. Preventive diplomacy acknowledges both causes and effects of a crisis and acts to limit and contain any negative outcomes.[21] It was a mainstay of the Hawke–Keating Labor governments and, while it will not be overtly labelled as such, we may be seeing a nascent trend towards this form of engagement in the Howard government.

Within Australia, there was bipartisan support for the East Timor and Solomons interventions and for enhanced engagement with Papua New Guinea, and this is not likely to change with a change of government. Furthermore, there is a strong domestic constituency supporting intervention—there was no mainstream criticism of the Solomons operation, other than that it should have occurred earlier.[22]

A real problem with disentangling the government's intervention in Iraq and the South Pacific is the tone of its rhetoric. The government has sent mixed signals about its policy towards the 'arc of instability'. Instances of state failure and the associated threat of terror 'from or through' the region have been used as a justification for action, thus linking intervention with Australia's responsibilities as a loyal ally to support the Bush-led 'War on Terror'.[23] Therefore, the proximate region is simultaneously a source of threat and a recipient of humanitarian and development assistance. We must see through this rhetoric to put the terrorism and humanitarian justifications in perspective.

AUSTRALIA'S RECENT INVOLVEMENT
IN THE PROXIMATE REGION

Australia has a long history of relations with the proximate region. The archipelago to the north and the South Pacific were the last bulwarks in the defence against the Japanese in World War II. Australian engagement has matured since then as the region has gone through the post-colonial nation-building period. In the case of Papua New Guinea, the links are even closer due to Australia's past role as colonial administrator.

In the South Pacific, Australia is the undisputed regional hegemon.[24] In the past twenty-five years, Australia has intervened to resolve regional disputes, to protect the sovereignty of island states, particularly their exclusive economic zones, to maintain regional law and order, to provide public goods in the aftermath of natural disasters and to exclude unwelcome strategic intervention by other powers. As such, the South Pacific could be described as an 'Australian Lake'.[25]

In the 1980s the Hawke government elevated the South Pacific to the same strategic significance to Australia as Southeast Asia.[26] The immediate result was expanded technical aid through the Defence Cooperation Program, including the provision of patrol craft under the Pacific Patrol Boat Program. Armed intervention was soon to follow.

Australian Defence Force (ADF) deployments were prompted by the coup in Fiji in 1987, civil unrest in Vanuatu in 1988 and in Papua New Guinea in 1989–90, the civil war in Bougainville in the mid-1990s, the East Timor Referendum from 1998, and civil unrest in the Solomon Islands from 2003. In addition to these events were a number of developments in the 1980s and 1990s that alarmed Australian decision makers, including Soviet 'fishing' arrangements and French nuclear testing.[27]

The gradual nature of the shift in strategic policy is illuminated by a brief overview of three of Australia's regional interventions: the intervention in Fiji during the Cold War, the post–Cold War intervention in Bougainville, and the recent intervention in the Solomon Islands. The focus will be on the most recent operation in the

Solomons because it was conceived after the 'War on Terror' was declared. In the interests of brevity, the East Timor operation is not discussed in depth. Suffice to say, it was largely organised and funded by Australia and the majority of troops were provided from the ADF. The fact that it was a UN-sanctioned operation sets it apart from the others, which is ironic considering it was the East Timor intervention that gave rise to the charge of 'Deputy Sheriffing' on behalf of the US.[28]

The Australian government's initial response to the Fiji coup in May 1987 was to cut diplomatic and military ties. Subsequently, a substantial task force was dispatched that included Royal Australian Navy (RAN) ships and an Operational Deployment Force rifle company. In September 1987 there was a second coup and the government again threatened intervention. This appears to be a classic case of 'gunboat diplomacy', as the ADF was stationed offshore but did not physically intervene. However, analysis by Matthew Gubb reveals that the situation stabilising was not the only reason for Australian restraint. Rather, operational problems actually removed the option of intervening. Deficiencies in the ability to deploy included helicopter breakdowns, equipment and training shortfalls and a lack of interoperability between the army and the navy.[29]

In the mid-1990s, the ADF was involved in a peace operation to halt the civil war between the Bougainville Revolutionary Army (BRA) and the government of Papua New Guinea. Australia's participation began with a PNG request for military assistance in 1990–91 under the terms of bilateral defence agreements. Increased police and military aid, including the provision of helicopters, led to criticism within and beyond Bougainville and did not resolve the crisis.[30]

Australia's bilateral military diplomacy was not sufficient and the South Pacific Forum, led by Australia and New Zealand, eventually brokered a cease-fire. In 1994 the ADF participated in the South Pacific Regional Peacekeeping Force, which monitored the Bougainville Peace Accords. The force was composed of personnel from Australia, Fiji, New Zealand, Tonga and Vanuatu. The ADF trained the combined force and provided logistic and communication support, RAN ships patrolled the maritime boundary between Bougainville and the Solomon Islands, and an Australian officer held overall command of the operation. Australia's commitment to the Bougainville operation (along with NZ, Fiji and Vanuatu) has cumulatively involved nearly 4000 personnel and more than A$150 million in aid. The conflict was significant because it risked the fragmentation of Papua New Guinea, which would seriously affect Australia's security interests. Economic interests were also at stake as the BRA stopped operations at CRA's Pangua copper mine in Bougainville.[31]

The Regional Assistance Mission to the Solomon Islands (RAMSI) was conceived, organised and run by Australia. The Townsville Peace Agreement brokered by Australia in 2000 was tenuous and often broken. The Solomon Islands was viewed by the Australian government as a failed state and decision makers concluded that intervention was necessary.[32] Great efforts were applied to establishing the legitimacy of the operation. The intervention had strong support from local political leaders and the general population. As early as 2000 the Solomon Islands government requested intervention, and Foreign Minister Laurie Chan requested UN intervention twice, but to no avail.[33] Australia asked for and received a formal invitation and the Solomons parliament was convened to pass enabling legislation. There was a small delay because of local political manoeuvring rather than serious dissent over the Australian-led intervention.[34]

As the UN was unwilling or unable to act, legitimacy was built on the participation of a regional multilateral organisation. Australia sought support from the Pacific Islands Forum, whose sixteen members unanimously endorsed the intervention. Papua New Guinea and Fiji offered troops. Most others offered police. France offered assistance but was rebuffed by Australia, which was not surprising considering both the tendency to exclude external powers from influencing regional events and also the lingering tension over the second Gulf War.

The government's Comprehensive Package of Strengthened Assistance to Solomon Islands (COMPSASI) represents a whole-of-government approach from Australia with close co-operation from regional states. The COMPSASI involves military security, policing, economic development and state capacity building. It forms a model for state capacity building that draws on Australia's experience in peacekeeping and peace-building. The Special Coordinator of

RAMSI, Nick Warner, has been responsible for strengthening the institutions of governance and the economy. It has been estimated to cost A$300 million per annum and up to A$2 billion over the coming decade.[35]

The operation began in July 2003. Its immediate aim was to re-establish law and order and to recover firearms. The second priority was to 'stabilis[e] the government's finances'. RAMSI has involved over 1700 ADF and Australian Federal Police personnel and more than 600 personnel from the Cook Islands, Fiji, Kiribati, New Zealand, Papua New Guinea, and Tonga. These forces are working closely as a regional task force.[36] The high operational tempo of the initial involvement quickly reduced. Within less than a year the military component of the operation had largely concluded.

The provision of armed peacekeepers highlights an important aspect of this operation that is obscured by the rhetoric used by Australian decision makers—there was no peace to keep. Soldiers and police imposed order on a lawless situation. The tragic shooting of Australian Federal Police (AFP) officer Adam Dunning in December 2004 highlights the tenuous situation. The swift redeployment of troops to protect AFP officers and track the killer(s) highlights the Government's resolve. While the initial deployment of forces was to be for six months, the government made it clear that the operation would continue in some form for the foreseeable future. Australia has intervened with an unprecedented military operation, and it was acknowledged that the outcome is uncertain without prolonged Australian civil involvement.[37]

Australia's ongoing humanitarian intervention in the proximate region has involved (and will involve) greater military and economic resources than its operation in Iraq. The East Timor and Solomons operations and increased involvement in Papua New Guinea involve long-term commitments, measured in decades rather than in short federal election cycles. There is no question of 'cutting and running'. This commitment is significant considering that governments have changed and that the fashions relating to intervention have also shifted over this time.

Despite apparent similarities, these deployments differ in several important regards.

The main similarity in these operations was that they were aimed at 'encouraging South-West Pacific nations to see Australia as a neutral strategic partner'.[38] This strategy has been successfully maintained by Howard. For instance, at the 2004 Pacific Islands Forum meeting he described the Pacific as 'Australia's patch', and the PNG prime minister labelled Australia as the 'big brother' to regional states.[39]

Australia's hegemonic behaviour is evidenced in attempts to exclude other powers from the South Pacific. The reluctance to support proposals for a permanent regional peacekeeping force that arose at the time of the Bougainville crisis,[40] and the exclusion of other bodies, in particular the UN or states such as France, point to an attempt to ensure that Australia can protect its interests. The emphasis on excluding other powers from Australia's area of primary strategic interest characterises both the Hawke–Keating and the Howard governments. It reinforces the point that close engagement with the proximate region should be added to the prevailing understanding of Australia's strategic culture.

The main differences in the operations point to how decision makers have strengthened Australia's ability to influence regional affairs.

A GREATLY ENHANCED CAPABILITY TO INTERVENE

In the 1980s the government was more willing than able to project military force to support Australian and Western interests in the South Pacific. By the 1990s this situation had reversed. Equipment deficiencies identified during the Fiji operation were rectified over the coming years, greatly improving the ADF's rapid deployment capability.[41] New acquisitions and enhancements came at a cost, leading to the conclusion that the ability to deploy force in such a manner was a priority. Some of this equipment could be used for low-level operations in the direct defence of Australia, but its prime use was to support operations further afield, whether in the proximate region or as part of a UN- or US-led coalition elsewhere.

The evolving orientation has involved expanding force projection concepts and capabilities. According to Gareth Evans, 'Australia certainly should not be embarrassed about using its politico-military capability to advance its own and the region's security interests'.[42] The growing confidence with which the government approached these actions gives substance to Evans' concept of regional 'military diplomacy'.[43] It is not surprising that commentators labelled Australia's South Pacific strategy 'solo-forward defence'. The Howard government continued this trend. For instance, Defence Minister Robert Hill noted that the ADF has been increasingly structured to cater for the types of contingencies posed by failed states.[44]

A SHIFT FROM INDEPENDENT OPERATIONS TO 'COALITIONS OF THE WILLING'

The Fiji and Vanuatu 'virtual' interventions were unprecedented examples of a willingness to take unilateral action,[45] while the Bougainville, East Timor and Solomons operations show a preference for regional multilateral diplomacy, independent of either a 'great and powerful friend' or unwelcome powers. The creation of ad hoc peacekeeping/making forces for both operations typifies regional multilateralism that conformed to the approach taken in *Australia's Regional Security* and was continued by the Howard government.[46]

Despite the facade of multilateralism, by using the South Pacific Forum (and later the Pacific Islands Forum)[47] to oversee the operations, respective Australian governments chose a mechanism over which they could exercise a good deal of control. Australia ensured that it remained the most powerful actor in the South Pacific, but not one that would be expected to respond to all potential crises alone.

Ideally, Australia would like to be invited to intervene— international, regional and domestic legitimacy demands an invitation. The importance of legitimacy was underscored by Howard's comments at the formal farewell of forces going to the Solomons operation. He said the intervention 'will send a signal to other countries in the region that help is available if it is sought'.[48] Clearly,

Australia will intervene if it is in its interests and if it is invited (and past practice has been to engineer an invitation when it is not forthcoming).

ENLARGED STRATEGIC INTERESTS IMPLIED BY JUSTIFICATIONS FOR REGIONAL DEPLOYMENTS

The ostensible justification for the deployments in the 1980s was to evacuate Australian citizens if the need arose. Australian interests came to include its (and its allies') citizens in the proximate region, and the maintenance of regional stability.[49] The justification provided for support to Lini (Vanuatu) and Namaliu (PNG) in 1988 shifted from protection of Australian citizens to support for 'a legitimate government'.[50] Defence Minister Beazley also revealed that there was also an expectation that Australia would protect the interests of the Western strategic community in the region.[51]

By the dawn of the twenty-first century the justification for intervention enlarged again to include the potential local humanitarian costs of state failure and the implications for Australia's security of terrorists taking advantage of state failure.[52] Therefore state failure provides a justification for intervention based on both humanitarianism and Australia's national interests.

Over the last twenty years successive Australian governments have become more willing to intervene in the proximate region and the ADF has become more capable of intervention. Governments have become more inclined to use ad hoc coalitions to respond to regional security crises, but the interest in multilateralism does not extend to inviting other major powers to resolve regional problems.

Australia's interventionism does not support the contention that alignment with the US was the primary objective. 'Deputy-Sheriffing' for the US is only a partial explanation for the policy, and one that leaves intervention in the proximate region inadequately explained.

Operations in the 'arc of instability' are not simply a case of 'Deputy-Sheriffing'. Australia believes that it is the sheriff, charged with maintaining order. United States policy makers may support

Australia's initiatives, but US attention is focused elsewhere.[53] Australia does not have the luxury of turning away from its proximate region—geography equals necessity. Successive governments have decided that it is in Australia's national interests to take on the role of regional sheriff in its area of primary strategic interest.

The addition of 'sheriffing' in the region to our understanding of strategic culture seems to preclude humanitarianism from being the primary reason for intervention, but does not exclude the possibility that these motives coexist. Australian decision makers have consistently sought to shape the regional security environment and the humanitarian costs of state failure and subsequent threat of terrorism have challenged the maintenance of stability in the region. As Australia is concerned with maintaining regional order, the implications of operating in a region populated by failing or failed states demand further attention.

WHAT IS A FAILING STATE AND WHY DOES IT MATTER TO AUSTRALIA?

State failure is a relatively new conceptualisation of an enduring condition in international affairs. A full examination of the concept and its implications is beyond the scope of this chapter. For our purposes, a brief overview will suffice.[54] Westphalian statehood requires states to fulfil obligations to their citizens and to the international community.[55] If a state cannot fulfil these obligations, then it could be considered a failing or failed state. Zartman notes that 'collapse means that the basic functions of the state are no longer performed, as analysed by various theories of the state'.[56] A failed state is characterised by political, economic and social crises spiralling out of control. Conflict, famine and pestilence are often united in failed states.[57] Examples of failed or failing states include Somalia from 1992, Rwanda in 1994, the former Yugoslavia in much of the 1990s or more recently the Solomon Islands in 2003.[58]

Clearly, failing states have the potential to cause great local suffering. Any of the implications of state failure could be viewed primarily as a domestic crisis that is not the responsibility of other states. However, their combination has international significance, but the response to the crisis is dependent on an external state or states having the political will and capacity to intervene. The latter qualification partially explains the patchy record of humanitarian intervention in international affairs.

There are many implications of state failure for other states which highlight the link between 'hard' military and 'soft' humanitarian security issues.[59] Decision makers generally treat 'hard' security issues differently because they are perceived to directly threaten their state or its core interests. 'Soft' security issues generally focus on a different referent of security: human beings rather than states. Most 'hard' military threats spring from the failure to maintain what is termed a 'monopoly of violence' within a given territory. That is, a failing or failed state is unable to protect its borders, to uphold international law and order, or to uphold domestic law and order.[60] The most serious form of international instability caused by state failure is that another state could take advantage of the situation and invade. This form of 'hard' security threat is a remote prospect in the South Pacific and in the interests of brevity is excluded from the discussion.

Failing and failed states can become what one author has called a 'petri dish for transnational threats', a perspective reiterated by the Australian government as a justification for intervening in the Solomons.[61] Prime Minister Howard made the case by arguing that, 'if the Solomons becomes a failed state, it's a haven potentially for terrorists, drug runners and money launderers. We don't want that on our doorstep.'[62] That is, non-state actors such as drug or people smugglers or terrorist groups could take advantage of the breakdown in law and order. These groups invariably reach beyond the borders of the failed state within which they operate and as such they can have a broader destabilising effect that can threaten the security of other states. This was the principal argument used to support intervention against the Taliban regime, due to its close relationship with al-Qaeda, in Afghanistan.

A failing state is one that is struggling to fulfil its obligations but is not necessarily beyond remedial action. Much of the literature on failed states marries discussion of state collapse with reconstruction. This perspective is significant because it informs the decision by external states to shore up the failing or failed state.[63] The more a state struggles to meet its obligations, the greater the likelihood that the endemic problems will lead to its collapse. Traditional avenues of external influence, such as aid, become less effective. At this stage, international forces of law, order and development—states, non-government organisations (NGOs) and donors with the capabilities to intervene[64]—may also be discouraged by the sense that the situation is spiralling out of control. Military force may be needed to maintain law and order because NGOs are unable or unwilling to act in these circumstances. By the same token, state-sponsored humanitarian and development agencies may be unable to sustain the level of involvement needed to demonstrably improve living conditions, and NGOs are often more suited to this role than government organs.[65]

The belief that external intervention can resolve these problems and improve living conditions provides the impetus for many co-operative acts in international relations, including humanitarian military intervention. Therefore, there is a sense of altruism fuelling external interventions, but the record of inaction shows that often altruism alone is not enough to ensure action. The implications of this are that a whole-of-government approach focused on governance, the economy and society must operate alongside more traditional instruments to ameliorate the problems that exist in fragile states and to counter threats created by them.

At first glance, state failure seems a credible reason for intervention. However, the patchy record of intervention in the region, historically or, more importantly, presently, raises questions about the transference from theory to policy. We must acknowledge how woolly the concept of state failure is, and therefore how woolly its implications are for decision makers seeking to use it to justify intervention.

FAILED OR FRAGILE STATES: THEORY AND PRACTICE

The most serious objection to using 'theoretical' state failure as a justification for intervention is that it does not provide a particularly accurate depiction of the dilemmas faced by decision makers. Much of the literature on state failure suggests that a continuum exists, with a strong state at one pole and a collapsed state at the other. This explains the many distinctions drawn using terms such as quasi-, collapsed, failed, failing, weak, and dangerously and safely weak.[66] From this perspective, most regional states have hovered on the brink of collapse for many years, but there is no indication of when or even if they are about to teeter over the edge.[67]

State failure involves a comparison with a strict sense of statehood that grew from Europe, and it may not be as relevant a measure of the success of statehood in the proximate region. In fact, attempts to maintain some of the trappings of statehood, such as national airlines and diplomatic corps, may actually exacerbate domestic crises. For instance, the Australian prime minister has noted that a number of island states were 'too small to be viable'.[68] This led to the call for some form of South Pacific Federation to make small states, such as the Cook Islands, Kiribati, Nauru, Tonga, and Tuvalu, viable.[69]

If the measures of state failure were rigorously applied to the proximate region, most if not all states would be considered failing or failed states, and there is no indication that their status will change suddenly. This points to a weakness in the state failure literature: if all states in a given region fail to measure up, then it is not an indicator of stability and security that can be used by decision makers to usefully predict when and how to intervene.

A more useful perspective would be to see the region as being populated by 'fragile states'. They are not necessarily on the brink of collapse, but they could provide greater security and stability for their citizens. A brief overview of the current situation in Papua New Guinea illuminates some of the weaknesses of using the theory of state failure to justify intervention.

A FRAGILE STATE ON AUSTRALIA'S DOORSTEP

Papua New Guinea faces many challenges emanating from the combined effects of decolonisation and globalisation. There is a sense that it is extremely fragile—that living conditions are slowly degrading and that indigenous efforts to halt this malaise are not working.[70] Issues such as endemic crime and corruption have undermined the capacity of the state to protect and further the interests of its citizens.

Most major social and economic indicators point to declining standards of living. Since independence in 1975 Papua New Guinea's gross domestic product (GDP) per capita has hardly grown, and over the last five years it has achieved zero or negative growth. The terms of trade have declined since independence and over the last five years the budget deficit has been rising. The Centre for Independent Studies notes that Papua New Guinea is facing a 'demographic time bomb' because the population is growing by 2.5 per cent per annum but 'job creation is totally inadequate'.[71] According to AusAID and the World Bank, Papua New Guinea also suffers from poor ratings of the strength of the rule of law, poor fiscal management and a failure to control corruption.[72] From a social standpoint, the outlook is also bleak. According to the UN's Human Development Index of per capita GDP growth, life expectancy and education, Papua New Guinea is not a healthy society. For instance, it experiences high levels of maternal mortality and low levels of adult literacy compared to the region.[73]

Even in the absence of the AIDS pandemic, Papua New Guineans would face an uncertain future. However, the work of Caldwell and others suggests that the risk factors that have exacerbated the pandemic in Africa are also present in Papua New Guinea, a point underscored by Peter Piot, the head of UNAIDS.[74] A brief overview of HIV/AIDS in Papua New Guinea makes stark reading: it has the highest incidence of reported cases of HIV in the Pacific. Somewhere between 6000 and 15 000 people are infected with HIV in Papua New Guinea.[75] This equates to more infections than in the whole of Australia, a country whose population is about four times as large. Infection rates are increasing by 15–20 per cent per annum.[76]

These predictions almost defy the imagination. AIDS will have a serious impact on the economy. Papua New Guinea spends only 3 per cent of its gross national product on health, a figure which has been declining since the 1980s. The cost of treating AIDS patients will drain already stretched resources. On current trends, AIDS will increase the budget deficit by between 9 and 21 per cent by 2020. Living standards will decline by between 12 and 48 per cent due to the impact of the epidemic.[77]

The conditions that make Papua New Guinea a fragile state have occurred over a prolonged period of time and have led to the decline in government capabilities in key areas affecting social and physical security. The onslaught of the AIDS epidemic will compound this weakness. Dennis Altman, Nicholas Eberstadt and others have established the linkages between increased vulnerability to AIDS and civil disorder (unregulated population flows, famine and crime).[78] There is a vicious circle between state fragility and soft threats, such as AIDS.[79] Alexander Downer has made the link between AIDS and state failure in the proximate region and noted that the 'Asia–Pacific region could become another epicentre of the epidemic, to rival Africa'.[80] If we are witnessing the 'Africanisation of the South Pacific' as some commentators suggest,[81] then the spread of AIDS must be viewed as integral to this process.

The implication is that Papua New Guinea is not capable of dealing with the problem of state fragility in the presence of the AIDS epidemic. Consistent with the logic of the state failure justification for intervention, the nature of the challenges that Papua New Guinea faces necessitates expanded intervention. It is reasonable to expect that Australia will continue and expand its already significant development and humanitarian intervention.[82] The annual aid package to Papua New Guinea is $300 million. The Australian government has recently announced that it will expand its $60 million AIDS prevention programme, and it aims to directly influence the declining PNG law and order situation by sending 200 Australian Federal Police and by tying the overall aid package to a number of reform measures.

However, simply spending more money on the problem may be a myopic solution. Papua New Guinea has received $28 billion in aid since independence in 1975.[83] Helen Hughes has noted that increased development aid could actually be counterproductive.[84] This raises the question of whether aspects of Australia's approach to the region may be implicated in Papua New Guinea's continuing state fragility.[85]

Many questions are yet to be adequately answered: precisely what role do 'soft' security issues such as transnational crime, terrorism or AIDS play in state fragility, especially in the proximate region? What strategies have been or could be employed to limit the impact of state fragility? Will regional leaders be receptive to this form of aid or intervention? How can intervention forces be tailored to deal with the unique problems posed by state fragility? These questions require innovative answers.

One answer to the latter question is provided by Hugh White, Director of the Australian Strategic Policy Institute, who has called for the development of a 2000-strong specialist police intervention force to undertake such operations.[86] The use of police force is probably more suited to the problems posed by fragile states in the region, but what of the underlying causes of state fragility that have gained ground despite the efforts of government and NGOs and billions of dollars in aid?

CONCLUSION

Is Australia's intervention in the proximate region an example of humanitarianism? The generous answer would be that Australia has obligations and responsibilities to act in its region and beyond, and is increasingly doing so, but the reality is that decision makers have exhibited mixed motives.

Despite rhetoric about terrorism, the threat perceptions revealed by decisions to intervene in the proximate region point to an acknowledgement that non-military issues arising from fragile states demand a response. Australia's interventionism shows that threats to human security in the proximate region can cause instability and therefore are no longer viewed as beyond (or below) the purview of national security policies. Asymmetric and transnational security threats such as AIDS, drug smuggling and, of course, terrorism are becoming more prominent in security policies, while the threat of invasion or high-level military conflicts is receding. These 'soft' threats particularly afflict fragile states.

The focus of recent interventions on state building and countering AIDS is an example of humanitarianism coinciding with self-interest—the exigencies of Realpolitik in a post–September 11 world. However, the shift towards a broader conception of human security implied by the humanitarian justification for intervention has been tentative and uneven. The implications of the shift are far from clear to decision makers, practitioners or academics, which explains some of the mixed signals sent. Asymmetric threats require more than the application of military force. If assisting fragile states in the proximate region is a core policy aim, then we will see more interventions based on a whole-of-government approach that attempts to resolve the underlying reasons for state fragility.

In interventions in the proximate region, decision makers have combined what have often been seen as two approaches to humanitarian crises: an 'emergency response' and a 'development intervention'.[87] While the policy tools are underdeveloped, it is clear that innovative approaches to 'soft' security threats, such as AIDS prevention, will continue to be a major part of any new interventionism. Armed intervention will restore law and order, and non-military engagement will be tailored to counter the 'soft' threats. Clearly there is a humanitarian aspect to Australia's intervention in the proximate region.

However, the perceived implications of state failure are not adequate to explain Australian intervention in the region. Assumptions about Australia's role in the proximate region are deeply ingrained in strategic culture. The humanitarian rationale for the Solomons operation is tempered by a good deal of self-interest. For instance, Howard's informal farewell to the forces going to the Solomons included these words:

> It is Australia being a good Pacific Neighbour and helping a small country that really does need help and has cried out for assistance, and we're going to provide it, as we should. Not only is it good that we do so for the wellbeing of the people of the Solomon Islands, but it's also important we do it for the long-term stability and security of our whole region. And in the end, that's in Australia's interests.[88]

David Carment has noted that 'anticipating state failure is as much a matter of being able to generate an effective response as it is of getting the analysis right'.[89] Australian decision makers have acquired the discourse of state failure and employed it to justify recent interventions in the proximate region. Strategic culture points to a necessity to intervene on the part of Australian decision makers and therefore they are likely to continue to use this justification for future intervention. However, the policy implications of responding to state failure are far from clear, in the literature or in the policy proposals for intervention.

Australian governments were intervening in the proximate region well before the term 'state failure' was developed, and the results of many emergency responses to crises and more general development interventions have not stopped the region from being populated by fragile states. These experiments have been based on a mixture of national interests and humanitarian intentions and may have done a great deal of good. However, unless the urge to intervene for reasons of Realpolitik can be more successfully married with humanitarianism, we are likely to see a continuation of existing trends. Furthermore, in separate but connected ways, the 'War on Terror' and the AIDS pandemic are likely to make it more difficult for regional governments to improve the living standards of their citizens, and also more difficult for external powers to intervene effectively.

It is in Australia's self-interest to ensure that order is maintained.[90] Some analysts have sought to describe Australia's interventionism as a 'new Pacific identity'; however, an expansion of Australia's approach is akin to a form of trusteeship that cannot escape some neo-colonial connotations. A long-term commitment to state capacity building seems to point to a form of neo-trusteeship akin to colonialism, but implemented by pliant multilateral organisations and NGOs.[91] The often heavy-handed approach is testament to the fact that Australia believes that it is the regional hegemon and is willing to impose its policy preferences on the region. Notable expressions of Australia's hegemony include the neo-liberal economic agenda imposed on the Solomons,[92] and the fact that one of the answers to the problem of unauthorised arrivals was the 'Pacific Solution'—Australia's Guantanamo Bay was in the South Pacific. Sensitivity to the charge that it is acting as a neo-colonial power is a clear signal that decision makers see some validity in this criticism.[93]

When attempting to judge intentions we must never exclude the possibility that issues completely distinct from the rational appraisal of policy options intruded on decision-making. For instance, domestic electoral considerations may have driven the decision to withdraw the bulk of Australian troops from Iraq. Sending them to deal with a pressing crisis in Australia's backyard allowed this to be done with honour. While these considerations cannot be excluded, we have enough evidence from the last twenty years to point to a shift in perceptions about Australia's role in the proximate region.

Australian decision makers have mixed motives. Australia is the self-appointed sheriff in its proximate region and decision makers will continue to intervene to maintain order. Humanitarianism plays a part in Australian foreign policy and the prescriptive value of the literature on state failure needs to be clarified to ensure that intervention has lasting benefits for Australia and regional states.

6 THE DOCTRINE OF HUMANITARIAN INTERVENTION AND THE NATO AIR STRIKES AGAINST THE FEDERAL REPUBLIC OF YUGOSLAVIA

PAUL MUGGLETON

In the absence of substantiating state practice and opinio juris sive necessitis,[1] [a] right of [humanitarian intervention], which can only be deduced by an elaborate legal sophistry, is nothing more than an artificial effort at realizing a moral fiction.[2]

A traditional view of the UN Charter is that it has outlawed the use and threat of force subject to two remaining exceptions explicitly provided for in the Charter itself, namely, self-defence (Article 51) and armed force authorised by the Security Council (Chapter VII).[3] The centrepiece of the prohibition on the threat and use of force is provided by Article 2(4), complemented by the principle contained in Article 2(7) of non-intervention in matters essentially within the domestic jurisdiction of states.[4] The 1999 North Atlantic Treaty Organization (NATO) air strikes against the then Federal Republic of Yugoslavia (FRY), not in self-defence and without express Security Council authorisation, throw into sharp relief the efficacy of the above view.

The primary issue for this chapter is whether the NATO use of force against the FRY was consistent with, or in breach of, contemporary public international law. Addressing this issue involves: determining a theoretical framework for examining the status of the relevant elements of public international law; analysing the contemporary content of the general prohibition on the threat or use of force by states; analysing state practice in light of the theoretical framework; determining the status and content of the doctrine of humanitarian intervention, this doctrine being the principal pillar for those who support the lawfulness of the NATO intervention;[5] and, critically examining the NATO intervention and its implications. The chapter will not examine issues regarding subsequent agreements between NATO and the FRY ending hostilities and related Security Council resolutions.

CONTEXT

The NATO air strikes, which commenced on 24 March 1999, had the stated objective of averting an 'overwhelming humanitarian catastrophe' in Kosovo,[6] a province within the Republic of Serbia, itself an autonomous republic within the FRY.[7] There were allegations that ethnic Albanians in Kosovo were the victims of egregious human rights abuses. The air strikes ended by 10 June 1999 with the acceptance by FRY authorities of the general principles on a political solution to the crisis adopted by the G8 group of countries on 6 May 1999.[8]

The decision by NATO to commence air strikes was set against the background of regional diplomatic negotiations which had resulted in agreements on 15 and 16 October 1998 involving, variously, the FRY, the Organization for Security and Co-operation in Europe (OSCE) and NATO. The agreements provided for the establishment of ground and air verification missions in and over

Kosovo and for compliance with Security Council resolutions, which included cease-fire and security force withdrawals. After initial improvement, the security situation in Kosovo deteriorated, including an alleged massacre of ethnic Albanians by Serb security forces in Racak in mid-January 1999.[9] Diplomatic negotiations thereafter centred on the so-called 'Rambouillet Agreement' which had as its core substantial autonomy and meaningful self-administration in Kosovo and called for the deployment of a NATO-led multinational military force into Kosovo (KFOR) but with access throughout the FRY. FRY authorities accepted substantial autonomy and meaningful self-administration in Kosovo but wanted KFOR to be a UN-led force and for KFOR access to the FRY to be limited to Kosovo.[10]

The role of the UN Security Council leading to the 24 March 1999 military intervention by NATO was generally to support NATO, NATO member states and OSCE efforts to achieve a political solution. Resolution 1160 (1998), passed in March 1998, called on both parties, FRY authorities and ethnic Albanians, to reach a political solution and imposed on both parties under Chapter VII a mandatory arms embargo. Resolution 1199 (1998), passed in September 1998, determined that the Kosovo situation was 'a threat to peace and security in the region' and demanded a cessation to hostilities, an improvement in the humanitarian situation and the entering by the parties into negotiations with international involvement. Resolution 1203 (1998), adopted on 24 October 1998, affirmed the situation as being a threat to peace and security in the region, endorsed the 15 and 16 October 1998 agreements, and demanded full and prompt implementation of the agreements. No Security Council resolution, however, contained an express authorisation of an enforcement action.

NATO'S JUSTIFICATION FOR INTERVENTION

Statements by representatives of NATO and leading NATO member states identify two related grounds justifying NATO's threat and subsequent use of force regarding Kosovo. The first was the failure of the FRY to comply with extant Security Council resolutions,[11] specifically Resolutions 1160, 1199 and 1203. The second was, in the words of the UK Permanent Representative to the Security Council, as 'an exceptional measure on grounds of overwhelming humanitarian necessity'.[12]

The first ground, as an independent legal justification for a NATO military intervention, can be dealt with briefly but adequately. Extant Security Council resolutions did not expressly, or by reasonable implication, authorise the threat or use of force. Such an interpretation of the Security Council resolutions is 'untenable'. Certainly the German parliament in its deliberations on the issue in mid-October 1998 accepted that no express or implied Security Council resolution authorising the threat or use of force existed. Further, NATO Secretary-General Solana in a letter dated 9 October 1998 stated that no UNSC resolution containing a clear authority for enforcement could be expected, accepting therefore that none existed. It is also noted that in June 1998 the UN Secretary-General advised NATO of the necessity for a Security Council mandate for any military intervention in Kosovo.[13]

The second and more credible justification for the NATO threat and use of force regarding Kosovo has been taken by scholars to be the right of humanitarian intervention.[14] This conclusion is made notwithstanding that the expression 'humanitarian intervention' was rarely used by NATO spokespersons. It was, according to Bruno Simma, specifically referred to in the deliberations of the Parliament of the Federal Republic of Germany but not in, for example, the 24 March 1999 statement to the UN Security Council by the UK Permanent Representative. The UK Permanent Representative referred instead to the concept of 'humanitarian necessity'. An examination of his statement as well as the UK Ministry of Defence's *Kosovo: Legal Basis for Operation Allied Force* document indicates, however, that the UK justification for intervention essentially matches the doctrine of humanitarian intervention expounded by scholars.[15]

It is also noted that the UK government had, prior to the air strikes, presented to parliament a justification for coercive intervention that linked Security Council resolutions with 'humanitarian necessity'. A 'general doctrine of humanitarian necessity' was renounced. However, relying on the precedent of cases like that of northern Iraq in 1991, it was argued that a limited use of force was justifiable 'in support of purposes laid down by the Security Council but without the Council's express authorization when that was the only means to end an immediate and overwhelming catastrophe'.[16]

It has also been proposed that NATO's intervention had less to do with humanitarian intervention than other categories of self-help such as reprisals or forcible countermeasures to induce the FRY to comply with NATO proposals.[17] However, as humanitarian intervention has been used by publicists[18] and NATO countries as the primary justification for NATO's intervention, and as it subsequently appears to be the justification with a precedent effect,[19] it will be the basis for this chapter.

WHAT IS HUMANITARIAN INTERVENTION?

A leading pro-interventionist, Fernando Tesón, defines humanitarian intervention as 'proportionate trans-boundary help, including forcible help, provided by governments to individuals in another state who are being denied basic human rights and who themselves would be rationally willing to revolt against their oppressive government'. However, as highlighted by Thomas Franck and Nigel Rodley, 'a usable general definition' of humanitarian intervention is 'extremely difficult and virtually impossible to apply rigourously [sic]'.[20]

Certainly there is no doctrinal agreement as to the range of human rights and the degree of attack against those rights needed to give rise to a legal justification for intervention. Sir Hersch Lauterpacht, who provides the classic justification for humanitarian intervention, appears to establish a high threshold. For him, intervention is legally permissible 'when a state renders itself guilty of cruelties against and persecution of its nationals in such a way as to deny their fundamental human rights and to shock the conscience of mankind'. Wil Verwey refers to a 'serious violation of human rights'. Tesón talks of 'basic human rights' being protected and includes here the right to democratic government.[21]

In this chapter, the expression 'humanitarian intervention' is taken to exclude interventions to protect nationals and to further a right of self-determination,[22] as, although related, the supporting arguments for each can be distinguished in law and in principle. However, to properly address the full scope of state practice, the term includes interventions authorised by the UN and those conducted without such authorisation. The latter category of interventions will be termed 'unilateral', although they may have a multinational character.

EVALUATIVE FRAMEWORK

The start point for evaluating the existence and content of a right of humanitarian intervention is provided by Article 38 of the Statute of the International Court of Justice (ICJ). Article 38 'is generally regarded as a complete statement of the sources of international law'.[23] It provides for the application of: international conventions; international custom as evidence of a general practice accepted as law; the general principles of law recognised by civilised nations; and, as subsidiary means, judicial decisions and the teachings of the most highly qualified publicists of the various nations. However, although both supporters and critics of the existence of the right of humanitarian intervention share this evaluative framework, the content and weight given to elements of that framework vary.

Two elements of the evaluative framework are highlighted: the interpretation of the UN Charter, and international custom as evidence of a general practice accepted as law. State practice, for example, has been relied on by scholars who support the lawfulness of a general right of humanitarian intervention,[24] by those who reject it outright,[25] and by those who adopt a middle ground by rejecting a right of unilateral humanitarian intervention, but who support a right vested in organs of the UN pursuant to the Charter's peace and security framework.[26]

Interpreting provisions of the UN Charter is done in the context of its being both a constitutive and a law-making document. Due to its status as a constitution of the world community, 'resolutions and declarations passed by consensus play a major role in the formation and change of legal values which also influence the interpretation of the Charter'. According to Simma, the fact that the UN Charter is also a law-making treaty favours a dynamic evolutionary interpretation of the terms of the Charter. This view is reflected in the opinion of Judge Alvarez of the ICJ: 'the fact should be stressed that an institution, once established, acquires a life of its own … it must develop, not in accordance with the views of those who created it, but in accordance with the requirements of international life'. But Simma, while supporting a dynamic evolutionary interpretation of the Charter, concludes that the historical will of the parties contained in the *travaux préparatoires* is relevant in interpreting the Charter, 'although only of secondary importance'.[27]

Concerning the issue of analysing state practice, caution must be exercised, in part resulting from the absence of a compulsory system of jurisdiction in public international law. Consequently, the risk is that state practice, which in fact represents a violation, can be used to constitute 'practice accepted as law'. As Oscar Schachter states, 'infringements of existing rules reflect expediency and political motives: it would make a nonsense of customary law to treat them as repealing an accepted basic obligation'.[28]

One requirement for state practice to contribute to law creation is that the practice be uniform. Ian Brownlie indicates that complete uniformity is not required, but 'substantial uniformity is'. Another element relevant to the issue of humanitarian intervention is that the state practice be accompanied by the requisite *opinio juris*. Although Brownlie points out that some writers do not consider this psychological element to be a requirement for the formation of custom, he concludes that in fact 'it is a necessary ingredient'. As Malcolm Shaw indicates, it is necessary to distinguish behaviour undertaken because of law from behaviour undertaken because of a whole series of other reasons, from goodwill to pique. For Dino Kritsiotis, without substantiating state practice and *opinio juris,* pro-interventionists engage in 'legal sophistry'. Finally, the need for the psychological element appears clear from the terms of the Statute of the ICJ itself, which requires general practice 'accepted as law'.[29]

What constitutes evidence of custom appears at first blush uncontroversial. Brownlie says the material sources of custom are very numerous and include: diplomatic correspondence; policy statements; press releases; the practice of international organs; and resolutions relating to legal questions in the UN General Assembly. However, *opinio juris* may be difficult to establish as political and diplomatic statements can reflect pretextual rather than substantive reasons for state action or inaction. Proponents of humanitarian intervention tend to be dismissive of such statements, relying instead on the reality of state practice. Tesón argues that state motives are irrelevant; what matters instead are 'the legal *reasons*' that justify an intervention.[30] However, the Tesón approach does leave pro-interventionists open to the criticism of ignoring inconvenient evidence.

Simma raises a final point regarding sources of law relevant to the doctrine of humanitarian intervention. In interpreting the UN Charter, he highlights the significance of applying a teleological approach, an approach that determines the object and purpose of the Charter.[31] This approach is consistent with the Vienna Convention on the Law of Treaties Article 31(1).[32] Pro-interventionists argue that humanitarian intervention is consistent with the human rights purposes of the UN Charter, relying on provisions in the preamble and substantive articles.[33] Tesón addresses the possible tension between the entitlement to human rights protection and the prohibition of war purposes by arguing that it was intended that states be protected from being the target of coercive intervention on the assumption that they minimally observe individual rights.[34]

On the Tesón view, the UN Charter does not establish a hierarchy of purposes. This proposal, however, sits uneasily with the fact that the human rights components of the Charter appear aspirational only. In contrast, its peace and security provisions provide for specific and extensive executive mechanisms. The *travaux préparatoires* also support the fundamental nature of the peace and security purpose of the Charter. Simma relies on the Charter itself, specifically Article 1(1), to conclude that the 'paramount' purpose of the UN 'is to maintain international peace and security'.[35] Antonio Cassese holds a similar view:

> In the current framework of the international community, three sets of values underpin the overarching system of inter-state relations: peace, human rights and self-determination. However, any time that conflict or tensions arise between two or more of these values, peace must always constitute the ultimate and prevailing factor.[36]

In summary, the evaluative framework to be applied to the normative issues of this chapter includes the following elements: a dynamic evolutionary approach to Charter interpretation can be taken; the *travaux préparatoires* are a credible though subsidiary source of law; state practice to constitute custom accepted as law must be generally uniform and be supported by the relevant *opinio juris;* resolutions of UN organs are a credible source of evidence of *opinio juris* but diplomatic and political statements must be treated with caution; scholarly works are a valid but subsidiary source of law; and the fundamental purpose of the UN is the maintenance and restoration of international peace and security.

THE CASE FOR HUMANITARIAN INTERVENTION

The core arguments in support of a right of humanitarian intervention, which will be examined below, include:

- It is consistent with the UN Charter in that Articles 2(4) and 2(7) do not prohibit humanitarian intervention, and other provisions related to human rights give support.
- A customary law right of humanitarian intervention survives the UN Charter in situations where the collective security mechanisms of the UN are ineffective.
- State practice supports a right of humanitarian intervention.
- Scholarly writings support a right of humanitarian intervention as being correct in principle and morally right.

HUMANITARIAN INTERVENTION AND THE UN CHARTER

It has been said that the 'best case that can be made in support of humanitarian intervention is that it cannot be said to be unambiguously illegal'[37] in that no provision of the UN Charter refers to the doctrine of humanitarian intervention to expressly render it lawful or unlawful.

The start point for analysing NATO's use of force regarding Kosovo is the UN Charter, particularly Article 2(4), described as 'the heart of the United Nations Charter'[38] and the 'basic rule of contemporary public international law'.[39] The intention of Article 2(4) appears clear: to outlaw the use of force (and its threat) as a means of dispute resolution between states. However, 'the paragraph is complex in its structure and nearly all of its key terms raise questions of interpretation'.[40]

A fundamental issue is whether Article 2(4) indeed prohibits all uses of force other than the two expressly provided for by the UN Charter, namely, in self-defence[41] or pursuant to the collective security provisions of Chapter VII. Of particular relevance is how the prohibition on the threat or use of force 'against the territorial integrity or political independence of any state, or in any other manner inconsistent with the Purposes of the United Nations' should be interpreted. Pro-interventionists argue that the words 'against the territorial integrity or political independence of any state' qualify the prohibition. Tesón, for example, concludes that as a genuine humanitarian intervention does not 'result in territorial conquest or political subjugation', and as it is consistent with the UN Charter's human rights purpose, it survives the prohibited elements of Article 2(4).[42]

Simma, after referring to the Dumbarton Oaks Proposals, a precursor to the creation of the UN Charter, states that the '*travaux préparatoires*, as well as the broad formulation used in the third strand of the formulation, are being disregarded by those who, contrary to the predominant view, consider the references to territorial integrity and political independence as limiting the prohibition of the use of force'. He says that the word 'integrity' has to be read as 'inviolability'.[43] Shaw concluded that the weight of opinion probably favours the view that the words in question reinforced the primary prohibition, thereby rejecting the restrictive interpretation. He relied on the 1965 Declaration on the Inadmissibility of Intervention in the Domestic Affairs of States.[44] He also relied on the 1970 Declaration on Principles of International Law which reaffirmed the principle and indicated a breach would be a violation of international law,[45] and the *Corfu Channel* case where the ICJ rejected the British claim of a right to interfere in the territorial seas of Albania.[46] Yoram Dinstein bluntly says that the adherents of humanitarian intervention 'misconstrue' Article 2(4) on this point. For Shaw, the pro-interventionists' approach to the 'territorial integrity' provision of Article 2(4) is 'rather artificial'.[47]

It is considered, therefore, that the restrictive pro-interventionist view of Article 2(4) appears contrary to the UN Charter's *travaux préparatoires*, General Assembly resolutions,[48] ICJ decisions and the weight of scholarly opinion. Schachter, supported by Simma, concludes that the restrictive view neither represents the *lex lata* [what the law is] nor a desirable *lex ferenda* [what the law ought to be].[49]

Pro-interventionists face less of an obstacle with the Charter's principle of non-intervention at Article 2(7). It is expressly stated 'not to prejudice the application of enforcement measures under Chapter VII' so would not inhibit a Security Council authorised intervention to restore or maintain international peace and security. Further, the principle is limited to matters 'which are essentially within the domestic jurisdiction of any state'. As Simma indicates, 'the humanitarian interventions by the UN in the case of the Kurdish population in Iraq confirmed that a matter does not fall essentially within domestic jurisdiction when it involves systematic and massive violations of human rights'.[50]

HUMANITARIAN INTERVENTION AND EFFECTIVE OPERATION OF THE UN

Pro-interventionists argue that humanitarian intervention survives the UN Charter in that the Charter was premised on the effective functioning of the collective security system.[51] Should that system be ineffective, it is argued, states are morally and legally released from the Charter restrictions. Schachter is blunt and persuasive in his rejection of this argument:

> The legislative history of Article 2 of the Charter does not support the notion that effective enforcement of collective security was a pre-requisite to renouncing the use of force ... No evidence or logical reason supports the assumption that the drafters or the signatory governments intended this radical result. Rather, widespread affirmation of the rules on force as *jus cogens*[52] ... shows that states regard those rules as legally independent of the proper functioning of the UN organs.[53]

Notwithstanding, the notion that pre-Charter self-help mechanisms revive in the face of a UN that is 'deadlocked, emasculated or moribund'[54] has emotive appeal. However, it does not address the fact that the veto power, for example the exercise of which usually gives rise to the claim of ineffectiveness, was clearly a considered and deliberate element of the Charter system. The pro-interventionists' argument if accepted, and taken to an extreme, would fundamentally attack the Charter by permitting states to unilaterally bypass the Security Council if unhappy with a decision made in accordance with mechanisms provided for in the Charter.

HUMANITARIAN INTERVENTION AND STATE PRACTICE

Selected state practice since the adoption of the UN Charter will be examined below.[55] As admitted by Tesón, writers 'have hotly argued' the point whether the doctrine of humanitarian intervention had been accepted before World War II, although he concludes that 'there is little doubt, however, that the doctrine received considerable acceptance in the practice of states and in scholarly writings'. Brownlie is less certain, stating that 'state practice justifies the conclusion that no genuine case of humanitarian intervention has occurred, with the possible exception of the occupation of Syria in 1860 and 1861'.[56] In any case, the Charter has so affected the legal and political framework concerning international relations, including the use of force, to render an examination of pre-Charter practice of limited relevance.

Congo 1960–64

Faced with separatists, the breakdown of internal law and order, and Belgian interference following Congolese independence from Belgium, the President and Prime Minister of the Congo requested UN military assistance. The initial UN military mission was a broad one, namely to provide military assistance 'in consultation with the Government of the Congo'. Eventually it contained enforcement elements, including maintaining the territorial integrity and political independence of the Republic of the Congo, assistance in the restoration of law and order, prevention of a civil war and the removal of mercenaries. The Security Council in Resolution 161 determined that the crisis was a threat to international peace and security.[57] Brownlie has categorised the UN's involvement in the Congo as humanitarian.[58] This together with the broad view taken by the UN as to its peace and security jurisdiction is highlighted.

East Pakistan (Bangladesh) 1971

On 16 December 1971 Indian forces defeated Pakistani forces in the then East Pakistan, with the effect that the state of Bangladesh was established. The intervention followed massive human rights violations by Pakistani forces against 'all of the East Pakistan people', described as genocide.[59] The objective of the West Pakistan authorities was to suppress dissent amongst the East Pakistanis who were distinct ethnically, culturally and linguistically. It is estimated that at least one million people died, with as many as ten million East Pakistanis fleeing to India. The Indian intervention was also against the background of pre-emptive air strikes by Pakistan against Indian targets and inaction on the part of the UN.[60] Tesón says this case study is 'an almost perfect example of humanitarian intervention'.[61]

A key element of this case study is the evidence of *opinio juris*. Notwithstanding the seemingly obvious humanitarian benefits, Pakistan, China and the US accused India of aggression. Within the Security Council, Saudi Arabia, Argentina and Tunisia condemned India for reasons such as aiding 'secessionist movements in another (state)'. In the General Assembly most delegates considered the situation in East Pakistan to be an internal one, although, significantly for Tesón, the majority in the General Assembly did not flatly condemn India for violating Article 2(4).[62] Reportedly, India's representative at the Security Council initially justified the action as 'humanitarian intervention'; however, India subsequently altered the Official Records to remove this reference, highlighting instead India's need to respond to Pakistani aggression. Akehurst contends that this indicates a belief by India that a right of humanitarian intervention was insufficient to justify intervention.[63]

Also complicating this case as a basis for asserting a right of unilateral intervention are the geopolitical benefits that accrued to India by East Pakistan's secession, namely the opportunity to 'curtail Pakistan's power and to diminish the territory of its political and military rival'.[64] Tesón dismisses these concerns, arguing that what matters is not India's purposes, selfish or humanitarian, 'rather that the whole picture of the situation was one that warranted foreign intervention on grounds of humanity'. The Indian intervention could also be arguably justified on the basis of self-determination, although 'it is fairly well established that self-determination generally does not apply in non-colonial situations'.[65]

What then is the status of this case regarding a right of unilateral intervention? Francis Abiew supports the conclusion of the International Commission of Jurists that notwithstanding India may have balked at justifying its actions on the basis of humanitarian intervention and that grounds such as self-defence were available, 'India's armed intervention would have been justified if she had acted under the doctrine of humanitarian intervention, and further, India would have been entitled to act unilaterally under this doctrine'.[66] However, the assessment of the International Commission of Jurists has a Cold War backdrop and is based on a view that a right of humanitarian intervention predated and survived the UN Charter in circumstances of a 'deadlocked, emasculated or moribund UN'.[67]

Uganda 1979

On 20 January 1979 Tanzanian military forces entered Ugandan territory and by April, after combined operations with Ugandan rebels, had toppled the regime of Idi Amin. Tanzania initially justified its intervention on the basis of self-defence following Ugandan incursions into Tanzanian territory with continuing harassment of the Tanzanians in the border areas after Uganda's withdrawal. After the fall of Kampala it relied also on humanitarian motives. On 27 March 1979 President Nyerere of Tanzania argued that two wars were taking place: one in self-defence by Tanzania in southern Uganda, and the other by Ugandan revolutionaries in a war of liberation against a regime whose arbitrariness, ruthlessness and cruelty 'can hardly be overstated'.[68]

The Tanzanian actions were greeted with relief. They were supported by the US but on the grounds of self-defence and by the UK,

Zambia, Ethiopia, Angola, Botswana, Gambia and Mozambique. The Organization of American States (OAS), contrary to its normal practice of condemning interventions, remained silent, as did the UN.[69]

Tesón argues that the 'Ugandan case is perhaps the clearest in a series of cases which have carved out an important exception to the prohibition of article 2(4)'. He contends that 'considerations of humanity are the only conceivable legal justification for the overthrow of Amin' as self-defence is not 'punitive' and must be 'proportionate'. Michael Kelly agrees that Tanzania's actions went beyond self-defence.[70] However, it is considered that this takes too narrow a view of self-defence. Sean Murphy, for example, indicates that a state exercising self-defence may not only expel the aggressor from their own territory but also in some situations overthrow their government, if necessary, to prevent recurrence of the initial attack. Dinstein supports such a broad view, arguing that the coalition forces in the Gulf War would have been justified, on the basis of self-defence, in pursuing the Iraqi forces to the bunkers in Baghdad.[71] The continuing threat posed to Tanzania was from Uganda's ruler, so arguably the removal of that ruler was a necessary and proportionate response to the threat. Here it is noted that the casualties from the conflict were relatively light,[72] indicating focused use of force by the Tanzanians.

Attributing dominating humanitarian motives to the Tanzanian leadership, apart from not matching Tanzania's official position, is inherently speculative. It also fails to address the fact, as reported by Tesón himself, that after an initial improvement in the Ugandan human rights situation after Amin's overthrow, it dramatically worsened, with an estimated 200 000 killed during the next five years.[73] This occurred without further Tanzanian intervention.

Grenada 1983
On 25 October 1983, 8000 US troops and 300 men from six Caribbean countries landed in Grenada. This operation followed a military coup on 19 October 1983, which ousted Prime Minister Bishop and established a Revolutionary Military Council. The US intervention was justified on three grounds: in response to a request from a lawful authority, namely, the Grenadan Governor-General; as a collective

action under Article 52 of the UN Charter at the request of the Organization of East Caribbean States; and to protect US nationals. This latter ground was undermined by the continued presence of US troops after the withdrawal of US nationals. The US State Department Legal Adviser expressly stated that the US 'did not assert a broad doctrine of humanitarian intervention', although arguably as one objective for the UN intervention was to restore democracy, a narrow ground of humanitarian intervention based on a right of self-determination could have been asserted.[74]

The broadness of the doctrine of humanitarian intervention advocated by Tesón is highlighted by this case. He supports interventions to 'put an end to situations of serious, disrespectful, yet not genocidal, oppression'. In the case of Grenada, unlike other cases such as Uganda and East Pakistan, mass murder and genocide were not involved. However, Tesón justifies the US intervention on the basis that 'a very serious deprivation of human rights was imminent'.[75] Such a broad and inherently speculative approach is highly significant in light of a major concern of anti-interventionists being the potential for abuse of the doctrine.

The US action was heavily criticised, with the UN General Assembly voting 108 to 9 to condemn the invasion as a 'violation of international law'.[76] In light of this response, together with the position of the US that the intervention was at the request of a lawful authority and the position of the US itself regarding the humanitarian intervention justification, the Grenada invasion does little to support a broad right of unilateral intervention.

Liberia 1990

Following the end of the Cold War and the withdrawal of US aid and patronage to President Samuel Doe, Liberia descended into civil war, creating a refugee crisis in the West African subregion, with 700 000 people fleeing the country and about 500 000 being internally displaced.[77] The crisis prompted the Economic Community of West African States (ECOWAS) to intervene on 23 August 1990 with a force entitled the ECOWAS Monitoring Group (ECOMOG). The stated justification for the intervention was humanitarian, being: 'first and foremost to stop the senseless killing ... and to help the

Liberian people to restore their democratic institutions'.[78] The intervention was not by request of the Samuel Doe government, although he supported it subsequently.

The intervention, made without recourse to the UN, was met with cautious approval. The Security Council in Resolution 788 in November 1992 eventually commended the ECOWAS initiative and supported it through declaring the Liberian situation a threat to international peace and security and imposing an arms embargo.[79]

In terms of precedential value, the following elements of the Liberian intervention are highlighted. It was prompted by a failed state which created a humanitarian catastrophe such as to 'shock the conscience of mankind'. The intervention did not appear to have mixed motives. It was carried out by a multinational force which respected the sovereignty of Liberia in that it did not impose a government. It was carried out with the initially passive and eventually active support of the Security Council. Finally, the intervention was not such as to itself threaten international peace and security in that superpower interests were not involved.[80]

Former Yugoslavia 1991–

The violent disintegration of the Former Yugoslavia, particularly in Croatia from mid-1991 and Bosnia from early 1992, resulted in hundreds of thousands killed and in the order of two million refugees and internally displaced persons. By September 1991 the Yugoslav representative at the Security Council stated that 'Yugoslavia can no longer be simply repaired. It should be redefined.' In Security Council debates on the situation, India, China and Zimbabwe raised the issue of non-intervention in states' internal affairs. The US and UK representatives highlighted the international implications of the conflict, such as the spillover of fighting and refugee flows. Resolution 713 was passed expressing concern that the continuation of the war constituted a threat to international peace and security and imposing an arms embargo. Thereafter the UN passed a series of resolutions pursuant to Chapter VII, and on occasions did use force, including air strikes by NATO forces in 1995, to support its resolutions.[81]

Abiew indicates that the UN intervention in Bosnia could be justified on three grounds: the refugee crisis (and the possibility of a spillover of fighting), the humanitarian crisis, and the gross human rights violations. For Tesón, the intervention in Bosnia was 'over-determined' as it could be justified 'as an action both to restore peace and to stop the atrocities'.[82]

Northern Iraq and southern Iraq 1991

With the Iraqi government being distracted by the war over Kuwait against coalition forces and a Shi'ite rebellion in southern Iraq, Kurdish rebels in northern Iraq made significant military gains in their long-running rebellion. After the cease-fire with the coalition, Iraqi forces reversed the situation, but with indiscriminate attacks against Kurdish urban areas and large-scale massacres. Out of a Kurdish population of three to four million in Iraq, over 1.5 million became refugees. Initially for fear of fragmenting Iraq, the allied powers accepted Iraq's repression, but on 5 April 1991 the Security Council passed Resolution 688. This stated that the repression of the Iraqi civilian population, including the Kurds, threatened international peace and security, insisted Iraq allow immediate access by inter-national humanitarian operations in all parts of Iraq, and appealed to member states and humanitarian organisations to contribute to these humanitarian efforts. The UK, France and the US subsequently declared no-fly zones in northern and southern Iraq and armed forces were used to create humanitarian enclaves.[83]

Resolution 688 was subject to vigorous debate in the Security Council. France later argued that its concept of a 'duty to intervene' emerged from the Iraq intervention, contending at the time that the right to intervene in Iraq existed independently of the situation's international dimension. Other states supporting intervention, how-ever, relied on the effect of the flow of refugees. China and other states referred to Article 2(7), but Fine argues that China and Russia were not in a position to use the veto because of urgently needed trade benefits.[84]

Interestingly, Resolution 688 did not expressly authorise the use of force and the UN Secretary-General, although eventually acquiescing in the military intervention, initially stated that it required further Security Council and Iraqi approval. Resolution 688 (and Resolution 687) continued to be relied on by the US and the

UK to launch military strikes against Iraq up until the 'Coalition' invasion of Iraq in early 2003. This was notwithstanding criticism by nations including France, and scholars such as White and Cryer.[85] Fine states that, in time, the world will come to view the Kurdish enclaves 'as a curio of international law'.[86]

Somalia 1992–95

With violent rivalry between clans following the end of the Cold War, Somalia descended into a state of civil war. With no functioning government, by mid-1992 over 1.2 million Somalis were either refugees in Ethiopia, Yemen and Kenya or internally displaced. Starvation threatened about half the population and about 300 000 people had died. The armed factions were hampering humanitarian efforts. Eventually the Security Council in Resolution 794, adopted on 3 December 1992, determined that the situation constituted a threat to international peace and security, authorised member states 'to use all necessary means to create a secure environment for humanitarian assistance' and stated that impeding 'humanitarian relief violated international humanitarian law'.[87]

Resolution 794 resulted in the deployment of a US-led force of 35 000 troops commencing in mid-December 1992. UNISOM II eventually replaced UNITAF in May 1993. Operating under Resolutions 814 and 837, the UNISOM II mandate was expanded to include institution-building and the establishment of law and order,[88] matters traditionally essentially within the domestic jurisdiction of states.

Significant in the Somalia case is that there was no government to either request or reject the intervention. In a failed state, arguably the prohibition in Article 2(4) is not activated so an exception to it is not required. Tesón refers to but rejects this argument, saying that 'the fact there is no government does not mean there is no state'.[89] However, the Montevideo Convention on the Rights and Duties of States specifies that a state must include 'a government', and for Brownlie this means an 'effective government'.[90] Also, international *relations* are exercised through governments and the prohibition in Article 2(4) is against the threat or use of force in the *relations* between states.

The Somalia case does indicate the Security Council's willingness to categorise as a threat to peace and security civil war situations where there is no functioning government causing a humanitarian crisis, and to explicitly authorise a forcible intervention.

Rwanda 1994

Following the death of its president on 6 April 1994, Rwanda plunged into civil war accompanied by genocide. Up to one million Rwandans were killed, 1.2 million fled to neighbouring countries and 2.2 million were internally displaced. The Security Council reaction was slow and inadequate but included adopting Resolution 929 authorising in June 1994 unilateral French action to establish a security zone in south-western Rwanda. France argued before the Security Council that its 'initiative is exclusively humanitarian: the initiative is motivated by the plight of the people'. Although the French intervention was somewhat ambiguous, as arguably the intervention protected the perpetrators of the genocide previously supported by France, French troops withdrew after two months and did not interfere in the progress of the civil war.[91]

Tesón says that there 'is little doubt that the UN authorized French mission is best described as a case of legitimate humanitarian intervention'.[92] Perhaps it had humanitarian motives and a humanitarian benefit, but it occurred in the context of a genocide which clearly destabilised the region through refugee flows and the establishment of long-term refugee camps.

Haiti 1994–96 and the Comoros 1995

In September 1991 Haitian President Jean Bertrand Aristide was removed in a military coup. Haiti had had a history of dictatorial rule but Aristide had been democratically elected in December 1990 in internationally supervised elections.[93] Initially, the Security Council saw the situation as an internal matter that did not threaten the peace. The OAS and the General Assembly were more active, with the General Assembly condemning the 'illegal' replacement of the constitutional president and affirming as 'unacceptable any entity resulting from that illegal situation'.[94] In June 1993 the Security

Council invoked Chapter VII of the Charter to authorise member states 'to form a multinational force ... to use all necessary means to facilitate the departure from Haiti of the military leadership'.[95] The leaders of the coup agreed to relinquish power and a US-led force entered Haiti. The agreement and the intervention were well supported internationally, with Venezuela the only Latin American country to condemn the intervention.

As a precedent for the doctrine of humanitarian intervention, the Haiti case study is ambiguous. The Security Council had referred to the military regime's 'systematic violation of civil liberties' and the 'illegitimacy' of the regime.[96] However, one result of the coup was an influx of the refugees to the US. Cynthia Weber argued that the human rights violations in Haiti were not a priority for the US, rather 'it seems ... the focus on the protection of Haitian human rights served as a false cover for an issue closer to home—immigration'. Kenneth Regensburg suggests that international law played a minute role, if any, in the US decision to intervene and history may judge Resolution 940 an unwise decision. Additionally, an aim of the intervention was to restore a democratically elected government which the international community had a role in creating. Scheffer says that, in such a case, 'there arises a legitimate basis for the United Nations and the regional organization (instrumental in developing the government) to guarantee its survival ... when it has been overthrown by a military coup'.[97] If this is a case of intervention to protect a human right, it is suggested that it is much narrower than a general right of humanitarian intervention.

An intervention to restore a government removed by a coup also occurred in the Federal Islamic Republic of the Comoros in October 1995. France unilaterally intervened, at the request of the ousted prime minister, against the mercenary troops of Bob Denard. The intervention took place without UN approval or subsequent comment.[98]

Sierra Leone 1998
In 1991 in Sierra Leone a civil war erupted, with the Revolutionary United Front (RUF) opposing the government. In March 1996

Ahmad Kabbah became president in free democratic elections. On 27 May 1997 Kabbah was deposed in a coup by a group of military officers aligned with the RUF. The Armed Forces Revolutionary Council (AFRC) was formed, which was opposed by the UN, the Organisation of African Unity (OAU), ECOWAS, the Commonwealth and the European Union.[99]

Following the coup, the rule of law in Sierra Leone collapsed with widespread and egregious abuses of human rights. After pacific attempts to deal with the crisis, including diplomatic initiatives and economic sanctions and after requests from Kabbah to intervene, ECOWAS did intervene with the ECOMOG forces on 6 February 1998. The AFRC government collapsed and its forces withdrew.[100] The intervention was supported, after the event, by the UN Security Council. In Resolution 1162, the Council welcomed the efforts made by the democratically elected president of Sierra Leone since his return and that of his government to restore peace and security and commended ECOWAS and ECOMOG 'on the important role they are playing in support of the objectives related to the restoration of peace and security'.[101]

The precedential value of this intervention from the perspective of the doctrine of humanitarian intervention is similar to that for the Liberian intervention in 1990. It occurred in the context of what was essentially a failed state where human rights abuses were such as to shock the conscience of mankind. In the Sierra Leone case, the intervention was carried out at the request of a deposed but democratically elected head of state. Peaceful means to end the human rights abuses had been exhausted. The objectives of the intervention were limited to ending the abuses and restoring the democratically elected government. Finally, the intervention was carried out by a multinational force with the eventual support of the Security Council.

State practice: conclusions

Post-Charter state practice indicates that interventions with the authority of the UN and unilateral interventions must be distinguished.

Regarding UN authorised interventions for essentially humanitarian reasons, a supporting consensus has emerged. After a careful analysis of post-Charter state practice, Abiew accurately concludes that, although the emerging picture is marked by 'varied international responses and mixed results', a principle is clear, namely that 'massive human rights deprivations do constitute a threat to international peace and security either through transboundary refugee flows or spillage of internal strife across borders' and in such circumstances the Security Council 'can take appropriate action including the use of force'.[102] However, although UN practice indicates that state sovereignty is no impediment to intervention, it is on the basis of a broad definition of its peace and security power rather than on the basis of an independent right of humanitarian intervention. All cases of UN-authorised forcible interventions—the Congo, Somalia, Rwanda, the Former Yugoslavia, Haiti, and Northern Iraq—involved situations with transboundary implications.

Cases of unilateral non-UN-authorised coercive interventions, however, do not provide sufficient support for a proposition that a customary norm supporting a broad right of unilateral humanitarian intervention, save for the possible exceptions in failed state and genocidal situations, had emerged at the time of the NATO intervention in the FRY.[103] In the case of East Pakistan and Uganda, it is noted that evidence regarding the appropriate *opinio juris* was questionable, that a credible separate justification for the interventions was present, namely self-defence, and that self-interested motives were present. The Grenadan intervention was heavily criticised and could be justified on the basis of a broad right of humanitarian intervention only by speculating as to potential rather than actual human rights abuses. Liberia and Sierra Leone occurred in the context of a failed state and with the Security Council's initial acquiescence and subsequent approval. In short, it is considered that the position of a broad right of unilateral humanitarian intervention is best reflected in UK Foreign Policy Document No. 148, which states: 'The state practice to which advocates of the right of humanitarian intervention have appealed provides an uncertain basis on which to rest such a right'.[104]

Article 38 of the Statute of the ICJ includes, as a subsidiary source of international law, 'the teachings of the most highly qualified publicists'. Brownlie highlights that the writings of publicists not only provide evidence of the law, but also can have a formative influence on the law itself. He notes that notwithstanding the caution with which they should be approached these opinions are used widely, including by the ICJ.[105] It is considered that such writings are particularly significant in the area of humanitarian intervention as in many respects, as a legal concept, it is creation of scholarly advocacy.

Although it could accurately be said in 1986 that 'the overwhelming majority of contemporary legal opinion comes down against the existence of a right of humanitarian intervention',[106] this is perhaps now only the case regarding a right of unilateral intervention.

Certain key elements of the pro-interventionist case have already been examined, namely aspects of Charter interpretation, the broadness of the concept, and state practice. Further selected arguments by scholars in support of the doctrine will be critically examined below, with an emphasis on the writings of Fernando Tesón as an influential member of the pro-interventionist school who has comprehensively addressed both sides of the debate. The two remaining areas to be addressed are, first, the moral imperative underpinning the legal approach to the doctrine by pro-interventionists, and, second, the issue of whether UN practice supports an independent humanitarian intervention doctrine or merely reflects a broadening interpretation of the Security Council's collective security powers.

At the core of the interventionist approach is the belief that conventional methods of treaty interpretation are 'incapable of yielding a solution to the hard case of humanitarian intervention'. That solution can only be reached by 'presupposing an ethical theory of international law', by linking international law and moral philosophy. Tesón argues, for example, that as Article 2(4) and state practice can be interpreted either way, 'the only way to reach a conclusion is to appeal to moral-political values'. The Tesón approach requires treaties like the UN Charter to be interpreted 'in a manner consistent with our basic moral perceptions'. He relies for support in part on the fact that the allied intervention in World War II was a 'war of human rights' and it would be 'paradoxical ... to take the view that the United Nations Charter ... which was the direct result of World War II, outlaws the very type of war to which the Charter owes its existence'.[107]

Certainly the benefit of a legal-moral approach is that it can overcome the apparent restrictions of Article 2(4), and is by definition emotively appealing, but is it valid? Tesón says it is legitimate as non-interventionists are themselves 'making a value choice; they are giving priority to the rights of states over the rights of individuals'. However, the Tesón view of legal philosophy can be questioned without rejecting his position that 'when state sovereignty clashes with minimal human dignity, the former must yield'.[108] It is considered that rejecting a broad right of unilateral intervention does not follow from deciding in favour of state sovereignty in a battle between state sovereignty and the protection of human rights. Rather, the issue is which of the protection of human rights and peace and security imperatives has priority. As outlined previously, it is considered that the correct view, based on the drafting history and content of the Charter, is that the maintenance of peace and security is the pre-eminent purpose of the Charter.

Further, the legal-moral approach in part depends on a misinterpretation of history, overstating, for example, the allies' moral imperatives in World War II and understating issues of pragmatic geopolitics and conventional issues of security. The morality dimension to the Charter is thereby also inflated by pro-interventionists and its utilitarian aspects downplayed. The veto power, for example, is not a product of a sense of morality but a reflection of Realpolitik.

Other arguments for humanitarian intervention reflect misplaced idealism. Barry Benjamin, for example, argues for a relaxation of prohibitions on unilateral humanitarian interventions 'because [as] modern technology has significantly increased the ability to discern pretextual actions from altruistic actions, the potential abuse of unilateral humanitarian intervention is minimized'.[109] But the

NATO intervention in the FRY itself undermines faith in the accuracy of information, even in the information age. When reviewed after the conflict, NATO reporting during the conflict of the results of its air strikes was found to be significantly inaccurate.[110] A more recent example of the continuing uncertainty of the accuracy of information available at the relevant decision time is provided by Iraq and the allegations regarding weapons of mass destruction. The existence of such weapons provided the primary justification for an invasion of Iraq in early 2003, but, in more than a year since the invasion, no such weapons have been located. Benjamin's confidence that modern technology has increased our ability to discern pre-textual actions from altruistic actions, based on the availability of accurate information, is misplaced.

A final issue is whether UN practice supports a right of humanitarian intervention as a separate concept from that of peace and security. On one view, the Somalia intervention, for example, merely reflects a broad interpretation of Article 39 of the Charter. Tesón, however, argues that the intervention cannot be justified on the basis of Chapter VII as, notwithstanding the words used by the Security Council, the situation 'did not pose any serious danger to international peace'. He postulates that if Resolution 794 is not seen as being *ultra vires* by the Security Council it must be lawful on the basis of another, separate legal principle. He proposes that this principle is the right 'to authorize forcible measures in extreme situations of human rights violations'.[111]

The Tesón view, first, overstates the threshold issue for the Security Council in that a 'serious' threat is not required, and, second, provides an unreasonably restrictive approach to what circumstances may constitute a threat to international peace and security. It is considered that justifying the Somalia intervention, and similarly the interventions in northern Iraq and the Former Yugoslavia, on the collective security power of the Security Council is both reasonable and technically legitimate, being consistent with a dynamic evolutionary approach to interpreting the Charter. As the refugee crisis in the Great Lakes region of Africa has shown in the early and mid-1990s, for example, trans-border movements of populations can in fact have devastating and at least medium-term destabilising effects on regional peace and security.[112]

It is also argued by pro-interventionists that merely broadening the scope of the peace and security regime is insufficient. It shields from intervention cases of gross human rights violations that do not produce transboundary effects.[113] However, sufficiency is a matter of opinion not law. Further, it is considered that the fear of a deficiency in the breadth of the peace and security basis for intervention is one that exists in theory not reality. The state practice reviewed above shows no case of widespread human rights abuses that did not have actual or potential trans-boundary effects.

In summary, the pro-interventionist approach is dependent on a moral philosophy view of the UN Charter that sits uneasily with its clearly utilitarian components and it promotes humanitarian intervention as a stand-alone doctrine rather than accepting a reasonable broadening of the peace and security framework of the Charter. Although wars in 'defense of human rights may be just',[114] in principle at least, they are not necessarily lawful. The pro-interventionists are susceptible to the criticism that they adopt an evaluative framework that is biased towards producing a desired result rather than an objective assessment of the state of the law.

THE STATE OF THE LAW REGARDING HUMANITARIAN INTERVENTION

It is considered that Charter interpretation, state practice and, on balance, the content of scholarly works indicate that at the time of the NATO air strikes against the FRY a UN-authorised right of humanitarian intervention based on the Charter's peace and security regime had emerged, but a unilateral right had not. The state of the law in 1999 is considered to be generally reflected in the following statement: 'From a legal standpoint … neither the UN Charter nor the extensive government commentary thereon supports an interpretation subordinating the basic prohibition against unilateral use of force to ends other than self-defense or UN enforcement action'. To these clear exceptions may possibly have been added, as proposed by

Kelly, unilateral intervention in a failed state or interventions to prevent genocide. However, Kelly also counselled: 'It is preferable nonetheless that all interventionary action be carried out under the UN umbrella for the furtherance of international order'.[115]

It is also considered that a norm of customary international law supporting a broad right of unilateral humanitarian intervention has not yet emerged, notwithstanding that there has been an increase in the number of scholars advocating that it has. Support for the proposition that such a norm still has not yet emerged includes the General Assembly debate on the subject in September 1999 after the Kosovo air strikes. Of the states that took an explicit position on the issue, thirty-two were either 'overtly opposed or negatively inclined, while only eight states were generally supportive', with two opposed or negatively inclined, being members of the Security Council, namely China and the Russian Federation.[116]

Given the continued level of state opposition to unilateral humanitarian intervention revealed in the General Assembly debate, the limited and uncertain support for the norm provided by state practice linked with the necessary accompanying *opinio juris*, and the more recent 'degree of hostility or suspicion with which the intervention in Kosovo was received',[117] it cannot reasonably be concluded that a new norm of customary international law supporting unilateral humanitarian intervention has emerged.

NATO'S INTERVENTION: A BREACH OF INTERNATIONAL LAW?

The lawfulness of the NATO intervention in the FRY will be examined both against this chapter's view of the *lex lata* at the time of the intervention, and, as the case for a broad right of unilateral humanitarian intervention has emotive appeal and some 'in principle' support, also against the framework advocated by the pro-interventionists. The UK government's justification for intervention, which appears to sit somewhere between these two, will also be addressed.

Based on the legal framework supported by this chapter, the NATO intervention in the FRY commencing on 24 March 1999 was clearly unlawful. The situation did not support the use of force by NATO in self-defence, there was no Security Council resolution explicitly authorising the use of force, the government structures in Kosovo were intact, and there was no genocide. On this latter point, although the stated NATO objective was to avert a 'humanitarian catastrophe',[118] the situation was that, in the twelve months prior to the NATO air strikes, reportedly 2000 persons had been killed in Kosovo, with one-third being Serb.[119] This occurred in the context of an internal conflict of fluctuating intensity. It appears 'that the wide Serbian offensive against Kosovo Albanians began *after* NATO's attacks began'.[120] There were disturbing violations of human rights in Kosovo prior to the NATO intervention, but had the required threshold been reached?[121]

However, even if it were accepted that a new customary law norm had emerged, the NATO intervention is also regarded as being questionable when evaluated against the broad, unilateral interventionist framework advocated by publicists such as Tesón. Tesón summarises that framework as follows: 'the intervention must be necessary, proportionate and welcomed by the victims themselves'.[122] Although apparently supported by the Kosovo Albanians, claims that the NATO intervention complied with both the remaining principles of necessity and proportionality are problematic.

Regarding the principle of necessity, two issues are considered relevant. First, the justification for NATO bypassing the UN and, second, whether peaceful options had been exhausted. On the first issue, it was clear at an early stage that NATO would not obtain Russian support for a Security Council resolution expressly authorising force. It also appears that certain other members of the Security Council, including China and India, would have rejected such action. However, this was not a case of a 'deadlocked, emasculated or moribund' UN which in the Cold War period may have justified pro-interventionists arguing that the UN system could legitimately be bypassed. Arguably, in the post–Cold War period, at least up to the time of the Kosovo intervention, the collective security system of the UN was operating as it was intended, and, in the case of Kosovo, there were a number of legitimate reasons to question the utility of the NATO action.[123] The following view of Nigel White and

Robert Cryer is supported as being accurate at the time of the NATO action over Kosovo:

> It is no longer sufficient to point to Cold War politics to explain a lack of action from the Security Council. It may be there is simply no agreement on the necessity to use force ... the lack of a mandate from the Council is actually reflective of the balance of international opinion.[124]

Nor could it be argued that in failing to condemn the intervention that the Security Council had, as in the case of Sierra Leone and Liberia, acquiesced to it. Such an argument is both questionable in principle[125] and contrary to the statements by certain Security Council members condemning the NATO decision. For example, on 24 March 1999 the Indian Permanent Representative to the Security Council stated that '[the intervention is] a clear violation [of the Charter]. No country, group of countries or regional arrangement, no matter how powerful, can arrogate to itself the right of arbitrary and unilateral military action against others. That would be a return to anarchy where might is right.'[126]

It is also noted that the Uniting for Peace option[127] in the General Assembly was not utilised. Consequently, the key organs of the UN regarding the use of force were deprived of the opportunity to either legitimise or reject the proposed NATO action. The comments of White and Cryer are again apposite: 'To proceed unilaterally ... is to act only on behalf of self-interest, even if it is cloaked in a fictive claim of international approval'.[128]

It is commonly proposed by pro-interventionists that a genuine humanitarian intervention requires that certain criteria be met, including that 'all peaceful avenues which have been explored consistent with the urgency of the situation ... short of force have been exhausted'. In the case of Kosovo, whether NATO in fact complied with this requirement is hotly disputed. Cassese, referring to the Rambouillet process, argues that 'it cannot be denied that peaceful means had ... been tried and exhausted'.[129] However, a good case can be mounted that the Rambouillet process was fundamentally unreasonable, that it essentially constituted an ultimatum, and that it demanded more than was required to protect massive violations of human rights in Kosovo. NATO had demanded a NATO force be deployed in Kosovo rather than a UN force with access to the whole of the FRY not just Kosovo. It also required the institution of a particular civil and social structure in Kosovo. NATO's rejection of FRY counterproposals that arguably would have met the humanitarian needs taints its claim that 'NATO [had] been forced to take military action because all other means of preventing a humanitarian catastrophe [had] been frustrated by Serb behaviour'.[130]

Regarding the principle of proportionality, Tesón, for example, states that 'the intervention must always be proportionate to the targeted evil' and cautions against 'creating the same horrors that it is supposed to remedy'.[131] Although proportionality is a principle of inherently uncertain application, the NATO intervention in the FRY provides much material for critical comment. Although the human rights violations that prompted the intervention resulted from an internal conflict limited to Kosovo, between 24 March and 23 May 7000 air strikes on more than 500 targets throughout the FRY were carried out. The number of Serb civilians killed was at least 500 and perhaps up to 1500, this equalling the number of ethnic Albanians killed during the preceding twelve months in Kosovo. Reportedly, about 300 000 refugees and internally displaced persons were created at the height of the Serb offensives prior to the NATO air strikes. During the air strikes, 10 000 Kosovo Albanians were reportedly killed, with about 850 000 becoming refugees or internally displaced.[132]

A failure to achieve its stated objective of averting 'a humanitarian catastrophe'[133] does not of itself render the NATO intervention unlawful. However, if much of the above damage attributed directly to, or provoked by, the NATO intervention was predictable, this would go to the lawfulness of the intervention using the framework advocated by humanitarian intervention proponents such as Tesón.

What then of the UK government's justification for intervention which was not based on a claim of a 'general doctrine of humanitarian intervention', rather that 'a limited use of force was justifiable in support of purposes laid down by the Security Council but without the council's express authorization when that was the only means to avert an immediate and overwhelming humanitarian catastrophe'.[134] This reasoning is based on a misleading precedent, it being alleged there were 'cases' like that in northern Iraq. The northern Iraq case is the *only* similar case that has arisen prior to the NATO intervention in the FRY. Also, the Iraqi intervention can be distinguished. In a Memorandum of Understanding signed on 18 April 1991, Iraq accepted the international military intervention for humanitarian purposes,[135] whereas the FRY clearly did not consent to the NATO intervention. Also, it is significant that subsequent air strikes by the US and UK in the northern and southern no-fly zones established pursuant to Resolution 688 have been heavily criticised by scholars and states, including France, as being unauthorised.[136]

Although not a central issue, as it is subsumed by the use of force issue, NATO's actions in light of Article 2(7) are relevant. It is accepted that interventions to counter egregious breaches of human rights are matters not essentially within a state's domestic jurisdiction. However, as decided by the ICJ in the *Nicaragua* (Merits) case, 'Every State possesses a fundamental right to choose [and implement] its own political, economic and social systems'.[137] Here it is noted that the NATO intervention was to coerce the FRY to accept the Rambouillet document which affected, amongst other subjects, the political structure of Kosovo (Chapter 1), police/civil/public security (Chapter 2), and conduct of elections (Chapter 3).[138] Arguably, NATO was therefore in breach of Article 2(7) as it used coercive measures to influence matters that are considered essentially within the domestic jurisdiction of the FRY.

Also subsumed by NATO's actual use of force are the prior threats of the use of force by NATO. For example, in a statement on Kosovo by the North Atlantic Council on 30 January 1999 it was noted that: 'NATO is ready to take whatever measures are necessary … [it] may authorize airstrikes'.[139] The threat of force prohibited by Article 2(4) 'requires a coercive intent directed towards specific behaviour on the part of another state'.[140] As the NATO intent regarding the FRY was coercive requiring specific behaviour, it comes within the Article 2(4) prohibition, and, as for the eventual use of force, without there being an applicable exception.

NATO'S INTERVENTION:
UNLAWFUL BUT LEGITIMATE?

Following the intervention, a central element of the ensuing debate was a perceived gap in the area of humanitarian intervention between the concepts of legality and legitimacy. The Independent International Commission on Kosovo, for example, concluded that the NATO intervention in the FRY was unlawful as it breached the UN Charter. However, it found it was nonetheless legitimate 'because all diplomatic avenues had been exhausted and because the intervention had the effect of liberating the majority of the population of Kosovo from a long period of oppression under Serbian rule'. The International Commission on Intervention and State Sovereignty (ICISS), an initiative of the Canadian government prompted principally by the NATO intervention over Kosovo, also raised the issue of there being a distinction between legality and legitimacy.[141]

The assessment of the Independent International Commission on Kosovo that the NATO intervention was illegal is reasonable, but its claim that the intervention was otherwise legitimate can be contested. As described above, NATO's actions contained disturbing elements. For the purpose of highlighting the fact that the legitimacy of those actions is not free from doubt, the following elements of an argument that NATO's actions lacked legitimacy are raised:

- NATO essentially took sides in an internal conflict and became, in effect, the air force of the Kosovo Liberation Army (KLA), an organisation described in a UK Defence Select Committee Report on Kosovo as being a 'shadowy organisation' associated with 'outlaw elements' and being involved in a campaign of 'shootings and murder'.[142] As a precedent, intervention on behalf of insurgents against an established government has its risks.
- Human rights abuses in Kosovo prior to the NATO air campaign were not, in the context of an internal armed conflict, such as to shock the conscience of mankind, with the intervention itself arguably converting a humanitarian emergency into a humanitarian catastrophe.[143]

- The claims that the intervention was a 'last resort' are open to question.
- NATO adopted a military strategy that employed means and methods of warfare that, if not in breach of international humanitarian law regarding protection of civilians and civilian objects, sit uneasily with the protective imperative underpinning the concept of humanitarian intervention. An element of this strategy involved the transfer of risk from their own forces to civilians, including engaging targets from high altitude and thereby increasing the risk that those targets were civilian rather than military.[144] Another was the general strategy of engaging targets which were, at best, of an indirect military nature with the apparent intention of putting pressure on government decision makers through affecting the civilian population. Representative of this strategy was the 25 April 1999 *Washington Times* report that NATO planned to hit 'power generation plants and water systems, taking the war directly to civilians'. Adam Roberts refers to this concept of the US, and with it NATO, as having been developed over recent decades and designed to put pressure not just on the armed forces of the adversary state but also on its government. He highlights that this approach is in tension with an underlying principle of the laws of war 'that the only legitimate object which States should endeavour to accomplish during war is to weaken the military forces of the enemy'.[145]
- The motives of NATO in intervening in Kosovo had as much to do with the protection of NATO's credibility as it did with a humanitarian imperative. The UK Defence Select Committee's report following the intervention in Kosovo states: 'Once made, the threat of military action had put NATO's political and military credibility at stake. In its After Action Report to Congress, the US Department of Defense made it very clear that "maintaining NATO's credibility" was one of the three core objectives of the bombing campaign that was eventually adopted.'[146]
- The intervention has failed to produce a stable outcome, replacing the oppression of one ethnic group by the oppression of others and placing Kosovo in a sovereignty twilight zone.[147]

Given the moral ambiguity of the context and content of the NATO intervention over Kosovo, not surprisingly 'no overwhelming consensus emerges as to either the legality or the legitimacy of the action'.[148] The failure to arrive at a consensus regarding the intervention highlights weaknesses in the current formulations of the doctrine of unilateral humanitarian intervention in principle and in application. It is a doctrine that in effect avoids reasonably clear prohibitions contained in the UN treaty for the sake of a moral imperative. In practice, however, it is a doctrine that is uncertain in content, being variously formulated by scholars and bodies such as the ICISS. Further, the world of Realpolitik does not sit well with the purity of motive and action underpinning the doctrine.

LEX FERENDA: SHOULD A RIGHT OF UNILATERAL HUMANITARIAN INTERVENTION EXIST?

A right of unilateral humanitarian intervention is not part of the *lex lata*. The proposition that a genuine humanitarian intervention does not breach Article 2(4) is artificial and to argue on the basis of the emergence of a new customary law norm of international law that overrides Article 2(4) is to create a 'moral illusion', limiting the law to a 'mere description of reality so that making the law coincide with the state practice would be at a cost of completely renouncing any regulation of states' behaviour by international law'.[149] Stated bluntly, the latter proposition places a greater burden on examples of state practice regarding unilateral humanitarian intervention, such examples being small in number and equivocal in nature, than they can reasonably bear.

It is also true, however, that there is a common notion that interventions such as that over Kosovo are 'unlawful but nevertheless legitimate'.[150] For there to be a perceived gap between what is legal and what is legitimate is destructive of the rule of law. What then is a desirable *lex ferenda*? Not surprisingly, scholarly opinion is divided as to what the law should be regarding the use of force. Tesón says that a right of humanitarian intervention exists and that it should exist as there 'is something deeply wrong with an international legal system that protects tyrants like Amin'. Dinstein is equally clear in rejecting a right of humanitarian intervention: 'this is not only the law as it is, but also the law as it should be'.[151]

Prior to the NATO intervention over Kosovo, there was certainly a clear trend in support of humanitarian intervention. For example, the historically anti-interventionist OAU in its summit in July 1992 resolved that it was prepared to sanction interventions in internal conflicts on humanitarian grounds but highlighted the lack of clarity in international law. However, as Abiew indicates: 'not all states are supportive or in favour of a proactive international interventionist stance. International support has been forthcoming mainly from Western states. France has been in the forefront.' Even support for an expanded view of peace and security itself is of concern to certain third world countries that fear 'the spectre of a modern Holy Alliance of the Great Powers'.[152]

Whatever the content of *jus ad bellum* in the future, two related elements are considered essential. First, that international peace and security remain the paramount object, and, second, that 'it is the task of states to render it so'. That is, it must be a product of the global community of nations, not a regional collection of states whose interests coincide, nor an epistemic community. If there is a perceived gap between legality and legitimacy regarding humanitarian intervention, it is for the community of nations to bridge it. The unilateralism displayed by NATO regarding Kosovo is disturbing. The comments of White and Cryer relating to UK and US air strikes against Iraq in the 1990s have general application: 'This unilateralism should not be encouraged: it is dangerous'.[153]

Tania Voon refers to two contrasting proposals to close the perceived gap between legitimacy and legality, one being to codify the norms of intervention in an international treaty and the other being to allow the jurisprudence surrounding the UN Charter to develop without amendment to the text. She argues that the better view is that the law should be reformed to ensure a clear and consistent response to humanitarian crises according to agreed principles.[154] If the current legal framework is to be altered, this approach is supported as the contemporary situation, which arguably is following the second track, and is undermining of the apparently clear proscriptions in the UN Charter without providing a well-defined and generally accepted alternative. As Ralph Zacklin suggests, humanitarian intervention, as presently conceived, 'is an instrument of dubious legality, inequitable in implementation, and represents a weakening of the foundations of organised international society'.[155] This situation is both undermining of the rule of law generally as well as of the credibility of the doctrine of unilateral humanitarian intervention specifically.

In the area of use of force by states, the danger of unilateralism is particularly high in the absence of the checks and balances provided by a compulsory review mechanism. If each state is the 'final arbiter of the legality of it own acts ... the international legal endeavour would have been an exercise in futility'. The absence of a compulsory review jurisdiction is highlighted by the inability of the ICJ to decide the merits of an application by the FRY concerning the NATO air strikes against the US and Spain for want of jurisdiction. Similar applications by the FRY against Belgium, Canada, France, Germany, Italy, the Netherlands, Portugal and the UK are also being resisted on the basis of jurisdiction.[156]

The events in the FRY in the mid-1990s have implications for the conduct of future armed interventions where policy makers and publicists seek to justify them with a so-called right of humanitarian intervention. Many of the problems raised by the Kosovo intervention remain unresolved, and in a number of ways have been compounded by the recent interventions in Afghanistan and Iraq.

CONCLUSION

This chapter's contention is that there was not only a 'thin red line' separating NATO's actions from legality, but that the NATO threat and use of force regarding Kosovo also 'radically departed' from the UN Charter and assaulted the core of the international peace and security system accepted by the world community after World War II. As Simma, the proponent of the 'thin red line' thesis, concedes:

'should such an approach become a regular part of [NATO's] strategic programme for the future, it would undermine the universal system of collective security'.[157]

The counsel of Abiew is endorsed: 'if future humanitarian interventions are to be successfully developed, then they must be collectively underwritten by the international community as a whole'.[158] It is suggested this be through the Security Council or the General Assembly pursuant to the Uniting for Peace framework, or through the development of new treaty law. If this is not the case, then little exists to constrain states other than their own relative military capacity and the level of domestic popular support. Unilateralism, other than in self-defence, is not only unlawful, it is also dangerous. Tesón may be correct when he argues that a legal system that supports an Idi Amin would be flawed, but a strong case can also be made that a system that permits or condones interventions with a profile of that of the NATO intervention over Kosovo must be avoided.

The final word is left, however, to the UN Secretary-General Kofi Annan, who on 18 May 1999, at the height of the NATO air strikes, stated:

> For this much is clear: unless the Security Council is restored to its pre-eminent position as the sole source of legitimacy on the use of force, we are on a dangerous path to anarchy. But equally importantly, unless the Security Council can unite around the aim of confronting massive human rights violations and crimes against humanity on the scale of Kosovo, then we will betray the very ideals that inspired the founding of the United Nations.[159]

7 DOMESTICATING MILITARY INTERVENTIONS AND THE CREATION OF A UN STANDING FORCE

Lutz Unterseher

Armed interventions on behalf of the international community differ from traditional peacekeeping missions (using 'blue-beret' contingents) in at least one vital aspect: the role of lethal force. Whereas in blue-beret missions weapons have been normally (and ought to be) confined to personal self-protection, the kind of military expeditions discussed here cannot, as a matter of principle, rule out the use of force above the individual level. Indeed, they imply the systematic application of combat power, if necessary.

This is not to suggest that traditional peacekeeping operations are going out of fashion. On the contrary, there likely will be a steady demand for 'neutral' agents, symbolically representing the world community, to supervise armistice, demilitarisation and similar agreements after combatants have laid down their arms. In this role of quiet undramatic stabilisation, blue-berets have usually performed well—and it is deplorable that their contribution has not been sufficiently appreciated in the international arena.

Problems can arise, however, when troops trained, structured and equipped for traditional peacekeeping (with its restrictive rules of engagement) are employed in missions such as the protection of humanitarian sanctuaries and convoys *under acute threat*. As shown by the events in Bosnia-Herzegovina from 1992 to 1995, placing excessive military demands on blue-beret soldiers means abusing them. Predictably, the result is poor performance and, rightly or wrongly, a loss of respect for the ultimate authorising agency, the United Nations (UN).

This state of affairs has encouraged those who favour lowering the threshold for employing maximum force in peace operations. This position has also called forth its opposite: critics who maintain that 'overkill' approaches, while possibly suppressing conflict in the short term, will only stimulate long-term revanchist sentiments and undermine the prospects for a stable peace.

Lost in this polarised debate is another possibility: the use of armed intervention above the level of traditional peacekeeping, but substantially below that of intensive 'war-fighting'. Associated with this is a unique principle of 'adequacy': an employment of armed forces and (possibly) forceful measures that is sufficient to deal with and discourage military challenges, while not being of a character or magnitude that compromises the primacy of political conflict resolution.

The theory and profile of such forces that would neatly fit in with a 'holistic' concept of political stabilisation have so far not been properly understood by the wider expert community. Yet in practice there have been improvisations leading in the right direction. In the context of several recent missions authorised by the international community, attempts were at least made to tailor military contingents to the needs of 'robust peacekeeping': to be able to fight, if necessary, but not in an escalatory manner. Examples are the UN and EU/ NATO 'peace support' regimes in Bosnia-Herzegovina (years after the Dayton agreement), postwar Kosovo (albeit with serious shortcomings), Macedonia, postwar Afghanistan and in Central Africa.

Apparently, the official understanding of military intervention lags behind established practice. Concepts that guide long-term military planning are, as we shall see, still very much influenced by quasi-imperialist thinking and dreams of power projection with massive force. This is why soldiers out in the field, on peace support duty, are only rarely provided with an adequate equipment mix and often lack up-to-the-task leadership. Tailoring forces for such missions has all too often been characterised by makeshift approaches.

PACIFIST FALLACIES

Pacifists in Central Europe and elsewhere often argue that armed intervention of any kind, regardless of authorising agency, cannot lead to a resilient peaceful transformation of a crisis. Any armed intervention, they contend, has incalculable effects, too often leading to the destruction of those values, assets or people that the intervention was supposed to protect.

They make a strong case for conflict prevention and resolution by peaceful means and for the strengthening of supranational institutions, representative of international law. These, they say, should be given the support and resources they need to develop effective capabilities for monitoring and mediating crises.[1] These prescriptions are laudable, important and entirely reasonable. Unfortunately, they are not enough.

What should the world community do when international efforts to stabilise a crisis situation or prevent a humanitarian disaster by peaceful means fail? What should we do when such efforts come too late or are not accepted by the parties directly involved? Are we to be left then with only two options: do nothing or yield to military doctrines of 'decisive' force? This dilemma is especially acute because the competency of international agencies is presently so underdeveloped.

When the pacifists, especially the Greens of Austria and Germany, were confronted with media reports of mass rape, torture and murder during the 'ethnic cleansing' of Bosnia-Herzegovina, they immediately split into factions along the lines suggested above. One faction, the so-called 'Fundies' or fundamentalists, continued to resist even considering military action. They had no other answer but to stick to their naive tabooing of armed intervention, while grave crimes ensued across Bosnia.

The other faction, the so-called 'Realos' or realists (pragmatists), called for international punitive action, eventually acquiescing to most of what NATO prescribed: a very substantial and traditional military response. Driven by moralistic and humanitarian concerns, but unable to imagine a differentiated use of military instruments, the Realos could see no alternative to embracing a type of action and a role for NATO that they previously had opposed strongly.

In 1998, when the so-called red-green coalition was formed, the Realos became the German Greens' dominating faction. Soon after, in the spring of 1999, they joined their partners in government, the Social Democrats, in supporting NATO's bombing campaign against Yugoslavia (Serbia-Montenegro). There had been allegations, which later turned out to be false,[2] that Serb regular and paramilitary forces were embarking on a major operation to drive out the Albanian population from Kosovo. In the Greens' perception this prospect weighed more than the fact that NATO's military commitment to punishing the alleged wrongdoers had no legitimation by the UN Security Council.

Caught on the horns of a dilemma, torn between humanitarian concerns and anti-war sentiments, left and liberal political forces in many modern countries, from Austria to Australia, have, one way or the other, handed the initiative on security issues over to conservative leaders and their followers in the politico-military establishment.

INCREASING POWER PROJECTION CAPABILITIES AND NATIONALIST SENTIMENT

The post–Cold War trend of development in many Western militaries is towards increased 'power projection' and intervention capabilities, despite some substantial reductions in overall defence spending. And this development has gone forward essentially unhampered by political opposition. Reviewing the case of the UK, a British defence analyst close to New Labour, and with reference to Tony Blair's Strategic Defence Review, observes that:

> [our] expeditionary capability, which aspires to be nationally autonomous, would be a balanced force for operations of choice … This nationally autonomous force would have strategic significance. Operational autonomy is … useful if coalition partners are various and variable … All indications are that the Strategic Defence Review will formalise … an expeditionary strategic concept with a primary emphasis on flexibility and strategic mobility … Things might have been otherwise. A safe island nation might have opted for a comparatively cheap concept that emphasised territorial autonomy, or minimal defence. Or national autonomy could have been sacrificed in favour of a menu of contributions to NATO or European forces. Or the moral consciousness of a fairly wealthy, unthreatened nation could have been discharged through ground forces specialising purely in peacekeeping … But it has not been so.
>
> … Issues of the direct defence of the UK have not been central to the Review. The fundamental questions have gone beyond matters purely of defence and security. They are: 'What future role does the UK wish to play globally and in Europe?'; 'Will a relationship with the US continue to be a means to influence power events?'; and 'What instruments of national power need to be developed to fulfil this role?'. Of these instruments military capability is a strong and widely respected suit for the UK. A final and crucial question is therefore: 'How much military force is enough to command international respect and in what form will this military force be most influential?'.[3]

And, indeed, the Strategic Defence Review conducted by the Labour government did formalise an expeditionary strategic concept.[4]

Statements similar to Michael Codner's could be cited from other countries, NATO and non-NATO, although most (especially the official sources) are less frank about nationalist motives.[5] All in all, one gets the strong impression that the current build-up of intervention forces is a matter of international status competition. Paraphrasing the British source's 'crucial question': it is all about who has got the longest reach or who can project more power over greater distances.

PROBLEMS WITH PROPER TIMING

The formation of modern intervention contingents has been indicative not so much of a growing sense of international responsibility, but rather of the continuation of national profiles and interests. This suggests that joint action by a group of states, or by a military pact such as NATO, is not easy to achieve. Very much depends on whether or not an accord can be reached and sustained at least for a period of time, and even the best developed institutional mechanisms currently available for fashioning such accords seem clumsy.

The difficulty in forging co-operation is due not only to the fact that states may have different calculi of interests and power with respect to an intervention site, but also to the fact that they usually operate under different domestic constraints—for instance, the sentiments of their respective publics. Indeed, domestic public opinion seems to be of growing relevance in making decisions about intervention. Taking into account both factors, while trying to build an international consensus, can turn out to be a time-consuming business. The public, for instance, may be willing to send their soldiers into a conflict situation only after atrocities there have reached a high threshold; or publics may remain reluctant until they have been convinced that there are low-risk options for intervention forces.

Besides these problems, which concern the difficulty of forming intervention regimes, there are also other complications inherent in crisis situations. Take, for example, the case of Kosovo. The media, in Europe at least, and numerous political analysts have pointed to the danger of violent escalation there ever since the early 1990s.[6] Nonetheless, the international community did little or nothing for years, mainly for two reasons:

- Kosovo is a part of the Federal Republic of Yugoslavia (Serbia and Montenegro), which makes intervention without authorisation by the UN Security Council (required by international law) a tricky political business.

- In order to facilitate the negotiations leading to the Dayton accord for Bosnia-Herzegovina, which were a close-run, touch-and-go affair, the actors involved agreed clandestinely to postpone the Kosovo question, lest it impede reaching an agreement on Bosnia.

Whatever their source, delays in addressing a crisis allow processes of conflict escalation to spiral upward unhampered. And, as the situation gets worse, the option of a modest, well-tempered application of outside military force comes to appear less and less feasible. In the end, a massive counterstrike may seem the only option. This can be taken as kind of self-fulfilling process (or prophecy).

FOCUS ON PUNITIVE ACTION

When outside intervention to end an already well-developed conflict takes the form of a massive strike, such action almost automatically has the character of punishment, rather than denial. Massive strikes to stop the exchange of fire normally cannot be directed against zones where the conflicting parties are closely intermingled because such an operation would lack any discriminatory effect: the 'good' guys would get hit as well as the 'bad'. Instead, the strikes are directed at the military (and sometimes also the political and civilian industrial) infrastructure of the party identified as the aggressor. But often such strikes against an aggressor's 'backyard' are perceived by the people in the target area, themselves often victims of domestic oppression, as counter-civilian retaliation or even as an attempt at merciless subjugation.

With reference to the recent history of the Middle East, and to other conflict-prone areas, it has been argued that punitive or retaliatory military action is likely to evoke the desire for revenge.[7] The development of affairs in Bosnia-Herzegovina gives evidence to this hypothesis: with the NATO air strikes of 1995, the armed clashes on the ground soon came to an end (although they were not actually over until Croat troops had driven Serb forces and civilians out of the Krajina region). Quite a few observers have considered the

NATO strikes to be what prompted the peace process. Others disagree, with substantial arguments. According to these voices, the strikes were merely coincidental or, at least, not the main reason for the cease-fire.[8]

They believe it was more important that the conflicting parties had already achieved most of their goals of ethnic disentanglement and that they had largely exhausted their human and material resources. Also important in this view is the fact that the Clinton administration reversed its previous position in early 1995, showing itself ready to accept the new status quo. In other words: the results of ethnic cleansing.[9]

Seen against this background, the NATO air strikes take on a different connotation. Since they were almost exclusively directed against the military infrastructure of the Serbs, it is plausible to assume that they would have the effect of deepening Serbian resentments, rather than creating the conditions for a stable peace. Such negative reactions were further substantiated when—after the insertion of IFOR (Implementation Force) and SFOR (Stabilisation Force) to safeguard the Dayton accord—the Serbs gained the impression that the West, especially the US, gave preferential treatment to the Federation of Bosnia and Herzegovina (the Croats and Muslims). Today an international military presence continues to be needed to guard the peace in the Balkans. This includes the need for foreign troops in Kosovo where, in the wake of the bombing campaign against rump-Yugoslavia, Albanian self-confidence grew to such an extent that now the Serbian minority legitimately demands protection.

There is good reason to believe that punitive action can contribute to the development of conditions that demand 'more of the same': prolonged military presence or even another massive strike, then a third, and so on. At best, punishment can momentarily, or for a very limited period of time, stop hostilities; but it is unlikely to produce a stable peace. In this way, the reliance on military punishment by means of intervention forces is likely to give violent conflict a longer lease on life. This outcome, the product of myopic policies, would neatly preserve a central axiom of 'realism', that influential school of political science: namely, the belief that war cannot be 'disinvented'.

PROMISES OF HIGH TECHNOLOGY

Punitive strikes, which we have identified as problematic, are more likely to occur if the military culture of the intervening states centres on high-technology and the promises of its aficionados. The potential of high-technology applications appears to be greatest with respect to long-range, precision-guided fire using air-launched (stand-off) or ground-/sea-based missiles. For this reason, high-technology lends itself more to the improvement of strike capabilities than to the optimisation of military performance in other areas.[10] Currently, investments in high-technology equipment are mainly driven by three considerations:

- First, military strategists hope to minimise the collateral damage caused by punitive strikes in order to assuage public opinion and avoid challenges to the legitimacy of such strikes.
- Second, since modern societies are 'casualty averse' (especially with respect to their own youngsters sent abroad), there is increased reliance on machines that promise to do the job from safer, stand-off distances.
- Third, high-technology aficionados have successfully induced military hierarchies to believe that cutting-edge technologies make possible a quantum leap in cost-effectiveness.

These hopes are questionable, however. Many high-technology applications tend to be over-complex and, thus, susceptible to 'Murphy's Law'. High rates of mission capability are maintained only by Herculean maintenance efforts. Moreover, these systems, like all others, are vulnerable to countermeasures, but their high cost and long development cycles impede any quick adaptation to such countermeasures. Although the precision-guided weapons used in the 1990 Gulf War were given the highest ratings by Pentagon officials and were made to look good by militarily censored TV reports, their actual performance fell far short of initial claims and their cost-effectiveness proved quite low.[11] In some cases—for instance, the efforts to interdict Iraqi SCUD missiles and to find their launchers—their performance was abysmal.

Admittedly, in the recent war against Iraq, the large-scale use of newly introduced GPS-guided bombs (sporting satellite navigation) by the US Air Force and Naval as well as Marine Aviation led to a drop in complexity and cost. But this novel type of precision-guided munitions is not as accurate as older ones with on-board target seeking and is by no means proof against countermeasures. Future conflicts with forces employing more sophisticated jamming techniques than those used by Saddam Hussein's troops may set in motion new and expensive counter-countermeasure responses.

As for the limitation of collateral damage by high-tech means: one would have to be short-sighted and narrow-minded to conclude that the picture is good. On the one hand, by World War II standards, the rate of *immediate* civilian casualties per target destroyed was very low in the 1990 Gulf War and the Kosovo conflict. On the other hand, in absolute terms, thousands of civilians were directly killed by coalition attacks in the Gulf War; hundreds (and perhaps many more) were killed in the strikes on Serbia (in 1999). And with respect to the recent war against Iraq, the number of immediate casualties has been estimated to amount to 12 000–15 000 uniformed personnel and civilians.[12] These are not insignificant numbers, especially for relatively small countries and short wars.

Much more significant are, in certain cases, the indirect and intermediate effects of such bombings, unfolding in the days and months following the attack, which in the case of second Gulf War involved a genuine humanitarian disaster. After this war, a team of investigators from the Harvard School of Public Health estimated that there were 70 000–90 000 postwar civilian deaths, principally due to the lack of electricity for water purification and sewage treatment. Even one-tenth this number would be significant.

Also pertinent to the issue of damage limitation and cost-effectiveness is the question: what was gained by these attacks? In the case of the Gulf War, the official US Gulf War Air Power Survey found that the campaign against 'strategic' (meaning 'non-battlefield') targets did not have a compelling operational impact on the battlefield. The air strikes conducted in early 1999 against Saddam Hussein's regime and his arms production facilities may deserve a better marking. They appear to have, in addition to the international arms embargo, further weakened Iraq's military potential, thus conditioning it for the successful intervention of spring 2004 which combined strategic and tactical air assets with a powerful ground component.

In the case of the Kosovo conflict, many have said that 'air power won the war'. A much higher percentage of the air strikes were of the so-called 'strategic' sort than in the Gulf War and many more of the munitions used were of the precision type: 35 per cent, versus 8 per cent in the Gulf War. But proclaiming the victory of high-technology air power ignores several relevant points.

First, the US did not achieve its goal of victory within four days, as estimated beforehand, or anything approaching it—and this short-fall imposed a high political cost. Second, rather than bringing immediate relief to the Kosovars, the over-reliance on long-range strategic attack left them at the mercy of enraged Serbian forces for ten long weeks. Third, factors other than long-range strikes probably played as great a role in ending the conflict, if not a greater role. Among these factors were the Kosovar *ground offensive* late in the war and the mounting prospect of a NATO ground campaign, the role eventually afforded the Russians in mediating and enforcing the final accord, and the easing of some of the peace terms originally put forward at Rambouillet.

If we pay proper attention to operational effects, ultimate aims, and long-term consequences, the promises of high-technology and strategic air power advocates ring hollow. And we are reminded that, in attempting to conduct truly adequate military interventions, there is no substitute for human beings (inter)acting 'on the spot'.[13] High-technology strikes, per se, cannot oust a bloodthirsty dictator, keep warring factions apart or stop ethnic cleansing.

EXPEDITIONARY MISSIONS AND THEIR NATURE

Having criticised essential aspects of the current practice, let us now consider a better, more effective concept of military intervention. There are a variety of important tasks that armed interventions (above the level of traditional blue-beret missions) might undertake on behalf of the international community:

- military back-up for economic sanctions, arms embargoes, and so on (preferably only hurting a targeted regime and not the respective population);
- preventive, stabilising deployment of troops to a country (territory) under acute threat;
- evacuation of foreigners from a country torn by civil war;
- creating and defending a demilitarised zone to keep warring factions apart;
- protection of humanitarian convoys;
- defence of sanctuaries declared by the world community;
- punitive action to end escalatory processes;
- offensive retaking of territory seized by an aggressor; and
- occupation of territory to keep conflicting parties under control.

With respect to this catalogue of typical military missions, three interesting observations can be made:

- First, most types of missions have to do with control and protection—functions which cannot be regarded as punitive or offensive, per se. (Even if George Bush Jnr's recent wars in Afghanistan and Iraq are taken into account, as developments during the last fifteen years show, international control and protection missions have occurred more often than punitive operations or acts of reconquest.)
- Second, if the functions of control and protection can be performed in an optimal manner, enhancing political stability, the demand for punitive action or reconquest is greatly reduced.
- Third, the requirements for stability would be met best if the necessary military measures are well timed, immediately effective, and aimed at minimising provocation.

DEFENSIVE SUPPORT AS A KEY CONCEPT

A new concept of interventionary action that is attuned to the afore-mentioned points is 'defensive support'. It derives from that school of thought known as 'alternative', 'non-offensive', or 'confidence-building' defence.

As a mission concept, defensive support covers both protective and control functions. Its principal design insight is to structure expeditionary forces in a way that would 'decouple defensive from offensive mobility'. This means, on the one hand, giving troops a high degree of strategic mobility to allow for the speedy allocation of defensive combat power to 'the right spot' at 'the right time'. On the other hand, 'defensive support' prescribes organising, equipping and training these troops for holding ground and for patrol and escort missions, tangentially ruling out the capability to move offensively under heavy fire.

Typically, defensive support would require light, mechanised infantry formations (with organic air transport) riding on wheeled armoured carriers and being equipped with monitoring and counter-mobility gear (probably backed up by some artillery capable of firing advanced ammunition). Details concerning such a structure are available from a rich collection of recent alternative defence literature,[14] and from some innovative armies (such as the Finnish forces) whose leadership well understands that adequate crisis response demands modern, well-tailored contingents with a strong human element rather than high-technology gadgetry.[15]

Critics of alternative defence often have asserted that the school of thought fails to comprehend the mobility requirements of the new military era. More generally, it has been argued that the high degree of mobility necessary for intervention forces precludes the possibility of their being 'defensive'. However, a detailed analysis shows that there are different kinds of mobility, serving different ends—force allocation, offensive or defensive action—and that the competencies associated with each of these do not necessarily have to be combined.[16] In other words, even with long-range intervention forces, it is possible to structurally limit offensive capabilities.

The key innovation is to combine strategic mobility, which ensures optimal force allocation, with a tactically defensive mode of force structuring and deployment. This is entirely consonant with the fundamental rationale of non-offensive or confidence-building defence. Its central principle, with roots in ancient Chinese military philosophy,[17] is that a posture geared to directly deny aggressive aims has a much better chance of contributing to de-escalation and war avoidance than does a posture that aims to deter or defend by posing the threat of retaliatory punishment.[18]

Recent empirico-analytical studies of historical cases have produced evidence that the outbreak of armed conflict is more likely when at least one party believes that victory is both possible and relatively easy. In other words, the war temptation is greatest when an offensive strategy or option seems to be feasible and to promise success in a relatively short time at an acceptable cost in 'blood and treasure'.[19]

In this light, the best strategy for defusing crises and avoiding war would usually consist of measures that make territorial conquest more difficult: time- and resource-consuming. By contrast, in most cases, threats of retaliation are not equally promising because they can provoke pre-emptive moves. This is not an unlikely response, if one assumes that potential aggressors believe in the feasibility of the offensive.

POLITICAL AND INSTITUTIONAL REQUIREMENTS

If an act of military intervention is to have a stabilising effect, one important precondition is that it receives a mantle of 'international legitimacy' based on overwhelming support in the world community. Without this, even good-hearted interventions are likely to precipitate a cycle of unilateral or unipolar interventions and counter-interventions, with individual nations or groups of nations simply posing their interests in universal terms. Moreover, the failure to develop a true and resilient international consensus supportive of an interventionary act is likely to make success on the ground more difficult and costly. This is because one or more of the parties to the local dispute may hold out hope of gaining some significant outside support.

A second important prerequisite to effective intervention, as we have learned, is prompt action: timeliness. However, these two preconditions taken together can pose something of a dilemma. The broadening of the support base requires time, especially if it involves the integration of disparate national contingents and operational concepts: the more participants involved, the less likely that they will be able to act in concert in due time.

The need for legitimacy raises other difficulties as well. The legitimacy of interventionary acts has hinged on the approval or authorisation of the UN Security Council. Indeed, such authorisation is required by international law, especially in those cases where the intervention concerns a conflict inside the borders of a sovereign state. However, positive action by the Security Council has often been neutralised by the excessive use of the veto power given to its permanent members. This may eventually change: the admission of more permanent members to the Security Council may also involve some modification of traditional veto privileges.

Former UN secretary-general Boutros Boutros-Ghali expressed his concern, however, that the already long-overdue admission of new permanent members, along with a reformulation and differentiation of veto rights, might take more than a decade.[20] In his view, before key countries of the northern hemisphere (especially the US) would be ready to really share power with representatives of other regions, there has to be much more progress in the process of globalisation—the development of ever tighter cultural, social and economic networks—and the feeling of worldwide interdependence has to intensify considerably. But Boutros-Ghali contends that in the long term there is no viable alternative for the world community: greater co-operation, a necessity, requires a broader sharing of responsibility and authority.

And there is one more problem. If we assume that the UN will someday be capable of better (and more legitimate) decision making, there still remains the question of capability: does the world community have adequate means of implementation at its disposal? Currently, the UN is totally dependent on the goodwill of the member states which, particularly in cases where an armed intervention involves substantial risks, costs precious time.

Quite a few countries have earmarked selected 'stand-by' armed formations (or elements thereof) for military missions authorised and commanded by the UN. In most cases, however, the governments involved have linked their commitment to restrictive conditions. In spite of this, the designation of national forces for international use represents a step in the right direction. But there is a better solution yet: the development of a permanent UN legion.

PLEA FOR THE CREATION OF A UN LEGION

Several analysts have proposed that a standing 'UN Legion' could be allocated more flexibly to potential crisis spots and tailored more adequately to the world community's needs than could a force consisting of different national elements operating under different political constraints.[21]

Carl Conetta and Charles Knight formulated their proposal for the creation of a UN Legion in the context of a debate among experts (mainly in the US) whose concern was to provide the UN with more adequate means of military intervention.[22] And they have been particularly inspired by a systematic presentation of the problems involved by Boutros Boutros-Ghali.[23] They point to the fact that it was the malfunctioning of the UN stand-by system during the Rwanda crisis that induced the Netherlands to consider the possibility of setting up a standing UN brigade. In this context, their quotation from a speech which Hans van Mierlo, then Dutch Minister of Foreign Affairs, gave to the UN General Assembly in September 1994 is of particular interest.[24] The Minister reflected on a UN official's assessment that a *single* mechanised brigade deployed to Rwanda during the crisis might have averted the tragedy there:

> If the deployment of a brigade could have prevented the indiscriminate slaughter of many hundreds of thousands, what then prevented us from doing so? Let us face it: the reason was that under the circumstances no government was prepared to risk the lives of its citizens … If member states are not in a position to provide the necessary personnel, will it then not become unavoidable for us to consider the establishment of a full-time, professional, at all times available and rapidly deployable UN Brigade for this purpose: a UN Legion at the disposal of the Security Council?

With the demand thus stated, the future UN Legion could take on a profile such as the following.[25]

PROFILE OF A STANDING UN FORCE

Personnel
The Legion would comprise 15 000 internationally recruited soldiers and civilians (on a contract basis).

Force structure
The main organisational elements would be:

- 2 brigade headquarters
- 2 motorised infantry battalions
- 2 light mechanised infantry battalions
- 1 light mechanised cavalry regiment (battalion size)
- 1 light armoured cavalry regiment (37 light tanks)
- 2 armed scout helicopter companies (18 aircraft each)
- 6 field artillery batteries (eight 155-mm field pieces each)
- 2 air defence companies (12 mounted air defence systems each)
- 2 strong combat engineer companies
- 2 signal companies
- 2 field intelligence companies
- 2 military police (MP) companies
- 2 civil affairs companies
- 2 field logistics bases.

Deployment
Having two types of infantry and cavalry allows for a relatively precise tailoring of deployment packages. Most demanding would be missions aiming to protect large humanitarian sanctuaries or to separate (and disarm) warring factions. Such a mission could require the deployment of a reinforced brigade numbering up to 5000 soldiers. This is about as many troops as the proposed legion could keep out in the field at any one time. Among the assets of such a reinforced brigade would be 18 light tanks, 16–24 155-mm field pieces, 32 medium-heavy mortars, 12 mobile air defence systems, 18 armed

scout helicopters, and approximately 200 other combat vehicles or armoured transporters.

A brigade-sized deployment package of normal dimensions (3300 to 3500 persons) could be transported from its home base to a site 10 000 kilometres away within twelve days. This would require less than 500 C-141 sorties (and a fleet of only 36 C-141s or its equivalents). A lead element of such a force—a reinforced light mechanised infantry battalion—could be 'on the spot' within only three or four days.

Cost estimates

The initial capital expenditures for equipping the proposed force, including base construction or renovation, would amount to approximately US$1.9 billion (at 2003 prices). And the long-term average annual budget for a UN Legion has been estimated to be US$900 million. Incremental costs associated with field operations might add another US$720 million per year. It should be noted that the estimate of these incremental expenses is for one year of full utilisation. The costs of strategic lift are included (rental basis), on the assumption of two separate deployments (in each case 50–60 per cent of the force would be transported by air).

AVOIDING A PECULIAR KIND OF LEGIONARY'S DISEASE

The profile of the proposed UN Legion shows us a force that is somewhat dominated by infantry. And there are additional elements —such as engineers, MPs, and those for civil affairs—which also place particular emphasis on human actors and their performance. This emphasis is totally adequate because the envisaged force does not just have to be tactically and technically efficient, but also has to engage in numerous human interactions in order to have a truly stabilising, confidence-building effect in the crisis region. Think, for instance, of soldiers who, having suppressed hostile sniper action by their own high-precision counterfire, are ordered to disarm the village where the shots had come from! In such cases, very much depends on the UN soldiers' social skills, on their ability to stand firm and to avoid provocation.

Such virtues could erode or might not fully flourish, however, if the members of the UN standing force develop an esprit de corps with a decidedly elitist touch. Of course, the UN legionnaires would quite likely constitute an elite. The question is: would this quality be unduly emphasised or not? In this regard, the history of the French Foreign Legion teaches an interesting lesson.[26] In order to overcome the divisive tendencies inherent in the Foreign Legion's multicultural recruitment base, and to generate (as well as to maintain) the high degree of group cohesion necessary for combat effectiveness, a veritable cult of being 'special' and 'superior' was developed. This often led to very serious problems of interaction with the indigenous civilian population in the regions of deployment. At present the Foreign Legion seems to pose less of a human relations problem than was the case during the period between 1830 (the Legion's founding date) and the Algerian war. The reasons for improvement may be better political control and a greater degree of professionalisation.

One good thing about the concept of a UN Legion is that human relations problems can more easily be made a topic of international public concern and a subject of concerted measures aiming to minimise inappropriate behaviour. It would be far more difficult to address similar problems in the context of a peace mission comprising various national contingents from individual UN member states. It is well known, although seldom discussed in the political area, that not all soldiers participating in UN peace operations have behaved as appropriately as, for instance, the ones from Scandinavia.

What to do in order to achieve the best results concerning the human potential of a UN Legion should be subject to further study. For now, the following short-list of measures may provide a sense of direction:

- careful screening of applicants
- firm politico-military control
- introduction of an ombudsman system
- professionalisation partly linked to civilian education

- establishment of obligatory language courses
- exercises in multicultural understanding
- thorough information on potential deployment regions.

GENERAL ASSESSMENT

Provided that the human relations problems inherent in the creation of a UN Legion can be dealt with in a satisfactory manner, the concept is quite promising. It envisages a relatively light force that lends itself optimally to quick allocation and flexible adaptation to different environments. Its costs are by no means outrageous. Note, for instance, that of July 2004 arrears in payments of contributions to the UN peacekeeping budget amounted to US$2.479 billion, of which the US owed 34 per cent (US$837 million)![27] The estimated initial capital expenditures for a UN Legion would be lower than current overall arrears.

A special assessment of the Legion's fighting value shows that it would have considerable bite as long as it stayed on the defensive. Wherever needed it could mount a denial-type posture of respectable firepower stemming from a mix of direct- and indirect-fire weapons (in which high-precision artillery and mortars would play a key role).

A UN Legion could help overcome both the 'casualty aversion' of modern societies and the status-seeking impulses associated with the building up of nationally autonomous intervention forces. To the world community, notoriously lacking in resources, this option could be sold on grounds that a timely, non-escalatory insertion of adequately structured forces would promise success in peace operations at relatively low cost in 'blood and treasure'.

NEGATIVE EXAMPLE: IRAQ

The war against Saddam Hussein's Iraq does not fit in with a concept of stabilisation which holistically combines political and military means in a non-provocative manner: seeking legitimation by the world community and being aware of the problematic after-effects of an intervention. This military campaign has been praised as the 'New American Way of War'[28] and is widely regarded as the first 'pure' application of the 'Rumsfeld doctrine'.

This doctrine, ascribed to the US defense secretary and, along with Vice-President Cheney, key inspirer of the Iraq war, is assumed to imply that the United States should in principle be capable of going it alone: to conduct full-scale, aggressive interventions without any justification by the UN Security Council and win quickly by employing only a lean force and not needing much help from allies. (It should, for instance, be possible to go to war without being able to count on the massive assistance of a 'fifth column' or local ground forces, as in Afghanistan at the end of the year 2001.)

Supposedly, the reason why such a strategic approach has found support among the (neo-) conservative elite in Washington is as follows:[29] the members of this power group view the US as a hegemon of global reach that in relevant dimensions of influence has lost substance, as other centres of the world—Europe, China and India, for example—are in a process of political and economic emancipation.

To compensate for a relative loss of status in the economic and political sphere, the diagnosis goes on, the administration of George Bush Jnr relies more than its predecessor's on the exertion of military might: boosting one's political standing by the ability and willingness to coerce, and improving one's economic position by reaching for the control of increasingly scarce natural resources.

Such an approach only makes sense if the US continues to be capable of fighting and winning encounters like the recent war against Iraq or even more challenging ones. Leaving aside the question of whether or not the aftermath of the Iraq war—strong US forces being tied down by armed resistance and terror—works as a deterrent of its own, it should be asked what the military chances are that the exercise of armed intervention could be easily repeated. To answer this question, two assessments are required: of the war against Iraq and of potential future foes of the United States.

The war constituted a departure from the previous American pattern of military intervention: attempting to win through the application of strategic air power alone. The US leadership was obviously willing to take risks, namely by committing ground forces.

And these ground forces appeared to be just designed for the job, in other words, did not march into Iraq in overwhelming (numerical) strength as was customary in the US Army. Swift operations and a decisive military victory at relatively low cost in (one's own) 'blood and treasure' were the result of three interacting factors:

- the superiority of the aggressor, especially through advanced technology (70 per cent of all air-delivered munitions were precision-guided) and the close co-ordination of land and air operations;
- terrain conditions favourable to the invader (relatively good main roads, no destruction of strategically important bridges, and wide alleys leading into the centres of major cities); and
- the inferiority of the defender as a result of a weak military infrastructure (due to the UN embargo and measures of disarmament as well as to allied bombing raids before the war), plus the demoralising effect of a brutal and corrupt dictatorship.[30]

But what about other potential foes? A list of countries eventually to be targeted in the future was published by a member of Donald Rumsfeld's immediate entourage.[31] It contains twenty countries which allegedly are not properly developing, not open to free trade and globalisation and therefore suspected to be involved in international criminal activities, breeding, hosting and spreading terrorism or working on weapons of mass destruction.

The list comprises several weak nations and 'failed states'. In these cases, a demonstration of US military power may just be overkill and would not much, if at all, contribute to status-boosting. Other cases on the list represent military capabilities significantly more developed than Iraq's just before the war (such as Iran and North Korea). It is not likely that these countries could be successfully invaded *at calculable risk*.

And there also are nations which, apart from their military profile, appear so complex that any attempt at 'taking' them seems bizarre from the outset (such as Brazil and Pakistan). In other words, the number of countries focused on which would have to plausibly fear an American onslaught is very limited.[32]

PERSPECTIVES

Sooner or later, the political class in the United States may learn that hegemonic war is not an instrument lending itself to easy repetition. Of course, such wisdom would mainly stem from the violent aftermath of the Iraq war and the impression it continues to make on the American public. In the expert community, however, this insight may be increasingly substantiated by those analyses which demonstrate that the astounding victory in Iraq was the result of a rather unique constellation of factors, unlikely to be found elsewhere. As a consequence, sooner or later, the pendulum may swing back to those policies that seek international status in domestic reforms combined with a more co-operative, less dominant attitude towards the rest of the world.

In other centres of power around the globe, the political elites may learn from the American experience in that they cease to merely copy the basic patterns of orientation the US Armed Forces have come up with. Europe, in particular, whose nations either through NATO or in the context of the new Euro Army have in vain tried to somewhat narrow the military gap vis-à-vis the US, might come to the conclusion that military power as such is not a guarantee of equal partnership. What in the end counts is whether or not a given foreign-cum-security policy can be supported by truly adequate means of power projection.

It is near-inconceivable that the nations forming the European Union could consent to breaking international law, calling illegal preventive war pre-emption (as was done by the US, the UK and Australia). What the Europeans can consent to instead (and they often do) are policies and military missions intended to cautiously stabilise crisis regions. Such an orientation would demand an increasingly tight linkage with the UN and, apart from that, a military policy along with a congenial, affordable force design of the kind suggested in this study.

8 FOREIGN INTERVENTION IN CÔTE D'IVOIRE: THE QUESTION OF LEGITIMACY

MOYA COLLETT

Côte d'Ivoire's civil war began in 2002. The war erupted just as hope was emerging that the conflicts in nearby Liberia and Sierra Leone might be nearing definitive conclusion, thus bringing an end to large-scale and prolonged warfare in West Africa. The growing assumption that the international community has a moral responsibility to prevent humanitarian tragedy, and the hope that peace in West Africa was within reach, combined to guarantee foreign intervention in Côte d'Ivoire.

The attempt to enforce peace before full-scale war had really begun was taken up by France, the ex-colonial power; the Economic Community of West African States (ECOWAS); and the United Nations (UN). Initially, it appeared that the peacekeepers and political mediators would be successful, as a comprehensive peace agreement was signed after only four months of conflict. However, the strength of divisive feeling grew over the following year as the peace process uncovered longstanding inequalities which it was unable to adequately address. By the beginning of 2004, French and ECOWAS troops were beginning to lose control. The situation was finally considered serious enough to merit the deployment of a greatly enlarged UN peacekeeping force. As in many other African states where conflict recurs and spreads through neighbouring countries, the international intervention forces appeared only able to postpone a bloody conclusion to the politically and economically motivated civil war.

Distrust of the real motivations of humanitarian intervention forces is reinforced by their general inability to effect more than a temporary peace or to prevent extensive and lasting damage. One of the setbacks facing such forces is the continual conflict between the will to defend internationally accepted human rights and the older legal norm of non-interference in the affairs of independent states. These problems were particularly resonant in Côte d'Ivoire, where the question of the effectiveness of foreign involvement is thus tied up with legitimacy. The persistent challenge is to determine whether humanitarian intervention is best undertaken by a unilateral, regional or global force, in this case France, ECOWAS or the UN. In order to address this question, both theoretical and practical dilemmas must be explored. Different understandings of state sovereignty will first be used to examine expectations regarding the theoretical legitimacy of foreign forces in Côte d'Ivoire. However, given that the ultimate aim of intervention is to secure peace, practical considerations must then be appraised so that potential for success may direct legal norms and influence considerations of legitimacy.

DILEMMAS OF SOVEREIGNTY

State sovereignty, one of the bases upon which the concept of an anarchical international society was built, has existed as a term of reference since seventeenth century Europe. Relating as it does to the independence of states, giving them both the freedom to act at will in international society and the freedom from interference in their internal affairs, sovereignty is a deceptively simple concept.

Arguments over its implications have persisted over centuries but it has been given particular eminence since general decolonisation in the 1960s, and the idea is once again in a state of evolution.

The concept can be broken down into four separate but interconnected definitions.[1] Juridical sovereignty denotes recognition that a certain territorial entity constitutes a state and assumes that official authority is held by a central government, whereas empirical sovereignty relates to the exercise of permanent control by the state apparatus over its citizens. Westphalian sovereignty essentially excludes external actors from interfering in the internal affairs of a state, while interdependence sovereignty describes control over the flow of ideas, goods and people across state borders.[2] It is important to differentiate between these different types of state sovereignty as they are undermined by different actions.[3]

JURIDICAL AND EMPIRICAL SOVEREIGNTY

The links between juridical and empirical sovereignty are particularly important as they respectively denote the existence of official and real control by a government over internal state affairs. At the beginning of the 1990s, as intervention for humanitarian reasons began to increase, the Secretary-General of the UN, Boutros Boutros-Ghali, claimed that juridical sovereignty was dependent on empirical sovereignty.[4] According to this understanding, however, many Sub-Saharan African countries would at some point have ceased to exist, and yet state weakness and lack of control have not caused any African state to be involuntarily altered or nullified. While the increase in humanitarian intervention over the past decade would appear to indicate that Westphalian sovereignty is becoming more dependent on 'good governance' and adherence to human rights norms, juridical sovereignty has continued to be upheld without reference to the existence of any other form of sovereignty.[5]

There is a sense in which the loss of empirical sovereignty should entail the loss of juridical sovereignty. Emphasising the importance of juridical sovereignty presupposes a solution to internal conflict, namely the maintenance of the existing structure. By striving to uphold juridical sovereignty at all times, international society in the guise of the UN has in many cases helped to perpetuate the rule of incompetent governments that possess little control over their official jurisdiction, thus increasing the likelihood of future conflict.

The mandate authorising a UN peacekeeping force in Côte d'Ivoire emphasised the need to respect the sovereignty, independence, territorial integrity and unity of the state, even as it was being torn apart by four separate warring factions.[6] As violence escalated in the months following the September 2002 failed coup d'état, a statement by the President of the Security Council called for respect of the 'elected' and 'legitimate' government, despite the nature of President Laurent Gbagbo's rise to power through unresolved elections in 2000 during which only 13 per cent of the Ivoirian population voted and from which the major opposition candidate was barred.[7] Gbagbo's refusal to follow the terms of a January 2003 peace agreement, involving delegation of some presidential powers to a consensus prime minister, formed part of the reason for the disintegration of the Government of National Unity and the peace process more generally, and yet Gbagbo remained head of state, thus retaining juridical sovereignty and legitimacy in the eyes of the international community.

Gbagbo's status exemplifies the general fear of disrupting the established order of international society. In Sub-Saharan Africa, the basis of this fear dates back to the 1960s when most countries gained their independence and self-determination was enshrined as an unconditional right. While the state structures may have been artificial, with nations within and across European-determined boundaries denied the right to self-determination, they were also legitimising. Nationalism constructed within predefined borders was important to attaining independence, and was thus to become an important part of African tradition. African states, feeling the need to prove their validity independent of European jurisdiction, became jealous of their sovereignty and unwilling to consider valid the self-determination of interior nations, which could have a destabilising and delegitimising effect.[8] The attempt of the UN and the ex-colonial powers to preserve juridical sovereignty without reference to the viability of internal structures has thus been consolidated by African aims. Further evidence of the delinking of empirical and juridical sovereignty is the international prevention of 'state failure'. When empirical sovereignty is lost, it is the holder of juridical sovereignty, namely the official government, that has the right to invite foreign support to restore order and often to deny self-determination. The importance ascribed to juridical sovereignty in this way has major consequences for the significance of governmental expectations.

When General Robert Gueï staged a coup against Gbagbo's government on 19 September 2002, inciting a civil war, Gbagbo did not hesitate to ask France for protection.[9] His government expected France to act on its behalf, following the precedent of French involvement in the country since independence in 1960. French neo-colonial influence in Côte d'Ivoire had since this time been characterised by support for the Ivoirian government in return for co-operation with French military, political, economic and social policy.[10] Militarily, the document that defines the French role in Côte d'Ivoire is the defence agreement of 1961[11] which gave France extensive influence, mostly through the establishment of a permanent military base and the exclusive right to train the Ivoirian army.[12] Similar agreements were made between France and almost all of its Sub-Saharan African colonies when they became independent. Félix Houphouët-Boigny, the president of Côte d'Ivoire from independence in 1960 to his death in 1993, apparently felt strengthened by the presence of French troops as they were instrumental in deterring coups and defusing vocal opposition. According to the Ivoirian Ambassador to the US, Pascal Kokora, Houphouët kept the Ivoirian military to a minimum 'because he was sure the French would always defend the country in case of a foreign invasion'.[13] The 1961 agreement remains valid and was the basis of Gbagbo's expectation that France would respond to his call for protection.

Intervening by way of this agreement effectively predetermined France's mandate. Despite the internal nature of Côte d'Ivoire's conflict, France agreed to support the Ivoirian army with 'transmissions, transport and general provisions'[14] as well as 1200 troops, thus legitimising the assumption of juridical sovereignty and consolidating the expectation that its intervention would be biased. After initial deployment, however, France began co-operating with both ECOWAS and the UN in carrying out impartial peacekeeping and political mediation. After helping to engineer the cease-fire agreement of 17 October 2002, France refined its mandate and increased its troop strength to 3900 in order to focus on defusing aggression and protecting civilians on all sides of the conflict.[15] As French impartiality became more apparent, government supporters became more disillusioned with their former colonial masters, and one government supporter is reported as saying, 'We are calling on the heart of France. We feel like a child abandoned by his protector. We want to see at our sides "our ancestors the Gauls"!'[16]

French political mediators were instrumental in bringing about the comprehensive Linas-Marcoussis peace agreement of January 2003.[17] However, it was as a result of this agreement that government supporters became particularly angry, feeling that the French had forced them into giving way to rebel demands, and they began to attack French schools, businesses, cultural centres and other symbols of neo-colonial influence. Government supporters also issued a cry of help to the US 'which governs the peace of the world',[18] but the US had no interest in helping this bastion of French neo-colonial influence in West Africa. France's right to intervene stemmed from the invitation of a juridically sovereign government on the assumption that it would be returned empirical sovereignty. France's consequent failure to unequivocally support the government, as per the terms of the 1961 agreement, undermined its legitimacy. However, for the realisation of peace, Côte d'Ivoire remained dependent in major part on France and the UN, which also disappointed the expectations of the Ivoirian government.

As the central arbiter of sovereignty in the international system, the legitimacy of the UN is dependent on its reputation for impartiality. It continually attempts to preserve its image as a non-aggressive organisation that strives to prevent war, human rights abuses, state collapse and the loss of empirical sovereignty.[19] However, the UN's process for dealing with conflict, and states in general, tends to involve negotiation primarily with the group in control of juridical sovereignty. For example, while the 2000 Brahimi report on peacekeeping emphasised the importance of gaining the consent of warring parties in order to gain their goodwill, in practice the UN is mainly concerned about its legitimacy in the eyes of the official government and may not wait for the consent of insurgent groups.[20] It is often initially only possible to liaise with the government, particularly as different rebel groups are continuously splitting and re-forming, and authorities do not necessarily have control over their fighters. This reinforces the perception that a government such as that of Gbagbo is the legitimate representative of its country, thus giving it a distorted understanding of the extent and nature of UN impartiality.

Bias towards the government and official state structure in the lead-up to deployment, juxtaposed with the constant use of rhetoric concerning 'consent' and 'impartiality', leads to the expectation that this discrepancy will continue. Once on the ground, UN peacekeepers that act with true impartiality incite anger. By taking action in response to human rights violations on any side, they undermine governmental authority, and this may be perceived as bias towards the rebel force. In Côte d'Ivoire, this perception was manifested by outrage at the UN report condemning Gbagbo's violent suppression of a peaceful opposition protest against his failure to implement the terms of the Marcoussis agreement.[21] Government supporters also accused the UN of bias for not forcing the rebels to disarm as provided for by the same agreement.[22] However, the UN continued to recognise Gbagbo as President of the Government of National Unity and to prevent the rebels from gaining control. Whereas in the case of France, the Ivoirian government expected bias and subsequently accused it of impartiality, in the case of the UN, it expected impartiality and accused it of bias. International reliance on the existence of juridical sovereignty, and the attempts by the UN in Côte d'Ivoire as elsewhere to prop up juridical sovereignty and restore empirical sovereignty to the state, make governmental expectations particularly important. Not only are there problems with upholding the norms of sovereignty, but the institution which promotes them also undermines and contravenes them.

Like the UN, ECOWAS was expected to be impartial. However, expectations and subsequent perceptions by Côte d'Ivoire are of minimal importance because of the precedent set in Sierra Leone and Liberia of its limited real power and tendency to be superseded by unilateral and UN involvement. In Côte d'Ivoire, ECOWAS was initially involved in political mediation but, unable to bring about a lasting cease-fire, allowed France to take responsibility for both political mediation and peacekeeping. After the instigation of the Marcoussis agreement, command of peacekeeping was symbolically returned to ECOWAS, and France declared its intention to withdraw militarily.[23] However, ECOWAS was unable to undertake the entire mission, and there were no French troop reductions. Instead, ECOWAS peacekeepers were integrated into the full-scale UN peacekeeping operation when it was deployed in 2004.[24] Governmental expectations of ECOWAS thus have little bearing on ECOWAS legitimacy.

As a result of the loss of empirical sovereignty, Côte d'Ivoire exercised its juridical sovereignty to invite foreign intervention. It then became disillusioned when the intervening forces did not consider themselves subject to governmental jurisdiction but instead acted according to their own policies, thereby undermining Westphalian sovereignty. Westphalian sovereignty in Côte d'Ivoire has, however, since colonial times been subject to the existence of interdependence sovereignty. Interdependence sovereignty can be undermined not only by the flow of fighters, weapons, refugees and goods, initiated by the citizens of neighbouring states, but also by the ability of foreign powers to infiltrate domestic social systems.

WESTPHALIAN AND INTERDEPENDENCE SOVEREIGNTY

The neo-colonial nature of French influence in Côte d'Ivoire after independence in 1960 resulted in interdependence between France and Côte d'Ivoire taking on an asymmetrical character. The Ivoirian government had little control over the French ability to infiltrate its country, but France was free from the influence of Côte d'Ivoire. Kwame Nkrumah, the first Ghanaian president, described the neo-colonial state as one that is 'in theory, independent [with] all the outward trappings of international sovereignty',[25] but in reality dependent on the ex-colonial power, and Côte d'Ivoire was one country where French neo-colonial influence remained particularly important. Lack of ability, coupled with lack of will, to restrain the French influence in Côte d'Ivoire led to French control over the education system, the judicial system, the content of the constitution and the language of Côte d'Ivoire.[26] Perhaps most important, however, was the influence over economics and the military.

The French military presence in West Africa, pursuant to the 1961 agreements, led France to intervene both in civil wars and in response to external threats, with or without the consent of host governments. While military support tended to aid official governments, it also enabled France to significantly influence the choice of regime, prop up or restore favoured presidents and control the establishment of alliances between African states.[27] Côte d'Ivoire was hindered by remaining dependent on France rather than developing its own army or co-operating with its neighbours. Similarly, in the economic arena, the French trade advantages that helped to prop up Houphouët's government did so at the cost of balanced growth and co-operation with neighbouring states. Ivoirian export crops, of which cocoa and coffee have been the most significant, were chosen according to French needs in the early colonial period. Côte d'Ivoire benefitted from a protected market for its produce in France, but the constant overvaluation of the Communauté Financière Africaine (CFA) franc led to high prices and difficulty attracting alternative customers. The lack of industrialisation, another side effect of catering to French needs for specific resources, led to extensive imports of French manufactured goods and ultimately further dependence on France.[28]

French influence over Côte d'Ivoire at all levels has had far-reaching effects, even to the extent of contributing to the outbreak of civil war. However, as it results mainly from long-term policies that have remained unchanged since the colonial period, rather than from the recent imposition of French directives, continuous but covert interference over the past forty-five years has led to the acceptance and naturalisation of a lack of interdependence sovereignty. The asymmetrical nature of interdependence between France and Côte d'Ivoire represents a continuous erosion of Westphalian sovereignty, but it is not until this is epitomised by a direct undermining of governmental authority that it becomes contentious, as has occurred in the civil war with the discontinuation of French military support for the government.

Ivoirian Westphalian sovereignty was further eroded by the UN presence. Chapter VII of the UN Charter, to which Côte d'Ivoire subscribes, gives the UN the authority to use peace enforcement measures to maintain international peace and security, even if this involves intervening in the domestic affairs of an independent state. From the late 1980s, the humanitarian impact of the internal security dilemmas of developing countries led to increasing pressure on the UN to intervene in what were often essentially domestic conflicts, and there is thus a precedent for the principles of sovereignty and non-intervention to be overridden by UN authority.[29] Unlike the French influence, UN involvement was not presupposed, but the historical legal precedent led to a similar normalisation of one-sided interdependence sovereignty. This is significant in that it entails accepting the presence not only of UN peacekeepers, but also of civilian personnel and analysts with the ability to produce reports damaging to the credibility of the Ivoirian government, which has limited ability to influence UN policy. As in the case of France, it is when the results are not as expected or desired that acceptance turns into resentment.

ECOWAS poses less of a problem for sovereignty, and not simply because its comparatively weaker power defuses its potential impact on Côte d'Ivoire. The compromising of interdependence sovereignty by the ECOWAS presence is of a reciprocal nature in that the Ivoirian position as a member of ECOWAS gives it equal rights vis-à-vis other members should conflict within or between them necessitate action on a regional level. In addition, as Côte d'Ivoire forms a part of the ECOWAS structure, there is a sense in which ECOWAS peacekeepers should not be seen as a foreign intervention force but as friendly troops helping to carry out Ivoirian policy determined prior to state disintegration. While this may seem unrealistic in light of the West African climate of suspicion between authoritarian and unrepresentative governments, it demonstrates the possibilities of an integrated regional security community.

The basic reason for exploring the benefits of a regional solution is that conflict in West Africa occurs at a regional level. This is not to say that interstate wars are prevalent, but rather that official domestic struggles have an impact on neighbouring states, with insurgents operating from foreign bases, leaders supporting rebels in the states of their rivals, and war creating a general flow of refugees, arms, mercenaries, resources and child soldiers across borders, leading to the spread of conflict and conflagration across the subregion.[30] Links at the regional level and interaction between peoples have occurred in West Africa for centuries and continue to take place despite the twentieth century imposition of state borders. In order for a regional solution to be effective, however, there is a need to strengthen reciprocal interdependence and lessen the importance ascribed to juridical sovereignty. Enforcing juridical sovereignty on unviable structures can hamper rather than strengthen the development of empirical sovereignty.[31] Just as state borders do not confine conflict, neither should they confine peace.

The concept of a regional security community, uninhibited by state sovereignty, was first identified by Karl Deutsch and has since been refined by Emmanuel Adler and Michael Barnett.[32] A security community occurs where trust and common identification across a region have led not only to the absence of war, but also to a situation in which states do not even expect nor prepare for conflict. In its most advanced form, a security community will involve the loosening of state boundaries with some transfer of responsibility to a regional command. Communication and interaction, coupled with the need to fight common problems, highlight similarities between states that will then find it easier to trust each other to maintain peace. This process could be hastened by solidarity in the face of a mutual threat. While it is generally assumed that such a threat will come from outside the region, in West Africa stability is threatened more by internal problems, common across the region.[33]

The lack of interstate conflict in West Africa points to the possibility that some form of security community already exists. There is now a need for regional integration to be developed so that it can become as effective in preventing domestic conflict and addressing its causes as it can be in battling an external threat. Calling for a regional solution to the Ivoirian conflict, Nigerian President Olusegun Obasanjo said, 'A threat to Côte d'Ivoire is a threat to all of us',[34] thus demonstrating an understanding of the need to fight regional problems on a regional level, but Nigeria was prepared to contribute no troops to the ECOWAS mission, thereby demonstrating the need for greater commitment and extensively increased co-operation between ECOWAS member states.

In Europe, a security community has been built on the basis of strong states, but in West Africa there is a need for regional co-operation even while many states remain weak and divided. The lack of state-based unity may, however, be more of a help than a hindrance to regional strength. In Côte d'Ivoire, for example, state borders are part of the problem, both in their arbitrary delineation and in the violent consequences of the nationalism constructed within them. The idea of regional integration and a loosening of the importance of state sovereignty is not new. During the 1960s, Nkrumah advocated integration on a Pan-African scale, incorporating an African rapid reaction force, but his ideas gained little support from the majority of his peers. African leaders were not ready to give up the sovereignty they had just gained and had more faith in bilateral agreements, both with the ex-colonial powers and between themselves. West African states are still not ready to give up their sovereignty, but over forty years of experience has led many to rethink their attitudes and consider addressing the problems of African Union (AU), successor to the Organisation of African Unity (OAU) formed in 1963.[35] One problem with these Africa-wide organisations is that it has been difficult to identify common goals for the whole continent. Common concerns are much more evident in West Africa and perhaps Nkrumah's ideas could be used to develop Pan-Africanism on a subregional scale.

An assumption of the security community literature is that civil society will gain power through links across the region according to interests rather than on the basis of state borders. In West Africa, where civil society has traditionally lacked political influence, this could strengthen peaceful opposition and reduce the perceived need for violence. A stronger civil society may also lead to more general acceptance of ECOWAS peacekeepers as legitimate mediators.

The principle of non-intervention is not so deeply embedded in the ECOWAS ideology as it has been in that of the OAU or AU. Instead, its treaty envisages the 'gradual pooling of national sovereignties to the Community' and encourages 'the removal between Member States, of obstacles to the free movement of persons, goods, service and capital, and to the right of residence and establishment'. However, these terms are yet to be ratified by the member states. As the erosion of juridical sovereignty is not yet a reality, and as states remain the only actors with the authority to enact legislation, ECOWAS remains inevitably state-centric; yet the loss of empirical sovereignty and the danger of social, political and economic collapse in West African states remain a constant threat.

State sovereignty causes problems for the attempt to arrest conflict in West Africa. This is not only due to the resulting reluctance on the part of international actors to intervene for humanitarian reasons, but mostly because of the confusion and hypocrisy that it tends to entail. It does not follow, however, that sovereignty should be ignored, because as a concept it is important for state legitimacy, the international rule of law, and to prevent unjust domination. Success in bringing about peace is also more likely if intervention forces possess legitimacy both internationally and from the point of view of the warring parties, as fewer obstacles are likely to be placed in their path.

The challenge, then, is to find a humanitarian force that possesses both legal legitimacy and the potential to succeed. The need to consider the practical ability of the three levels of foreign intervention to contribute to a lasting peace in Côte d'Ivoire is thus pressing. Their legitimacy will ultimately be judged by their success, rather than by their respect for varying types of state sovereignty.

PRACTICAL DILEMMAS

FRANCE

As the old colonial power, France was well placed to conduct a unilateral peacekeeping and political mediation mission in Côte d'Ivoire. Its past involvement led to the Ivoirian and international expectation that it would lend its support to ending the conflict, it had numerous longstanding bilateral agreements with Côte d'Ivoire that facilitated intervention, and its troops were already stationed in the country ready for rapid deployment. France also had responsibilities to become involved in the Côte d'Ivoire civil war. The responsibilities it recognises stem from the special relationship that has been maintained between the two states and France's implied duty to protect Côte d'Ivoire's future. Although it does not admit fault, France's responsibility in the country also stems from the part it played in the economic and consequent political decline in the lead-up to the civil war.

Continuing French influence in the post-independence period had lent Côte d'Ivoire a semblance of strength and even contributed to the apparent Ivoirian miracle of economic development, and yet French involvement in all areas of Ivoirian policy was determined more by French interests than by benefits to Côte d'Ivoire. The extent of disproportionate dependence on the old colonial power in all areas of the economy was ultimately to mean that when the prices of coffee and cocoa fell sharply at the end of the 1970s and France was unwilling or unable to continue to guarantee a market for Ivoirian produce, there was little to prevent a recession that was to continue through to the 1990s.[36] When Houphouët died in 1993, France began to distance itself from Ivoirian affairs, and the continuing economic problems and competition for resources led to the individual power struggle following Houphouët's death becoming a contest of ethnic allegiances, which in turn diverted attention away from an attempt at economic recovery.

Despite the responsibility that stems from such extensive involvement in Côte d'Ivoire's demise, there is little to suggest that French policy may have changed to reflect anything other than French interests. France may talk of the need to respond to cries for help 'between countries that know and love each other',[37] but it also had significant reasons of its own to become involved in the Ivoirian conflict. In terms of economics, its conglomerates owned most of the infrastructure and controlled most of the production in Côte d'Ivoire, and were likely to suffer from prolonged conflict. An escalation of the civil war also had the potential to destabilise the economy of much of the region. Symbolically, France needed to prevent a repeat of Rwanda or Congo to maintain international respect. It also wished to restore stability to the country once known as the 'shop-window' of successful French decolonisation in order to preserve remnants of belief in the benefits of French colonialism.[38]

Even when French interests do not appear to come into play, but action is called for, involvement or disengagement is determined by the internal fluctuations of French policy. Thus, after nearly thirty years of neo-colonialism, the decade following Houphouët's death has been characterised by wavering commitment to Ivoirian difficulties. The problems began with the rule of President Konan Bédié who succeeded Houphouët in 1993 and proceeded to change the electoral code to exclude his most powerful rival, Alassane Ouattara, from standing in the presidential elections of 1995. Ouattara's father was from Burkina Faso, and the law Bédié passed to ensure his exclusion effectively limited Ivoirian citizenship to those whose parents had both been born in Côte d'Ivoire. This law gave rise to the concept of Ivoirité, according to which only 74 per cent of the Ivoirian population could claim to be Ivoirian, but it was not contested by France who recognised Bédié as the legitimate president.[39]

Partly as a result of this law, in December 1999 Côte d'Ivoire experienced its first coup d'état, successfully led by General Robert Gueï with the assistance of Gbagbo. While France gave Bédié sanctuary at its Abidjan garrison, its decision not to demand his restoration was facilitated by its new policy of 'influence but not interference'.[40] Initiated by left-wing Prime Minister Lionel Jospin in 1997, the policy claimed that France did 'not want to interfere in the internal affairs of states',[41] but as a Western diplomat put it, 'the point was that France would not bail you out anymore'.[42] French troops in Africa were immediately reduced from 430 000 to 300 000 and France announced its intention to close its African bases in entirety.[43] However, while the Central African Republic military base was closed, those of Djibouti, Senegal, Chad, Gabon and Côte d'Ivoire remained and the agreements of 1961 were not revised. Gbagbo gained power in the presidential elections of 2000, but the undemocratic and unresolved nature of the elections was again uncontested by international actors.

With hindsight, it is clear that France's passivity when faced with the first clear symbols of the deteriorating political situation may have hastened further political deterioration and civil war. By failing to react to the instigation of Bédié's Ivoirité law and his consequent re-election, by not preventing Gueï's military rule after his coup in 1999, and by according Gbagbo all the status of a legitimate president, France was setting itself up for future problems. As each successive step towards deeper political disintegration was not countered by international action, civil war and the necessity of foreign intervention became more likely. When Gueï staged his second and fatal coup on 19 September 2002, triggering civil war, and Gbagbo requested help from France, it was too late to question his legitimacy. Moreover, by this time a right-wing French government had been elected with President Jacques Chirac who favoured a return to an interventionist strategy in Africa.[44] He initially supported the Ivoirian government without analysis of its questionable legitimacy or the history that had given it power.

France is well placed in terms of its military and political resources to help bring peace to Côte d'Ivoire, and its part in bringing about the Marcoussis agreement and in quelling the violence between government and rebel forces was significant. However, French involvement is continually determined by self-interest based on a mixture of domestic politics, international image, economic considerations and wavering commitments to different levels of sovereignty, all of which give it the appearance of neo-colonial interference and reduce faith in France's long-term commitment. In view of the potential for internal division and changes to undermine French attempts at a normative solution to conflict, a multilateral solution is justified.

THE UNITED NATIONS

The UN is generally considered as a legitimate actor in both interstate and intrastate warfare. Its resolutions are taken to denote agreement in the international community, its reports are assumed to be impartial and its peacekeepers are seen as having the most potential to defuse violence. However, in the peacekeeping arena, it has problems that stem from both constitutional and operational difficulties.

UN involvement in Côte d'Ivoire began as statements condemning the September coup d'état and subsequent violence, and commending the French action in the country. Following the January 2003 Marcoussis agreement, a small liaison committee, called the United Nations Mission in Côte d'Ivoire (MINUCI), was established. Its primary roles appeared to be to monitor the situation, lend support to the Government of National Reconciliation and demonstrate the UN's commitment to post-conflict reconstruction. In April 2004, the United Nations Operation in Côte d'Ivoire (UNOCI) was finally established with 6240 military personnel and a mandate to monitor the cease-fire of May 2003, liaise with the various armed groups and the Government of National Reconciliation, assist with the disarmament campaign and support the implementation of the peace process.[45] Each stage of UN involvement has demonstrated some of the limitations of the UN process for dealing with domestic armed conflict.

In legal terms, the UN's limitations stem from the difference between its rhetoric and its actions. Often, this is a result of the UN's inclination to shrink from the capability to undermine state sovereignty given to it by the peace enforcement provisions in Chapter VII. Instead, multinational peacekeeping and its attendant limitations, not even provided for in the Charter, has become the most common form of foreign intervention.[46] Peacekeeping operations tend to push their own boundaries with regard to the use of force, while striving to maintain a certain image and articulating unrealistic aims. For example, UN information regarding peacekeeping continues to emphasise *post*-conflict situations involving *ex*-combatants, but even after an official cease-fire, conflict tends to continue, and even as the UN disarms ex-combatants in the aftermath of conflict, thousands of weapons are hidden as commanders distrust the sincerity of their erstwhile enemies.[47]

Consent of the warring parties is another concept important to peacekeeping, but it relies on trust and assumes continued co-operation. However, 'a party may give its consent to the United Nations presence merely to gain time to retool its fighting forces and withdraw consent when the peacekeeping operation no longer serves its interests'.[48] The tone of the Brahimi report suggests that consent is important only in the initial stages of the deployment of peace-keepers, after which the UN should be free to act at will. This suggests that the principle of consent is simply a way in which the UN can become involved militarily while hiding behind the rhetoric of non-intervention in the internal affairs of sovereign states.

Another hindrance to peacekeeping as identified by the Brahimi report is the insecurity of situations in which peacekeepers find themselves. It emphasises the need for impartiality, which is important to the UN image, but there is a fear that peacekeepers will be limited by their inability to use pre-emptive force.[49] While Chapter VII relates only to peace enforcement missions, it has been used to justify the mandates of peacekeeping operations such as that of Côte d'Ivoire. By calling the mission a 'peacekeeping' operation, the UN retains legitimacy as an objective body, but by acting under Chapter VII, it is able to authorise a greater use of force than would traditionally be implied. These examples demonstrate the discrepancy between UN principles and the realities faced by peacekeeping operations. This discrepancy has ramifications both for the effectiveness of UN operations that must negotiate the legal hurdles, and for the continued acceptance of UN credibility.

Despite the UN Charter beginning with the words 'We the Peoples', the international system has difficulty dealing with peoples that are not represented by states. When coups d'états occur, the UN has a tendency to condemn the violence before considering the possible legitimacy of the insurgents' claims. By becoming involved earlier, before the outbreak of conflict, the UN would be in a position to address the social and economic problems faced by disadvantaged groups before they took recourse to violence to express their political needs, as occurred in Côte d'Ivoire. However, both peacemaking prior to conflict, and peace-building in its aftermath, require additional funding.[50] This funding is not forthcoming, despite the potential of such missions to prevent the outbreak of conflict and the consequent need for peacekeeping with its more excessive cost.

Earlier involvement also requires co-operation by member states that need to be convinced of the urgency of the situation. In an area with a recent colonial history such as West Africa, working with ex-colonial powers that are more likely to be willing to contribute troops, funding and other essential resources could negate this problem. However, experience co-ordinating with major powers in such a way during peacekeeping operations demonstrates the additional difficulties that may arise. If there is disagreement between major powers, or between the unilateral and the UN missions, this complicates deployment and can help to multiply rebel factions. When discussing the Ivoirian civil war, UN Secretary-General Kofi Annan with French backing constantly pushed for a larger and more comprehensive UN operation, while the US continually argued against it. The official reason for the US stance is based on funding problems, but its arguments were first made known shortly after Colin Powell told France it would suffer consequences for leading the opposition to war in Iraq.[51]

The self-interested and compartmentalised policies of external powers prevent a co-ordinated peacekeeping strategy across the West African subregion that could contend with conflicts that shift across borders and demonstrate many of the same difficulties. There is an increasing recognition of this, and the mandate for UN peacekeeping in Côte d'Ivoire flags the impact of the deteriorating Ivoirian situation on the economy of the region as a whole and recalls the importance of regional co-operation for widespread stability and peace. It calls for liaison between the UN missions in Côte d'Ivoire, Sierra Leone and Liberia.[52] However, increased co-ordination between West African peacekeeping missions tends to involve operations such as joint border patrols, effectively attempting to keep individual state crises separate, rather than dealing with the problems that inevitably spill across borders. As the regional body, ECOWAS should be in a better position to address issues affecting the area as a whole, and it has significant potential to do much more than act as an interim measure as it did in Côte d'Ivoire.

THE ECONOMIC COMMUNITY OF WEST AFRICAN STATES

ECOWAS was originally conceived as an organisation to further economic integration, but as economic problems and cross-border political conflicts are intrinsically linked in West Africa, it was perhaps inevitable that it would develop a common security initiative. While the Ivoirian civil war arose out of domestic economic and political problems, it has been stoked by violence spreading across the sub-region since at least the beginning of the 1990s. In 1989, Liberia's civil war was triggered by insurgents that launched an attack from their base in Côte d'Ivoire, allegedly supported by the Ivoirian and Burkinabé governments.[53] This rebel force also aided Sierra Leonean defectors to initiate their own civil war and together the militias threatened to disrupt peace in Guinea.

Côte d'Ivoire managed to avoid conflict in its territory until 2002. However, the country was the main destination for thousands of West African refugees, and these were ultimately to contribute to the political crisis and the Ivoirian civil war.[54] The coup of September 2002 was launched from Liberia, and Côte d'Ivoire's three rebel groups were allegedly sponsored by both President Charles Taylor of Liberia and President Blaise Compaoré of Burkina Faso. Even after Taylor was deposed, fighters still loyal to him continued to cause disruption in the west of Côte d'Ivoire.

The apparent disintegration of the Ivoirian peace process at the end of 2003 and into 2004 provoked fears that continuing conflict could stall the tenuous peace processes of both Liberia and Sierra Leone. Arms were being hidden from the UN Liberian disarmament process and smuggled across the border into Côte d'Ivoire where, if not used, they would attract more compensation with the commencement of Ivoirian disarmament, or could be smuggled back over the border if needed.[55] The Ivoirian conflict had also already had a negative effect on the economy of the region, with Mali and Burkina Faso particularly affected. The main source of trade for these countries is through or with Côte d'Ivoire, and this was halted after the beginning of the war.[56] The flow of both ex-citizens and new Ivoirian refugees into Mali and Burkina Faso also contributed to increased poverty and heightened tension. A regional solution is clearly warranted.

Integration of states in West Africa and the use of regional military forces are not unprecedented. During the colonial period, France used a force of *troupes coloniales* made up of soldiers from various colonies in French West Africa with no particular national affiliation to quell rebellion and prevent ethnic conflict in the subregion.[57] Prior to independence, the British used a Royal West African Frontier force in the region that was built on the same basis as the *troupes coloniales* and had the same aims. However, one problem for the military integration of West Africa stemming from colonial times is the need to overcome the tendency of its states to co-operate according to colonial heritage and linguistic affiliation. As Olu Adeniji noted, 'the language barrier created by the pattern of colonialism and the perpetuation of the vertical link with the former imperial power at the expense of the horizontal link with neighbouring states, discouraged much meaningful relations across the Anglo/Francophone divide'.[58]

Even in the early days after the formation of ECOWAS at the beginning of the 1970s, two separate associations were created, and each began campaigning to convince member states of the rival organisation to switch allegiances. Economically, the anglophone ECOWAS won out, but the French Communauté Economique de l'Afrique de l'Ouest was not dissolved, instead going on to initiate the non-aggression pact of 1977.[59] In 1981, the Mutual Defence Assistance Protocol was signed by both francophone and anglophone members of ECOWAS, marking the beginning of a co-ordinated security policy on a regional scale. It wasn't until Liberia in 1990, however, that the region saw its first co-ordinated security mission, and even today the linguistic hurdle has not been overcome. ECOMICI, the ECOWAS mission in Côte d'Ivoire, was made up of personnel mainly contributed by francophone states. Even so, although many of its terms are yet to be ratified, the ECOWAS treaty represents a strong attempt to overcome both state and linguistic divides. If its principle of free movement were to become a reality, with people able to move in accordance with the distribution of resources and employment, this would have the potential to reduce the inequality that is a cause of many West African conflicts.

West Africans are much more likely than an ex-colonial power or the UN to have an appreciation of the history, a knowledge of the participants, an understanding of the issues and a more immediate interest in conflict-ridden states in their region. ECOWAS peace-keeping operations thus have great potential; but regional co-operation does not dissolve many of the practical problems facing any peacekeeping operation. One of the problems of UN operations is their ad hoc organisation.[60] The UN tends to await the outbreak of conflict before calling for peacekeeping contributions, and the organisational phase in many instances takes too long for effective implementation. Countries like France with a permanent base in the country have an advantage, but the perceived legitimacy of such direct unilateral involvement is diminishing. To be effective, regional organisations must go further than ad hoc planning reliant on voluntary contributions, to establish a stable mechanism for monitoring peace, with possible inclusion of a joint peacekeeping force permanently ready for rapid deployment.[61] Such a force has been envisaged in West Africa, and has been advocated by France, the UK and the US who are willing to contribute, but is yet to become a reality.[62] As is often the case, innovative ideas are stalled by issues of finance.

France, the UK and the US contributed most of the initial US$13 million cost of the ECOWAS mission in Côte d'Ivoire, but the ongoing costs were not met, with the inevitable result that the mediation and peacekeeping operations were undermined by a gross lack of funding.[63] In principle, the fact that ECOWAS peacekeeping relies on voluntary contributions should not be a great hindrance as the states concerned are more likely to have a direct interest in the outcome, but in reality they simply lack the means to contribute. The real potential of ECOWAS to develop innovative ideas for peacekeeping is dependent not only on the will of sceptical governments and nationalistic populations, but also on capabilities for meetin g the monetary costs. ECOWAS legitimacy and regional security potential would gain significant strength and real ability if coupled with UN and French experience, resources, troops and administrative assistance.

CONCLUSION

The moral responsibility of the international community to intervene when civil war erupts in any state arises both from the part outside influences play in causing conflict, and from the recognition that preventable humanitarian tragedy is unacceptable. However, the ability of intervention forces to bring about real change is constrained by the power of the notion of state sovereignty and the distrust that can result from contradictory understandings of its consequences. Distrust of humanitarian forces renders them illegitimate and hinders the potential for an internationally manufactured peace, adding to the significant practical difficulties faced by international peacekeeping. However, the UN needs sovereignty or a similar legal mandate acceptable to all if it is to retain general recognition of its legitimacy. There must also be some constraint on unilateral actors whose self-interest often causes them to effect more harm than good.

In Côte d'Ivoire, France had the experience and practical capabilities for successful peace enforcement and mediation, but its legitimacy is waning as tolerance for neo-colonial interference diminishes. The UN possesses international legal legitimacy, but its ability to be effective in restoring peace is hampered by its need to conform to international peacekeeping norms. The deterioration of the peace process in Côte d'Ivoire suggests that a peacekeeping force that has both the legitimacy and the capability to rapidly bring about a lasting peace is still wanting.

ECOWAS is slowly gaining the legitimacy to disregard West-phalian sovereignty and even erode the importance of juridical sovereignty. This demonstrates a positive adjustment of legal norms to reflect the potential to achieve durable peace and stability. The operational problems of ECOWAS peacekeeping missions are significant, but the organisation has a strong ideological basis and a direct interest in peace throughout the subregion. The practical difficulties could be substantially overcome through support by other international actors, which in the case of Côte d'Ivoire would mean France and the UN. With increased integration, ECOWAS may demonstrate the potential of subregional organisations to become the most likely source of peace throughout Africa.

9 THE UNITED NATIONS AND THE HUMANITARIAN IMPERATIVE: SOME CHALLENGES

WILLIAM MALEY

At 4.30 p.m. on 19 August 2003, a flatbed truck carrying 1000 kilograms of high explosives was detonated by a suicide bomber in a service road adjacent to the Baghdad headquarters of the United Nations Assistance Mission for Iraq. Among those killed in the blast was Arthur C. Helton, Senior Fellow of the Council on Foreign Relations in New York and one of the most penetrating and insightful commentators on the dilemmas of humanitarian action in the post–Cold War world. In 2002, he had warned that the 'international system for delivering humanitarian assistance to needy populations around the world is badly fragmented'.[1] It was therefore a tragic irony that he died while investigating the roles that the UN could play in the aftermath of an invasion which itself had badly fragmented the understandings on which effective multilateral action depends.

The United Nations was founded in the aftermath of the most catastrophic conflict that the world had ever known, and the lives of countless millions at that very moment were in disarray. Thus, the

UN was charged very early in its own life with coping with humanitarian challenges and with the need to develop appropriate structures for addressing them. The Economic and Social Council established by Chapter X of the Charter of the United Nations was viewed as a major innovation, although in the immediate pre-war period, the League of Nations had taken some steps in this direction in the light of recommendations from a committee headed by Stanley Bruce. However, the following five decades were to highlight the importance of flexibility in the face of diverse challenges and, for a range of reasons, the UN system on occasion proved notably flat-footed. It is with the character of these challenges, the appropriateness of UN responses, and the way in which UN reform might facilitate humanitarian operations, that the remainder of this chapter is concerned.

HUMANITARIAN CHALLENGES

In recent years there has been a great deal written about 'complex humanitarian emergencies', but as Fiona Terry has pointed out, humanitarian emergencies have always been complex, and to the extent that things have changed in recent years, it has been in the intensity of the demands upon agencies and institutions to respond expeditiously and effectively. 'It is the international response', she argues, 'that is more "complex"; proliferation in the number and type of actors in the field has exacerbated inherent dilemmas in the provision of humanitarian assistance'.[2] It is also tempting to see the involvement of the UN in internal conflicts as a recent development, but that too is a suspect conclusion, as those who recall the Congolese crisis of 1960–63 would recognise. Rather, when one surveys the history of the UN, one witnesses a mixture of institutionalised and ad hoc responses to problems, with the level of initial understanding of a problem's complexity varying considerably. A number of specific cases help to highlight the nature of these problems.

Some forms of humanitarian challenge arise from territorial division. One of the early issues to confront the UN, one inherited from the League of Nations mandate system, was that of Palestine. The turbulent circumstances of the birth of the state of Israel, and the population displacements which accompanied it, left a legacy of hatred and despair which continues to haunt both the political and humanitarian agendas of the UN. The United Nations Relief and Works Agency for Palestine Refugees in the Near East (UNRWA), established in 1949, is one of the longest-standing UN relief agencies, and its activities are now integrally related to the mythologies of the Palestinian population. Bodies such as UNRWA can hardly play more than an ameliorative role. In this respect, UNRWA differs markedly from the office of the United Nations High Commissioner for Refugees (UNHCR), which has a general protective mandate in respect of refugees, and is much more heavily involved in promoting so-called 'durable solutions' to refugee problems.[3] However, as the more recent case of the breakup of Yugoslavia demonstrates, even a body such as UNHCR may have limited scope to shape the wider context within which humanitarian catastrophes unfold.

Of course, refugee movements are often symptoms of deeper problems of state disruption, which may create an apparently urgent need for humanitarian assistance. This was well illustrated by the case of Somalia. In the preamble to Security Council Resolution 767 of 27 July 1992, the Council recognised 'that the provision of humanitarian assistance in Somalia is an important element in the effort of the Council to restore international peace and security in the area'. Here one sees a certain ingenuity at work. Article 2.7 of the Charter provides that nothing in the Charter 'shall authorize the United Nations to intervene in matters which are essentially within the domestic jurisdiction of any state', but an exception to this is to be found in Chapter VII, which permits enforcement action to 'restore international peace and security'. Thus, by wording its resolution as it did, the Security Council implicitly brought humanitarian assistance within its mandate. The outcome in Somalia was not exactly a happy one, and this highlighted another serious challenge for the UN: restoring order in disrupted states is an exceptionally difficult and time-consuming undertaking, and may require considerably more patience than key states are capable of displaying.[4]

In the case of Somalia, the UN's involvement came at a time when there was a relatively high degree of optimism about the potential fruits of multilateral action. US President George Bush (1989–93) had spoken in visionary terms of a possible 'new world order', and UN Secretary-General Boutros Boutros-Ghali in his 1992 report, *An Agenda for Peace*, had called for the UN to consider a wider range of activities than simply classical peacekeeping as instruments for the prevention of conflict.[5] This optimism did not last long, for several reasons. First, the early 1990s witnessed a burst of intense internal conflicts which significantly stretched the resources of the UN system. Second, as major powers found themselves preoccupied with challenges such as the fragmentation of Yugoslavia, it proved difficult for other trouble spots to secure their attention. Thus, instead of being able to proceed proactively with adequate support from member states, the UN found itself increasingly confronted with the demand to clean up messes not of its own making. The frustrations which accumulated during the 1990s found voice in the blunt language of the 2000 Brahimi Report,[6] which warned against entanglement in ill-conceived operations. However, this is easier said than done. For example, despite the dubious legality of the US-led 'Operation Iraqi Freedom' in March and April 2003,[7] conducted by what former British Foreign Secretary Douglas Hurd has called a 'Coalition of the Obedient',[8] the UN was drawn into the provision of an Assistance Mission, largely because of pressure from the US. It took the killings of 19 August 2003 to drive Brahimi's warnings home. It is much easier to be a spoiler than a builder, and the old norms that protected humanitarian workers are breaking down. They are not so much angels of mercy as soft targets.

In the worst of circumstances, the UN is confronted with wholesale slaughter. The cases of Cambodia from 1975 to 1978, and Rwanda in 1994, saw millions killed in the face of an 'international community' that did nothing of benefit in response to the victims' cries. The failings of the UN in cases such as these, and in more limited but nonetheless agonising atrocities such as the 1995 Srebrenica massacre and the 1999 slayings in East Timor following the announcement of the results of a UN-run popular consultation on independence, have been documented in distressing detail.[9] It should therefore be repeated, in the UN's defence, that it has no military force of its own and, confronted with humanitarian challenges on a genocidal scale, it is entirely dependent upon the willingness of member states to take prompt action. One of the more unseemly spectacles of the 1990s was the gusto with which US political figures blamed the UN, and specifically the Secretary-General, for action which the US had given prior approval in the Security Council, or inaction resulting from the known reluctance of the US to support the kind of response required. Rwanda was one of the worst examples of the latter situation, as Samantha Power has documented in searing detail.[10]

What unites all these cases is the political element. Natural disasters can occur where political factors play no role, although ostensibly 'natural' disasters such as fires or mudslides may actually be a product more of inappropriate past policy decisions—on issues such as forest management—than of 'nature' on the rampage. Natural disasters can also give rise to political tensions. In the aftermath of the hugely destructive tsunami which struck a range of Asian and African countries following an earthquake near Indonesia on 26 December 2004, UN Humanitarian Relief Co-ordinator Jan Egeland's reference to developed countries as 'stingy' seemed to have the effect of galvanising into action a US administration which until then had been sluggish in its response.[11] Politics intrudes into these kinds of situations in a deeper sense as well. The losses in human and material terms from the December 2004 tsunami dwarf the costs of events such as the September 11, 2001 terrorist attacks, and the question of who will pay for reconstruction, and how, is inevitably political, as is the question of how to co-ordinate responses But in many cases where the UN's humanitarian agencies are drawn in, political factors are plainly at play in a *causal* sense.

From this, a sobering implication arises. If root causes of humanitarian problems are political, then the only solutions that are likely to prove durable will be political as well. The provision of humanitarian relief on its own is unlikely to address these root causes; indeed, it may have severe unintended consequences, the worst of which is the sustaining of unappetising political forces, as occurred in refugee camps in Zaire after the Rwandan genocide, when *génocidaires* actually found sanctuary. Here we see in stark form the paradox of humanitarian action, to which Terry and other writers have recently devoted considerable attention.[12] This can create acute tensions within the UN system, for the 'constitutional mechanisms' to ensure that relief does not aggravate political problems are weak. On occasion, different parts of the UN system have sent inconsistent signals to actors on the ground; this occurred in Afghanistan in May 1998, when a UN relief official actually signed a Memorandum of Understanding with the Taliban which provided that 'women's access to health and education will need to be gradual'.[13] Here, the humanitarian imperative to deliver relief overwhelmed basic common sense, which suggested that it was not a good idea to contradict in writing some of the key principles of gender equality which the UN system had been fostering.

RESPONSES

When looking at the UN's response to humanitarian challenges, it is important first of all to recognise that the UN has some splendid achievements to its credit. Its successes in providing succour to refugees, often with very little notice and limited cash resources, are remarkable. UNHCR, for example, helps around twenty million people, but has a total staff of only just over 5000. It is anything but a bloated bureaucracy. Too often, member states casually dump huge problems in the lap of the UN: Kosovo comes immediately to mind.[14] There are many outstanding staff on the UN's payroll, and without their dedication and commitment, countless evils of the world might never have been confronted. Those who scorn the UN should think of foot-soldiers of UN activity such as UNHCR's Bettina Goislard, who was callously murdered by the Taliban in the Afghan town of Ghazni on 16 November 2003 while working to help Afghans rebuild their lives. Some problems, for some people at least, *can* be ameliorated through well-crafted action.

The UN has also sought to fine-tune its mechanisms for the delivery of humanitarian assistance. In 1991, General Assembly Resolution 46/182 set out a mechanism for the raising of funds through consolidated appeals. This continues to the present, and on 18 November 2003, Secretary-General Kofi Annan launched the 2004 appeal, seeking US$3 billion for forty-five million people in twenty-one countries. The appeal, as usual, was the product of work in the UN Office for the Co-ordination of Humanitarian Affairs (OCHA). The OCHA is headed by the UN Emergency Relief Co-ordinator, a senior official directly responsible to the Secretary-General. Resolution 46/182 called for joint inter-agency needs assessment missions in response to requests for emergency assistance.

Nonetheless, on occasions, things have gone horribly wrong. The UN's inability to choke off the Rwandan genocide will forever stain the reputation of at least parts of the UN system, even though primary blame lay with member states rather than the UN as such. Unfortunately, this case was one in which the indifference of key states was matched by the wariness of the UN Secretariat about becoming involved in a situation which could turn into another Somalia. As a result, not only were vast numbers of Rwandans killed by ethnic Hutu extremists, but the UN's own Force Commander—a truly heroic Canadian, General Roméo Dallaire—was forced to bear witness to an orgy of killing which he was not authorised to stop. To deal with this problem was far beyond the capacity of Dallaire's foot-soldiers, and the case highlights the structural weakness of the UN in dealing with large-scale political problems which no great power has a great interest in solving.[15]

CHANGE

If such problems are to be overcome, some attention needs to be given to the architecture of humanitarian assistance. Resolution 46/182 was an important step in the right direction, but it remains the case that the UN system is constitutionally fragmented in areas where effective co-ordination is required. The biannual meetings of the UN System Chief Executives Board for Co-ordination highlight the ongoing problem of a multiplicity of chief executives rather than a single one. There is no prospect of the UN specialised agencies (such as the Food and Agriculture Organization, the World Health Organization, and the UN Educational, Scientific and Cultural Organization), or even the UN funds and programmes (such as the UN Development Programme, UNHCR, the World Food Programme, and the UN Children's Fund), being drawn back into the

Secretariat, and from time to time problems of co-ordination will surface as a result.

A more severe problem relates to resources. Whereas the UN Secretariat is financed from the dues paid by member states, the vital activities of UNHCR are almost entirely funded from voluntary contributions. As UNHCR has been increasingly driven into large-scale emergency relief operations, it has on occasion met with the displeasure of key donors as it attempts to discharge its other function of offering protection to refugees and asylum seekers in those donor countries. Separating the function of refugee protection in the strict sense from that of providing emergency relief to displaced populations might be a step in the right direction, but there is no indication that anything like this is about to occur.[16]

There is also a serious *global* problem of resources for addressing humanitarian problems, and a fashionable new emergency or political crisis can easily 'crowd out' a much needier 'at-risk' population. Here, the situation in Afghanistan is instructive. After the signing of the Bonn agreement in December 2001, there was not only a great deal of optimism that Afghanistan might at last have turned the corner, but also a desperate need for further measures to ensure that the momentum created in Bonn would not be lost. Yet, unfortunately, this was exactly what happened. With a view to conserving air-lift assets for future use against Iraq, the US responded dustily to suggestions that the new International Security Assistance Force be extended beyond Kabul,[17] and funds pledged for Afghanistan at a January 2002 Donors Conference in Tokyo simply failed to materialise.

The scale of the problem can be appreciated from work carried out by the Center on International Co-operation at New York University.[18] Figures compiled from the Government of Afghanistan Donor Assistance Database showed that, by November 2003, while US$5.37 billion had been 'committed', the amount spent on 'projects begun' was only US$1.78 billion (of which US$378.87 million was for the Afghan National Army), and the amount spent on completed projects was a mere US$112.5 million. And while the administration of George W. Bush trumpeted its intention to deliver further aid to Afghanistan, its actual behaviour belied its rhetoric. As Ivo Daalder and James Lindsay recorded, the 'White House's 2004 budget submission failed to include any funds for Afghan reconstruction',[19] and the Emergency Supplemental Appropriations Act for the Reconstruction of Iraq and Afghanistan of November 2003 approved just US$1.2 billion for Afghanistan, out of a total of US$87.5 billion. (By contrast, the amount for relief and reconstruction in Iraq was US$18.6 billion.) The UN simply has little say in what will be spent on humanitarian operations, and how.

Most serious of all is the problem of security. Humanitarian action is most often required in an environment rich with spoilers. On 2 July 2003, President Bush responded to threats to US forces in Iraq with the words 'bring 'em on'. Rarely can such a reckless plea have passed the lips of a prominent leader and, in the months that followed, spoilers lined up to meet his request. Many US soldiers died in the attacks which followed, but so did staff of the two leading humanitarian missions in Iraq: the UN and the International Committee of the Red Cross. In Afghanistan, the resurgence of Taliban groups, operating out of bases in Pakistan, created a similar climate of insecurity. In the long run, security sector reform, encompassing both military and police, may be required to provide a firm basis for future stability, but it offers no short-term palliative. Thus, if humanitarian action is to succeed, a neutral security force of adequate size and with a 'Chapter VII' mandate may be required—not to carry out humanitarian action itself, which can dangerously blur the distinction between aid workers and combatants, but to secure an environment in which humanitarian action can proceed.

Can structural reform of the UN system facilitate improvement in its handling of serious humanitarian challenges? In late 2004, a major report on the UN system was presented by a high-level panel chaired by former Thai Prime Minister Anand Panyarachun, based on extensive discussions with well-informed and interested parties.[20] The report took up a number of key ideas put forward in the earlier report of the International Commission on Intervention and State Sovereignty,[21] proposing five criteria—*seriousness of threat, proper purpose, last resort, proportional means, and balance of consequences*—for the Security Council to address when considering whether to authorise military action. Of greatest interest, however, were the panel's recommendations for changes in the structure and functioning of the Security Council. It endorsed an expansion of the Security Council from fifteen to twenty-four members (although not the extension to other states of the veto power enjoyed by the five current permanent members), and put forward two models that might give effect to such an approach: one involving six new permanent seats and three non-permanent seats with two-year non-renewable terms, and the other involving eight new non-permanent but renewable four-year-term seats and one non-permanent seat with a two-year non-renewable term. While not recommending any change to the formal powers of the Council under the Charter, it did propose one interesting procedural innovation, namely the introduction of 'indicative voting' whereby 'members of the Security Council could call for a public indication of positions on a proposed action', where '"no" votes would not have a veto effect, nor would the final tally of the vote have any legal force'.[22]

This proposal, if adopted, could be significant in its effect, especially in cases where permanent members are disposed to act in a selfish fashion which they realise is thoroughly immoral. A case in point occurred at the end of April 1994, in circumstances recounted by the then-President of the Security Council, Colin Keating of New Zealand, who had endured a month of agonising frustration as the Clinton administration prevaricated in the face of the Rwandan genocide: 'At the end of April, the Council finally agreed to a presidential statement addressing the true situation. It used words drawn specifically from the Genocide Convention. Sadly, it was still not possible to reach agreement on the use of the word "genocide". Indeed, even this outcome was possible only because of a draft resolution tabled by New Zealand, from the chair, threatening to force a vote that would have publicly exposed those countries that were resisting.'[23] Since an indicative vote of the kind proposed by the high-level panel would not be a veto, an issue could remain 'live' despite the desire of a permanent member to bury it, possibly creating room for domestic lobby groups to bring pressure to bear on key decision makers to shift their country's positions. However, this probably militates against the prospects of the proposal being accepted.

CONCLUSION

If the 1990s were not easy for the UN, they were not easy for humanitarian action either. While earlier crises such as the Biafran emergency had brought the paradoxes of humanitarianism into focus, it was in the 1990s that they appeared in a deluge. And, ultimately, there is no magic solution to the dilemmas which haunt contemporary humanitarian action. In modern humanitarianism, the tension between deontological and consequentialist ethics is fully on display. David Rieff, in a recent discussion, has argued that it is necessary for humanitarian action to recover its independence. Humanitarianism, he has argued, 'is neutral or it is nothing'.[24] His observations are based on both extensive field experience and deep reflection, and deserve to be taken seriously. Yet, if neutrality is necessary for humanitarian effectiveness, it is scarcely achievable within the framework of an integrated UN system with the Security Council in charge. Improving the efficiency of relief delivery does not begin to come to terms with this deeper structural and conceptual tension. The best, therefore, for which one can hope is an uneasy and compromising balancing of the UN's political and humanitarian responsibilities.

NOTES

PREFACE

[1] Carl von Clausewitz, *On War*, p. 87. To be fair to Clausewitz, it is worth remarking that his dictum was primarily intended to ensure that war was under political rather than military control. Nonetheless, it is often understood as also normalising the resort to war by making it merely one political means amongst others.

2 INTERVENTION, REALISM AND THE IDEAL OF PEACE

[1] Walzer, *Just and Unjust Wars*, pp. 101–8.

[2] For a fuller discussion of the consent problem, see Coady, *The Ethics of Armed Humanitarian Intervention*, pp. 10–11. Similar points are made in Coady, 'War for Humanity', p. 275.

[3] This matter is more fully discussed in Coady, *The Ethics of Armed Humanitarian Intervention*, pp. 11–13. See also Coady, 'War for Humanity', pp. 276–7.

[4] Bush, 'The National Security Strategy of the United States of America'.

[5] Schlesinger, 'The Necessary Amorality of Foreign Affairs'.

[6] Coady, 'Hobbes and the Beautiful Axiom'.

[7] Todorov, *Facing the Extreme*.

[8] Wotton cited in Morgenthau, *Politics among Nations*, p. 571.

[9] Coady, 'The Meaning of Moralism'.

[10] Some argue that the siding with the Northern Alliance was not motivated by moral objections to the Taliban, but by the need to make allies of the Northern Alliance troops in order to get non-American troops on the ground against al-Qaeda. There is a plausible case for this, but the alternative

I give has some support and usefully illustrates the point in the text. See Conetta, *Strange Victory*.

[11] Hehir, 'Intervention', pp. 5ff.

[12] Doyle, 'Kant, Liberal Legacies, and Foreign Affairs'.

[13] Walzer, 'The Politics of Rescue'.

[14] Galtung, 'US Foreign Policy as Manifest Theology', p. 119.

[15] Commager, 'Ethics, Virtue, and Foreign Policy', p. 132.

[16] Unterseher, 'Interventionism Reconsidered'; see also his chapter in this volume.

[17] See Finnegan, 'The Invisible War'.

[18] Weiss, 'UN Responses in the Former Yugoslavia', p. 231.

[19] Senior relief official in Sarajevo, October 1993, cited by Weiss, 'UN responses in the Former Yugoslavia', p. 231.

[20] Grant, *The State of the World's Children 1993*.

3 THE ETHICS OF INVASION

[1] Woodward, *Plan of Attack*. From Woodward's account it appears the decision emerged slowly over a period of months, long before the actual order was given to launch the attack itself.

[2] Freedman, *Kennedy's Wars*, pp. 208ff.

[3] White, 'Choosing War', p. 4.

[4] Singer, *The President of Good and Evil*, pp. 183ff.

[5] Charlesworth, 'What's Law Got To Do with the War?', pp. 38ff.

[6] Walzer, *Just and Unjust Wars*, p. 74.

[7] Singer, *The President of Good and Evil*, pp. 210ff.

[8] Bush, 'Graduation Speech at West Point'; Bush, 'National Security Strategy of the United States of America'.

[9] Walzer, *Just and Unjust Wars*, p. 81. Interestingly, in his recent writings on Iraq, Walzer seems to imply that it is only the advent of WMD that justifies an extension of pre-emption beyond Webster's limits (*Arguing about War*, p. 147). But his earlier arguments are more compelling: there has always been a legitimate right to go to war to forestall an attack. WMD may change the circumstances of judgements about prevention and pre-emption, but not the basis for them.

[10] Luban, 'Preventive War', pp. 221ff; Walzer, *Arguing about War*, p. 148.

[11] Walzer, *Arguing about War*, p. 147.

[12] Walzer, *Arguing about War*.

[13] Luban, 'Preventive War', pp. 213–14.

[14] International Commission on Intervention and State Sovereignty, *The Responsibility To Protect*, pp. 32ff.

[15] See, for example, Woodward, *Plan of Attack*; Mann, *The Rise of the Vulcans*.

[16] Harries, *Benign or Imperial?*, provides an excellent analysis of the ideas underlying this kind of thinking.

[17] Luban, 'Preventive War', p. 242.
[18] Luban, 'Preventive War', pp. 239–40.
[19] Luban, 'Preventive War', pp. 236ff.
[20] Kennan, 'The Sources of Soviet Conduct', p. 109.

4 COLLECTIVE RESPONSIBILITY AND ARMED HUMANITARIAN INTERVENTION

[1] See Weymouth & Henig, *The Kosovo Crisis*.
[2] Keane, *Season of Blood*, p. 29.
[3] See Kaldor, *New and Old Wars*, p. 64.
[4] Pollack, *The Threatening Storm*.
[5] Evidently in Kosovo the Albanians were the object of ethnic cleansing by the Serb armed forces, but the Serbs themselves became the object of ethnic cleansing by some Albanian armed forces (KLA). See Weymouth & Henig, *The Kosovo Crisis*, p. 239.
[6] For an insight into Saddam Hussein's strategies and policies in this regard, see Butler, *Saddam Defiant*. Of course, Saddam Hussein's policies took place as a response to, and in the context of, the sanctions imposed by the US and its allies. Given his response, the continued imposition of sanctions was surely both ineffective and immoral.
[7] See Walzer, *Just and Unjust Wars*.
[8] On the other hand, it could be argued that the media spectacle of significant numbers of body-bags containing dead NATO combatants might have created public pressure, in the US in particular, not to continue with the intervention, and thereby left the Albanian Kosovars to the mercy of their murderous Serbian enemies.
[9] For an earlier application of this notion of collective responsibility to genocide, see Miller, 'Collective Responsibility, Armed Intervention and the Rwandan Genocide'. See also Miller, *Social Action*, ch. 8.
[10] Cooper, 'Collective Responsibility'; French, *Collective and Corporate Responsibility*.
[11] Silber & Little, *Yugoslavia*, pp. 345–50.
[12] Weymouth & Henig, *The Kosovo Crisis*, p. 192.
[13] This mode of analysis is also available to handle examples in which an institutional entity has a representative who makes an individual decision, but it is an individual decision which has the joint backing of the members of the institutional entity (e.g. an industrial union's representative in relation to wage negotiations with a company). It can also handle examples such as the firing squad in which only one real bullet is used, and it is not known which member is firing the real bullet and which merely blanks. The soldier with the real bullet is (albeit unknown to him) individually responsible for shooting the person dead. However, the members of the firing squad are jointly responsible for its being the case that the person has been shot dead.

14 Silber & Little, *Yugoslavia*, p. 360. Arguably, if somewhat implausibly, the NATO bombing was not *intentional* support for the Croats. If not, then the example was not a paradigmatic case of joint action.

15 The co-operation between Croat land forces and NATO air power against Serbian forces is in sharp contrast to what happened in Kosovo. NATO forces were in some sense in alliance with the KLA who were engaged in fighting Serbian forces. The KLA were supposedly operating on behalf of the Albanian majority in Kosovo in their conflict with the Serbian forces controlled from Belgrade, but supposedly acting on behalf of the Serbian minority in Kosovo. However, NATO relied more or less exclusively on its own air power to destroy, or seek the capitulation of, the Serbian forces.

16 Shue, *Basic Rights*.

17 Shue, 'Eroding Sovereignty'.

18 These are individual moral responsibilities at one level of description (i.e. at the level of the nation-state conceived of as an individual entity). However, they are collective moral responsibilities in so far as nation-states or their governments are thought of as groups of individual human persons. The latter description is ultimately the correct one.

5   AUSTRALIAN INTERVENTION IN ITS NEIGHBOURHOOD

I would like to thank Dennis Altman, Andrew Cock, Anthony Jarvis and Robin Jeffrey for comments on an earlier draft of this chapter.

1 See, for instance, International Commission on Intervention and State Sovereignty, *The Responsibility To Protect*.

2 See Holzgrefe & Keohane, *Humanitarian Intervention*; MacFarlane et al., 'The Responsibility To Protect'; Rotberg, *State Failure and State Weakness in a Time of Terror*.

3 Cooper et al., *Relocating Middle Powers*.

4 Australian Government, *Transnational Terrorism*, pp. 107–8.

5 Australian Government, *Transnational Terrorism*, p. 17.

6 Howard, Transcript of the Prime Minister the Hon. John Howard MP Ministerial Statement to Parliament on Iraq.

7 The initial confusion arose over an interview with Howard in the *Bulletin* in 1999 (see Brenchley, 'The Howard Defence Doctrine'). For a recent example of the regional view, see Fickling, 'Australia Seen as America's Deputy Sheriff'.

8 The 'proximate region' is used throughout to denote the area described by the government as the 'arc of instability', 'crescent of instability' or 'nearer region'. It includes the archipelago to Australia's north (particularly PNG) and the South Pacific. Department of Defence, *Defence 2000*.

9 Macmillan et al., 'Strategic Culture'.

10 See Cheeseman, 'Australia'; Ball, *Strategic Culture in the Asia–Pacific Region*; Dutton, 'A British Outpost Facing North'.

11 Macmillan et al., 'Strategic Culture', p. 5; Allison, *Essence of Decision*.

12 The following section draws heavily on Cheeseman, 'Australia'.

13 See, for instance, Blainey, *The Tyranny of Distance*, p. 319.

14 See, for instance, Kelly, 'Punching above Our Weight'.

15 Compare the strategic summaries in Department of Defence, *The Defence of Australia 1987* and *Defence 2000*.

16 Garran, *True Believer*; O'Keefe, 'Enduring Tensions in the 2000 Defence White Paper'.

17 Macmillan et al., 'Strategic Culture', pp. 12, 13–14.

18 George, 'Australia's Global Perspectives in the 1990s'.

19 See, for instance, Garran, *True Believer*.

20 Evans & Grant, *Australia's Foreign Relations*.

21 Department of Foreign Affairs and Trade, *Australia's Regional Security*.

22 The Australian Strategic Policy Institute wrote a report just prior to the operation that detailed exactly how a successful operation could be undertaken (see Wainwright, *Our Failing Neighbour*).

23 This is a reference to the threat perceptions expressed in the Department of Defence, *Defence 2000*, p. 110, and Department of Foreign Affairs and Trade, *Australia's Regional Security*, para 47.

24 Department of Defence, *The Defence of Australia 1987*, p. 9.

25 This is a reference to Hayes et al., *American Lake*.

26 See Department of Defence, *The Defence of Australia 1987*, pp. 12–19.

27 See Department of Defence, *The Defence of Australia 1987*, pp. 17–18; Kiste & Herr, *The Potential for Soviet Penetration of the South Pacific Islands*, pp. 15–17.

28 Brenchley, 'The Howard Defence Doctrine'.

29 See Gubb, *The Australian Military Response to the Fiji Coup*, particularly pp. 13, 25–8; Admiral Hudson in Institute of Public Affairs, *Australia's Defence in Review*, p. 10.

30 Senate Standing Committee on Foreign Affairs, Defence and Trade, *United Nations Peacekeeping and Australia*, p. 119; *Australian*, 14 August 1989, p. 1; *Age*, 10 July 1990, p. 3; *Australian*, 9 December 1994, p. 5; *Age Extra*, 30 April 1994, p. 5.

31 Joint Standing Committee on Foreign Affairs, Defence and Trade, *Papua New Guinea Update*, p. 31.

32 Howard in *Australian*, 2 July 2003.

33 *Australian*, 1 July 2003, p. 2.

34 There was some dissent from former PM Manasseh Sogavare but the parliament voted unanimously to support the intervention (*Australian*, 11 July 2003, p. 2).

35 Howard in *Australian*, 23 July 2003, p. 1; *Australian*, 27 June 2003, p. 1.

36 Hill, 'Military Drawdown as Progress Continues in Solomon Islands', p. 1; Hill, 'Defence Personnel to Come Home from Solomons', p. 1.

37 See Downer, 'Solomon Islands'; Department of Foreign Affairs and Trade, *Solomon Islands*; Wainwright, *Our Failing Neighbour*.

38 Department of Defence, *Strategic Review 1993*, p. 13; Howard, Transcript of the Prime Minister the Hon. John Howard MP Address at Informal Farewell Reception for the Troops and Police Heading to the Solomon Islands.

39 *Australian*, 1 October 2004, p. 2.

40 Joint Committee on Foreign Affairs, Defence and Trade, *Australia's Relations with the South Pacific*, p. 156.

41 Department of Defence, *Force Structure Review*, p. 2.

42 Evans, 'Australia's Regional Security Environment', p. 381; Department of Foreign Affairs and Trade, *Australia's Regional Security*, p. 22.

43 Department of Foreign Affairs and Trade, *Australia's Regional Security*, para 71.

44 The term 'solo' forward defence was first used by King, 'Australia, Regional Threats and the Arms Race', p. 135. See also Thompson, *Australia's Strategic Defence Policy*; Hill, Keynote address, p. 1.

45 The term 'virtual' intervention is used here to recognise the true nature of the deployment. While the ADF did not physically intervene, forces were stationed offshore and the threat to do so was real.

46 Department of Foreign Affairs and Trade, *Australia's Regional Security*, pp. 22, 41–5.

47 The SPF changed its name to become the PIF.

48 Howard, Transcript of the Prime Minister the Hon. John Howard MP Address at the Solomon Islands Taskforce Farewell, p. 2.

49 For a fuller discussion, see O'Keefe, 'Enduring Tensions', pp. 523–6.

50 Beazley, 'Self-Reliance'; Department of Foreign Affairs and Trade, *Australia's Regional Security*, pp. 21–2.

51 Beazley, 'If you have to fight, you might as well win'. Seven states eventually asked Australia to rescue its citizens if need be. See Gubb, *The Australian Military Response to the Fiji Coup*, p. 6; Department of Defence, *The Defence of Australia 1987*, p. 3.

52 Howard in *Australian*, 2 July 2003, p. 1; Downer, 'Security in an Unstable World'.

53 Bush actually defended Australia by describing it as a 'sheriff'—Australia was willing to take responsibility for maintaining stability in its proximate region.

54 See Ignatieff, 'State Failure and Nation Building'; Crocker, 'Engaging Failing States'; Rotberg, 'Failed States in a World of Terror'.

55 See Zartman, *Collapsed States*, pp. 5–11.

56 Zartman, *Collapsed States*, p. 5.

57 See Chalk, *Non-military Security and the Global Order*.

58 Most analysis of state failure has occurred in the context of Africa and more research is warranted because it may not have universal application.

[59] See, for instance, Rotberg, *When States Fail*.

[60] Ignatieff, 'State Failure and Nation Building'. Persuasive arguments have been made against this construction of threat from the South Pacific (see, for instance, *Australian*, 21 July 2003, p. 9).

[61] Wainwright, *Our Failing Neighbour*, p. 19; Howard in *Australian*, 2 July 2003, p. 1; Downer, 'Security in an Unstable World'.

[62] *Australian*, 21 July 2003, p. 2.

[63] See, for instance, Milliken, *State Failure, Collapse and Reconstruction*. For an extended discussion of sovereignty, see Collett's chapter in this volume.

[64] Lindenberg & Bryant, *Going Global*, pp. 65–100.

[65] Horner, *Armies and Nation Building*; Harris & Dombrowski, 'Military Collaboration with Humanitarian Organisations in Complex Emergencies'.

[66] For instance, the former two are used by Rotberg, *State Failure and State Weakness in a Time of Terror*.

[67] On the latter point, see Fukuyama, *State Building*.

[68] Howard in *Australian* 23 July 2003, p. 4.

[69] *Australian*, 23 July 2003.

[70] See Windybank, 'Papua New Guinea on the Brink', p. 1.

[71] Windybank, 'Papua New Guinea on the Brink'.

[72] World Bank, *Governance Matters III*; AusAID, *Papua New Guinea and the Pacific*, pp. 7–9. See also Dinnem, *Law and Order in a Weak State*.

[73] UN Development Programme, *Human Development Report*; AusAID, *Papua New Guinea and the Pacific*, pp. 1–3; World Bank, *World Development Indicators 2002*.

[74] Caldwell, 'It's Everyone's Problem', p. 7; Piot, 'UN Says Pacific Faces New Wave of HIV'; Hauquitz, 'Looking down the Barrel of a Cannon'; Morrison, 'The Global Epidemiology of HIV/AIDS'.

[75] National AIDS Council (6103) and AusAID (10 000–15 000).

[76] AusAID, *HIV/AIDS in Papua New Guinea*; Centre for International Economics, *Potential Economic Impacts of an HIV/AIDS Epidemic in Papua New Guinea*.

[77] Centre for International Economics, *Potential Economic Impacts*; Morauta, 'Community Response to HIV/AIDS in Papua New Guinea'.

[78] Altman, 'HIV And Security'; UNAIDS, *2004 Report on the Global AIDS Epidemic*, pp. 175–81; Eberstadt, 'The Future of Aids'; Hankins, 'Transmission and Prevention of HIV and Sexually Transmitted Infections in War Settings'.

[79] Hankins, 'Transmission and Prevention'.

[80] Downer in *Australian*, 22 September 2003, p. 9. See also Downer's comments at the XV International AIDS conference in Bangkok in July 2004.

[81] Reilly, 'The Africanisation of the South Pacific'; and Piot, 'UN Says Pacific Faces New Wave of HIV. See also Fraenke, 'The Coming Anarchy in Oceania?'

[82] Downer in *Australian*, 22 September 2003, p. 9.

83 Windybank, 'Papua New Guinea on the Brink'.

84 Hughes, 'Aid Has Failed the Pacific', p. 1; Australian Strategic Policy Institute, *Beyond Bali*.

85 For instance, Australia's economic interests in Bougainville may have influenced the policy options applied to resolving the civil war. The provision of helicopter gunships to PNG is a case in point.

86 White in *Australian*, 2 October 2003, p. 2.

87 Putzel, *Institutionalising an Emergency Response*.

88 Howard, Transcript of the Prime Minister the Hon. John Howard MP Address at Informal Farewell Reception.

89 Carment, 'Assessing State Failure'. p. 407.

90 Howard in *Australian*, 2 July 2003.

91 See Vaughn, 'Australia's Strategic Identity Post-September 11 in Context', p. 111; Caplan, *A New Trusteeship?*. See Fearon & Laitin, 'Neotrusteeship and the Problem of Weak States', especially p. 7.

92 Downer, 'Solomon Islands'; Department of Foreign Affairs and Trade, *Solomon Islands*.

93 Howard in Harvey, 'Happy to "Patch" Things Up in the Pacific', *Australian*, 1 October 2004, p. 2.

6 THE DOCTRINE OF HUMANITARIAN INTERVENTION

1 *Opinio juris* means a belief by a state that particular state activity is legally obligatory. Shaw, *International Law*, p. 67.

2 Kritsiotis, 'Reappraising Policy Objections to Humanitarian Intervention', p. 1049.

3 Schachter, 'The Right of States to Use Armed Force', p. 1620.

4 Article 2(4) states: 'All members shall refrain in their international relations from the threat or use of force against the territorial integrity or political independence of any state, or in any other manner inconsistent with the Purposes of the United Nations'. Article 2(7) states: 'Nothing contained in the present Charter shall authorize the United Nations to intervene in matters which are essentially within the domestic jurisdiction of any state or shall require the Members to submit such matters to settlement under the present Charter; but this principle shall not prejudice the application of enforcement measures under Chapter VII'.

5 See, for example, United Kingdom, *Statement in the UN Security Council by the Permanent Representative of the UK*. Also see UN Security Council, *3988ᵗʰ Meeting*.

6 UK, *Statement in the UN Security Council*.

7 The two autonomous republics within the FRY at the time of the air strikes were Serbia and Montenegro. The FRY is now known as Serbia and Montenegro.

[8] UK, *Statement in the UN Security Council*; Letter of NATO Secretary-General of 10 June 1999.

[9] Simma, 'NATO, the UN and the Use of Force'.

[10] *Interim Agreement for Peace and Self-Government in Kosovo* and *Agreement for Self-Government in KOSMET*.

[11] See for example, UK, *Statement in the UN Security Council*; interview given by French Minister of Foreign Affairs, *Le Journal Du Dimanche*; US Secretary of State, *Statement*: 'let me repeat what Secretary Cohen said yesterday: he made quite clear that a resolution may be desirable but not required. We believe that there is existing Security Council authorisation and that we have inherent authority to do what needs to be done.'

[12] UK, *Statement in the UN Security Council*. Belgium also referred to the right of humanitarian intervention in its submissions to the ICJ in the provisional measures phase of the Case Concerning Legality of Use of Force brought by the FRY against NATO member states (International Commission on Intervention and State Sovereignty, *Supplementary Volume to the Report*, p. 168).

[13] Simma, 'NATO, the UN and the Use of Force'.

[14] See, for example, Simma, 'NATO, the UN and the Use of Force'; Cassese, '*Ex iniuria ius oritur*'.

[15] UK, *Statement in the UN Security Council*; UK, Ministry of Defence website.

[16] Baroness Symons of Vernham Dean, Statement to UK Parliament.

[17] Simma, 'NATO, the UN and the Use of Force'.

[18] See, for example, Simma, 'NATO, the UN and the Use of Force'; Cassese, '*Ex iniuria ius oritur*'.

[19] Former Australian foreign minister, Bill Hayden, referred to Kosovo and the establishment of the new right of humanitarian intervention when analysing the possible international intervention in East Timor ('Don't Forget We Are on Our Own').

[20] Tesón, *Humanitarian Intervention*, p. 5; Franck & Rodley, 'After Bangladesh', p. 305, quoted in Abiew, *The Evolution of the Doctrine and Practice of Humanitarian Intervention*, p. 31.

[21] Lauterpacht quoted in Abiew, *The Evolution of the Doctrine*, p. 42; Verwey quoted in Abiew, *The Evolution of the Doctrine*, p. 18; Tesón, *Humanitarian Intervention*, pp. 5, 189.

[22] Arguably, self-determination is a human right and therefore would be encompassed by the expression 'humanitarian intervention'. However, self-determination has been taken by authors such as Shaw to be a specific concept separate from that of humanitarian intervention. See Shaw, *International Law*, pp. 795, 802.

[23] Brownlie, *Principles of Public International Law*, p. 3.

[24] Tesón, *Humanitarian Intervention*, p. 15.

[25] Dinstein, *War, Aggression and Self-Defence*, p. 91.

26 Kelly, *Peace Operations*, p. 1–33.

27 Simma, *The Charter of the United Nations*, pp. 28, 36. Significant for Simma was the fact that the admission of the additional members to the UN makes the genuine will of the original parties of questionable relevance.

28 Schachter, 'In Defense of International Rules on the Use of Force', pp. 130, 131.

29 Brownlie, *Principles of Public International Law*, pp. 5, 7; Shaw, *International Law*, p. 58; Kritsiotis, 'Reappraising Policy Objections to Humanitarian Intervention', p. 1050.

30 Brownlie, *Principles of Public International Law*, p. 5; Tesón, *Humanitarian Intervention*, p. 171 (original emphasis).

31 Simma, *The Charter of the United Nations*, p. 42.

32 The United Nations Conference on the Law of Treaties, *Vienna Convention on the Law of Treaties*, Article 31(1) states inter alia that a treaty 'shall be interpreted in good faith in accordance with the ordinary meaning to be given to the terms of the treaty in their context and in light of its object and purpose'.

33 The Charter preamble states inter alia: 'We the peoples of the United Nations determined … to reaffirm faith in fundamental human rights'. See also Article 1 where a stated purpose of the UN is 'To develop friendly relations among nations based on respect for the principle of equal rights and self-determination of peoples'.

34 Tesón, *Humanitarian Intervention*, pp. 130, 153.

35 For example, in the Governments of the United States, United Kingdom, France, the Soviet Union and China, *Declaration of Four Nations on General Security*, it was stated '[the governments] recognize the necessity of establishing … a general international organization, based on the sovereign equality of all peace-loving States … for international peace and security'. Also of significance is that the US proposal at Dumbarton Oaks that the General Assembly should be able to study and recommend measures for promoting the observance of human rights was defeated due to British and Soviet opposition (Simma, *The Charter of the United Nations*, pp. 8–9).

36 Cassese, '*Ex iniuria ius oritur*'.

37 Harris, *Cases and Materials on International Law*, p. 873.

38 Henkin quoted in Simma, *The Charter of the United Nations*, p. 117.

39 Jimenez de Arechaga quoted in Simma, *The Charter of the United Nations*, p. 111.

40 Schachter, 'The Right of States To Use Armed Force', p. 1624.

41 Article 51 states inter alia: 'Nothing in the present Charter shall impair the inherent right of individual or collective self-defence if an armed attack occurs against a Member of the United Nations'.

42 Tesón, *Humanitarian Intervention*, p. 131.

43 Simma, *The Charter of the United Nations*, pp. 117–18.

[44] UN General Assembly, *Resolution 2131(XX)* states: 'no state has the right to intervene, directly or indirectly, for any reason whatsoever, in the internal or external affairs of any other state'.

[45] UN General Assembly, *Resolution 2625 (XXV)*.

[46] Shaw, *International Law*, p. 784. The ICJ stated: 'the alleged right of intervention [was] the manifestation of a policy of force, such as has, in the past, given rise to the most serious abuses and such as cannot … find a place in international law'.

[47] Dinstein, *War, Aggression and Self-Defence*, pp. 89–90; Shaw, *International Law*, p. 802.

[48] For example, UN General Assembly, *Declaration of Principles of International Law*, indicated that states were not to use or threaten force to violate existing international frontiers or to solve international disputes. Shaw, *International Law*, p. 781.

[49] Schachter, 'The Legality of Pro-Democratic Invasion', cited in Simma, *The Charter of the United Nations*, p. 118.

[50] Simma, *The Charter of the United Nations*, p. 146.

[51] Tesón, *Humanitarian Intervention*, pp. 137–42. Also Reisman, 'Coercion and Self-Determination', p. 643.

[52] A rule of *jus cogens* is a peremptory norm of international law, that is, it is a norm that is 'accepted and recognised by the international community of states as a whole as a norm from which no derogation is permitted and which can be modified only by a subsequent norm of general international law having the same character'. Article 53 of the Convention on the Law of Treaties, quoted by Shaw, *International Law*, p. 97.

[53] Schachter, 'In Defense of International Rules', pp. 125–6.

[54] Kelly, *Peace Operations*, p. 1–26.

[55] Case studies that do not assist in determining whether a broad right of humanitarian intervention exists are not examined. For example, the 1965 US Dominican Republic intervention had mixed motives together with there being consent for the intervention. It supports only the narrow right of intervention to protect nationals (see Abiew, *The Evolution of the Doctrine*, p. 112). Also, the Vietnamese intervention in Kampuchea in 1978–79, notwithstanding the clear humanitarian benefit that resulted, provides little support for a right of unilateral intervention. The absence of articulated support for the intervention on the basis of humanitarian intervention, the installation by Vietnam of a puppet government in Kampuchea and the fact that Vietnamese troops and advisers were still present in Kampuchea ten years after the invasion are all significant (see Kelly, *Peace Operations*, p. 1–27).

[56] Tesón, *Humanitarian Intervention*, p. 157; Brownlie, *International Law and the Use of Force by States*, p. 340.

[57] White, *Keeping the Peace*, pp. 259–60.

[58] Brownlie, referred to in Kelly, *Peace Operations*, p. 1–24.

59 Arend & Beck, *International Law and the Use of Force*, p. 118; Tesón, *Humanitarian Intervention*, p. 181.

60 Abiew, *The Evolution of the Doctrine*, pp. 113, 114–16.

61 Tesón, *Humanitarian Intervention*, p. 185.

62 Abiew, *The Evolution of the Doctrine*, p. 116; Tesón, *Humanitarian Intervention*, p. 188.

63 Arend & Beck, *International Law*, p. 119.

64 Abiew, *The Evolution of the Doctrine*, pp. 118–19.

65 Tesón, *Humanitarian Intervention*, pp. 183, 186. Relying on Section 6 of the UN General Assembly, *Declaration on the Granting of Independence to Colonial Countries and Peoples*, which states that, after providing self-determination of colonial peoples, 'Any attempt at the partial or total disruption of the national unity and the territorial integrity of a country is incompatible with the purposes and principles of the United Nations'. However, Tesón went on to argue that East Pakistan should be an exception as a right of self-determination arises due to the genocide.

66 Abiew, *The Evolution of the Doctrine*, p. 117.

67 Kelly, *Peace Operations*, p. 1–26; see also Abiew, *The Evolution of the Doctrine*: the Jurists referred to the 'inability of international organizations to take any effective action'.

68 Reportedly, there were at least 300 000 deaths: Tesón, *Humanitarian Intervention*, p. 163. See also Abiew, *The Evolution of the Doctrine*, pp. 120–3; Arend & Beck, *International Law*, pp. 123, 124.

69 Abiew, *The Evolution of the Doctrine*, pp. 122–4; Kelly, *Peace Operations*, p. 1–26.

70 Tesón, *Humanitarian Intervention*, pp. 163, 167; Kelly, *Peace Operations*, p. 1–26.

71 Murphy in Abiew, *The Evolution of the Doctrine*, pp. 124–5; Dinstein, *War, Aggression and Self-Defence*, p. 235.

72 Tesón, *Humanitarian Intervention*, p. 162. Fewer than 1000 Ugandans and 400 Libyans were killed in five months of fighting, with a lesser number of Tanzanians.

73 Tesón, *Humanitarian Intervention*, p. 163.

74 Tesón, *Humanitarian Intervention*, pp. 188–9, 193; Kelly, *Peace Operations*, pp. 1–28.

75 Tesón, *Humanitarian Intervention*, pp. 15, 197.

76 Arend & Beck, *International Law*, p. 127.

77 Abiew, *The Evolution of Doctrine*, pp. 200–2.

78 Kelly, *Peace Operations*, p. 1–28.

79 Abiew, *The Evolution of the Doctrine*, pp. 204–5.

80 Kelly, *Peace Operations*, p. 1–29.

81 Abiew, *The Evolution of the Doctrine*, pp. 177, 179–89.

82 Abiew, *The Evolution of the Doctrine*, p. 188; Tesón, 'Collective Humanitarian Intervention', p. 369.

[83] Abiew, *The Evolution of the Doctrine*, pp. 145–50.
[84] Fine, *Legal Times*, 13 May 1991, vol. 13, p. 20, cited in Abiew, *The Evolution of the Doctrine*, p. 157; see also pp. 149, 155.
[85] Cook, 'France's Chirac Begins US Visit'; White & Cryer, 'Unilateral Enforcement of Resolution 687', p. 243.
[86] Abiew, *The Evolution of the Doctrine*, p. 157.
[87] Abiew, *The Evolution of the Doctrine*, pp. 161–3.
[88] Kelly, *Peace Operations*, p. 1–31.
[89] Tesón, 'Collective Humanitarian Intervention', p. 353.
[90] Kelly, *Peace Operations*, p. 1–14.
[91] Abiew, *The Evolution of the Doctrine*, pp. 189–93.
[92] Tesón, 'Collective Humanitarian Intervention', p. 365.
[93] Abiew, *The Evolution of the Doctrine*, pp. 213–14.
[94] Tesón, 'Collective Humanitarian Intervention', p. 356.
[95] Abiew, *The Evolution of the Doctrine*, p. 216.
[96] Tesón, 'Collective Humanitarian Intervention'.
[97] Regensburg and Scheffer cited in Abiew, *The Evolution of the Doctrine*, pp. 217, 219.
[98] Kelly, *Peace Operations*, p. 1–33.
[99] Berger, 'State Practice Evidence of the Humanitarian Intervention Doctrine', pp. 615–17.
[100] Berger, 'State Practice Evidence', p. 622.
[101] UN Security Council, *Resolution 1162 (1998)*.
[102] Abiew, *The Evolution of the Doctrine*, pp. 229–30.
[103] See, for example, Kelly, *Peace Operations*, p. 1–34.
[104] Harris, *Cases and Materials on International Law*, p. 873.
[105] Brownlie, *Principles of Public International Law*, pp. 24–5.
[106] UK Foreign Office Policy Document No. 148 quoted in Harris, *Cases and Materials*, p. 873.
[107] Tesón, *Humanitarian Intervention*, pp. 129, 146, 158, 199, 245.
[108] Tesón, *Humanitarian Intervention*, pp. 146–8.
[109] Benjamin, 'Unilateral Humanitarian Intervention', p. 125.
[110] NATO, for example, had reported that during the air strikes between 5000 and 6000 FRY soldiers had been killed and over 300 FRY tanks destroyed, but after the conflict it was reported that in fact as few as 400 FRY soldiers had been killed and 13 tanks destroyed. Norton-Taylor, 'So Just What Was Achieved?', p. 14.
[111] Tesón, 'Collective Humanitarian Intervention', p. 354.
[112] Also it is noted that pro-Barre forces in Somalia in April 1991 and 1992 launched operations from the border region with Kenya (Abiew, *The Evolution of the Doctrine*, p. 161).
[113] Tesón, *Humanitarian Intervention*, p. 133.
[114] Tesón, *Humanitarian Intervention*, p. 245.

[115] Schachter, 'In Defense of International Rules', p. 143; Kelly, *Peace Operations*, p. 1–34.

[116] Zacklin, 'Beyond Kosovo', pp. 935–6. It is noted that those for and those against were divided along north–south lines.

[117] Zacklin, 'Beyond Kosovo', p. 937.

[118] UK, *Statement in the UN Security Council*.

[119] Thomas, 'NATO and International Law'.

[120] Hayden, 'Humanitarian Hypocrisy'.

[121] Simma, 'NATO, the UN and the Use of Force'.

[122] Tesón, *Humanitarian Intervention*, p. 242.

[123] From the viewpoint of countries such as China, Russia and India, there was much to question: an absence, arguably, of a situation in Kosovo such as to 'shock the conscience of mankind'; the ultimatum negotiation style of NATO; the breadth and reasonableness of the NATO proposals to the FRY.

[124] White & Cryer, 'Unilateral Enforcement', p. 281.

[125] Simma, for example, states: 'One especially dubious example is the view that the failure of the Council to disapprove regional military action amounts to [tacit] authorization'. Simma, 'NATO, the UN and the Use of Force'.

[126] Thomas, 'NATO and International Law'.

[127] Simma, *The Charter of the United Nations*, pp. 120–1. Prompted by Soviet use of the veto power in relation to Korea (having returned to its seat on the SC on 1 August 1950), the GA adopted the *Uniting for Peace Resolution* which states inter alia: 'if the Security Council, because of a lack of unanimity of the permanent members, fails to exercise its primary responsibility for the maintenance of international peace and security in any case where there appears to be threat to the peace, breach of the peace or act of aggression, the General Assembly shall consider the matter immediately with a view to making appropriate recommendations to Members for collective measures, including the use of force'.

[128] White & Cryer, 'Unilateral Enforcement', p. 281.

[129] Cassese, '*Ex iniuria ius oritur*'.

[130] *Interim Agreement for Peace and Self-Government in Kosovo*; *Agreement for Self-Government in KOSMET*; UK, *Statement in the UN Security Council*.

[131] Tesón, *Humanitarian Intervention*, pp. 238, 241.

[132] Human Rights Watch reports that it had been able to verify that around 500 Serb civilians were killed by the NATO air strikes ('Civilian Deaths in the NATO Air Campaign'); Hayden, 'Humanitarian Hypocrisy'; Thomas, 'NATO and International Law'; UK, *Statement in the UN Security Council*; Norton-Taylor, 'So Just What Was Achieved?'

[133] UK, *Statement in the UN Security Council*.

[134] Baroness Symons of Vernham Dean, Statement.

[135] *Memorandum of Understanding*, 18 April 1991, 30 ILM 860 (1991).

[136] White & Cryer report that China, Russia, Mexico, Pakistan, Malaysia and Egypt are critical of the UK and US position ('Unilateral Enforcement', p. 280).

[137] Tesón, *Humanitarian Intervention*, p. 215.

[138] *Interim Agreement for Peace and Self-Government in Kosovo*.

[139] Republic of France, Ministry of Foreign Affairs website.

[140] Simma, *The Charter of the United Nations*, p. 118.

[141] Independent International Commission on Kosovo, *The Kosovo Report*; ICISS, *Supplementary Volume*, p. 170.

[142] UK, Defence Select Committee, *Lessons of Kosovo*, p. 15. A Human Rights Watch report into humanitarian law violations in Kosovo in the period from February to early September 1998 refers to serious breaches of the law of war by the KLA, although on a 'lesser scale than the government abuses' (*Federal Republic of Yugoslavia*).

[143] UK Defence Select Committee, cited in Human Rights Watch, *Federal Republic of Yugoslavia*, p. 299. The report states that 'all the evidence suggests that plans to initiate the air campaign hastened the onset of the disaster'.

[144] Human Rights Watch, *Federal Republic of Yugoslavia*.

[145] Hayden, 'Humanitarian Hypocrisy'; Roberts, 'NATO's 'Humanitarian War' over Kosovo', pp. 142–3.

[146] UK Defence Select Committee, cited in Human Rights Watch, *Federal Republic of Yugoslavia*, p. 42.

[147] Human Rights Watch reported that seven weeks after KFOR entered Kosovo more than 164 000 Serbs and Roma had left Kosovo and many others had moved to Serb and Roma enclaves under KFOR protection within Kosovo, and it also reported a wave of arson and looting of Serb and Roma homes and a spate of abductions and murders of Serbs ('Abuses against Serbs and Roma in the New Kosovo'); UN Security Council, *Resolution 1244 (1999)* reaffirms the commitment of all member states of the UN to the sovereignty and territorial integrity of the FRY but provides for democratic and autonomous self-government in Kosovo.

[148] Voon, 'Closing the Gap between Legitimacy and Legality of Humanitarian Intervention', p. 60.

[149] Simma, *The Charter of the United Nations*, p. 117. This quotation relates specifically to the case of state practice relating to intervention in civil wars but the principle can be applied more generally.

[150] See, for example, Voon, 'Closing the Gap', p. 60.

[151] Tesón, *Humanitarian Intervention*, p. 167; Dinstein, *War, Aggression and Self-Defence*, p. 91.

[152] Abiew, *The Evolution of the Doctrine*, pp. 167–8, 235, 242.

[153] Arend & Beck, *International Law*, p. 136; White & Cryer, 'Unilateral Enforcement', p. 281.

[154] Voon, 'Closing the Gap', pp. 96–7.

[155] Zacklin, 'Beyond Kosovo', pp. 937–8.

[156] Dinstein, *War, Aggression and Self-Defence*, p. 204; ICJ website.

[157] Cassese, '*Ex iniuria ius oritur*'; Simma, 'NATO, the UN and the Use of Force'.

[158] Abiew, *The Evolution of the Doctrine*, pp. 280–1.

[159] United Nations, press release.

7 DOMESTICATING MILITARY INTERVENTIONS

[1] *Krisenprävention. Friedensbericht 1999.*

[2] Loquai, 'Medien als Weichensteller zum Krieg', pp. 112–16.

[3] Codner, *Aircraft Carriers*, pp. 3–4.

[4] Centre for Defence Studies, *The Strategic Defence Review*, pp. 5–7.

[5] Naumann, *Standortbestimmung, Informationen zur Sicherheitspolitik.*

[6] Pichler, 'Im Schatten von Dayton. Kosovo, Mazedonien, Albanien'; Libal, 'Kosovo nach dem Dayton-Abkommen'.

[7] Bunzl, 'Krisenherde im Nahen Osten'; Fischer, 'Krisenprävention'.

[8] Mutz, 'An den Verhandlungstisch gezwungen?'.

[9] Zumach, 'Dayton. Ein Friedensprozess' in Bosnien?'.

[10] Knight et al., 'Military Research and Development after the Second Gulf War'.

[11] General Accounting Office, *Operation Desert Storm.*

[12] Conetta, *The Wages of War.*

[13] Grin, 'Krieg ohne überflüssiges Blutvergießen'.

[14] For an overview, see Møller & Wiberg, *Non-Offensive Defence for the Twenty-First Century.*

[15] European Security and Finnish Defence, *Report by the Council of State to Parliament*, pp. 95–6.

[16] Unterseher, *Military Stability and European Security.*

[17] Watson, *Basic Writings of MO TZU, HSUN TZU, and HAN FEI TZU.*

[18] Møller & Wiberg, *Non-Offensive Defence for the Twenty-First Century.*

[19] Mearsheimer, *Conventional Deterrence*; Van Evera, 'Offense, Defense, and the Causes of War'.

[20] Boutros-Ghali, 'Interview mit dem früheren Generalsekretär', p. 130.

[21] Conetta & Knight, *Vital Force*; Conetta & Knight, 'A UN Legion for the New Era'.

[22] Urquhart, 'For a UN Volunteer Military Force'; Lewis, 'Peace Operations'.

[23] Boutros-Ghali, *An Agenda for Peace.*

[24] Conetta & Knight, 'A UN Legion for the New Era', p. 20.

[25] Conetta & Knight, 'A UN Legion for the New Era', pp. 24–30.

[26] Cadiou, *French Foreign Legion.*

[27] Global Policy Forum 2004, *US vs. Total Debt to the UN: 2004.*

[28] Boot, 'The New American Way of War', pp. 1–7.

[29] Altvater & Von der Währungskonkurrenz zum Währungskrieg, 'Was passiert, wenn der Ölpreis nicht mehr in US-Dollar fakturiert wird?', pp. 178–93.

[30] Unterseher, 'Krieg als beliebig einsetzbares Instrument', pp. 28–32.

[31] Barnett, 'The Pentagon's New Map', pp. 174–80.

[32] Unterseher, 'Krieg als beliebig einsetzbares Instrument', pp. 32–6.

8 FOREIGN INTERVENTION IN CÔTE D'IVOIRE

[1] Jackson & Rosberg, 'Why Africa's Weak States Persist', p. 1.

[2] Krasner, Sovereignty, p. 4.

[3] Jackson & Rosberg, 'Why Africa's Weak States Persist,' p. 4.

[4] Boutros-Ghali, 'An Agenda for Peace'.

[5] Taylor, 'The United Nations and International Organisation', p. 271.

[6] UN Security Council, Resolution 1528 (2004).

[7] UN Security Council, Statement by the President of the Security Council.

[8] Pelcovits, 'Peacekeeping', p. 263.

[9] Ayad & Jean-Dominique, 'L'opération Lucerne s'enferre dans ses contradictions'.

[10] Collett, 'Influence but not Interference', p. 10.

[11] 'Accord de défense entre la France et la Côte d'Ivoire'.

[12] Nwokedi, 'France, the New World Order and the Francophone West African States', p. 197.

[13] Luxner & Mbakwe, 'This is an Economic War', p. 26.

[14] 'transmissions, transport, et ravitaillement' in Leymarie, 'La Côte d'Ivoire à la dérive' (http://www.monde-diplomatique.fr).

[15] UN Security Council, Report of the Secretary-General on Côte d'Ivoire.

[16] 'Nous lançons un cri du cœur à la France. Nous nous sentons comme un enfant abandonné par son protecteur. On veut voir à nos côtés "nos ancêtres les Gaulois"!', Hofnung, 'Côte d'Ivoire' (http://www.liberation.fr).

[17] 'Les accords de Marcoussis'.

[18] Sengupta, 'Thousands Rally in Ivory Coast To Protest Peace Plan' (http://www.nytimes.com).

[19] Roberts, 'From San Francisco to Sarajevo', p. 14.

[20] United Nations, Report of the Panel on United Nations Peace Operations.

[21] Hofnung, 'Côte d'Ivoire'.

[22] Agence France-Presse, 'UN Mission Headquarters in Ivory Coast Besieged by Pro-Gbagbo Youth Rally'.

[23] Ministère de la Défense, Passation de commandement Licorne-ECOMICI.

[24] UN News Service, 'As UN Starts Peacekeeping Operation in Côte d'Ivoire, Annan Urges Reconciliation'.

[25] Nkrumah, Neo-Colonialism, p. ix.

[26] Corbett, The French Presence in Black Africa.

27 Corbett, *The French Presence in Black Africa*, p. 76.
28 Fieldhouse, *Colonialism 1870–1945*, p. 101.
29 Gelber, *Sovereignty through Interdependence*, p. 69.
30 Acharya, 'Collective Identity and Conflict Management in Southeast Asia', p. 203.
31 Malaquias, 'Peace Operations in Africa', p. 415.
32 Adler & Barnett, *Security Communities*.
33 Acharya, 'Collective Identity', p. 203.
34 Wax, 'Civil War Pushes Ivory Coast's Economy to the Brink'.
35 Welch, 'The Military Factor in West Africa', pp. 171, 175.
36 Masini et al., *Multinationals and Development in Black Africa*.
37 French President Jacques Chirac cited in French, 'Closing a Chapter', p. 21.
38 Ayad & Hofnung, 'Les représentants des rebelles et des partis politiques se réunissent dans l'Essonne pour neuf jours'.
39 Toungara, 'Francophone Africa in Flux', pp. 66, 67.
40 *Libération*, 'Pari risqué' (http://www.liberation.fr).
41 'ne veut pas s'immiscer dans les affaires internes des Etats', Gaulme, *Intervenir en Afrique?*, p. 31.
42 *Time*, 'Aftermath of Empire' (http://www.time.com).
43 Musah, 'Privatisation of Security'.
44 Ayad et al., 'La vitrine fêlée de la France en Afrique'.
45 UN Security Council, *Resolution 1479 (2003)*, and *Resolution 1528 (2004)*.
46 Barnett, 'Partners in Peace?', p. 417.
47 United Nations Peacekeeping, *Meeting New Challenges*.
48 United Nations, *Report of the Panel on United Nations Peace Operations*, p. 25.
49 United Nations, *Report of the Panel*, p. 9.
50 Boutros-Ghali, 'An Agenda for Peace', p. 323.
51 Lynch, 'US, France at Odds at UN'.
52 UN Security Council, *Resolution 1528 (2004)*.
53 Hirsch, 'War in Sierra Leone', p. 147.
54 Cour & Snrech, *Preparing for the Future*, p. 101.
55 UN Security Council, *Report of the Secretary-General on the United Nations Mission in Côte d'Ivoire submitted pursuant to Security Council resolution 1514 (2003) of 13 November 2003*, p. 5.
56 Gomez, 'Un pays en mal d'identité'.
57 Imobighe, 'ECOWAS Defence Pact and Regionalism in Africa', p. 115.
58 Adeniji, 'Mechanisms for Conflict Prevention in West Africa', p. 2.
59 Pelcovits, 'Peacekeeping', p. 273.
60 Diehl, 'Institutional Alternatives to Traditional UN Peacekeeping', p. 209.
61 See Unterseher's chapter in this volume.
62 Ministère de la Défense, *The RECAMP Program*.
63 UN Security Council, *Secretary-General Appeals to Security Council for Financial Support to Sustain West African States' Côte d'Ivoire Peacekeeping Force*.

9 THE UNITED NATIONS AND THE HUMANITARIAN IMPERATIVE

1 Helton, *The Price of Indifference*, p. 223.
2 Terry, 'Reconstituting Whose Social Order?', p. 280.
3 On UNRWA, see Bowker, *Palestinian Refugees*. On UNHCR, see Loescher, *The UNHCR and World Politics*.
4 See Maley, 'Twelve theses on the impact of humanitarian intervention'.
5 Boutros-Ghali, *An Agenda for Peace*.
6 United Nations, *Report of the Panel on United Nations Peace Operations*, also known as the Brahimi Report.
7 See Maley, 'Bypassing UN Sets Dangerous Precedent'.
8 'People and Politics', BBC World Service, 1 January 2005.
9 See Barnett, *Eyewitness to a Genocide*; *Report of the Secretary-General pursuant to General Assembly Resolution 53/35: The Fall of Srebrenica* (UN, New York: A/54/549, 15 November 1999); Maley, 'The UN and East Timor'.
10 Power, *'A Problem from Hell'*. Another episode which led to egregious attacks on the UN was the alleged 'oil-for-food' scandal, deriving from a Security Council—approved scheme to permit humanitarian relief to reach ordinary Iraqis before the March 2003 intervention. Here, once again, a credible case can be made that, in respect of such abuses as occurred, member states with oversight responsibilities were at least as culpable as any UN staff: see Ruggie, 'What about the Log in Your Eye, Congress?'; Thakur, 'Cheerleaders for War Round on the UN'.
11 Egeland's comments may also have hit home because they contained a very significant element of truth. While the United States in absolute terms is a major aid contributor, its contributions as a proportion of its gross domestic product are much smaller than those of many European states. See Harris & Wright, 'Aid Grows amid Remarks about President's Absence'; 'Are We Stingy? Yes', *New York Times*, 30 December 2004; Sanger & Hoge, 'US Vows Big Rise in Aid for Victims of Asian Disaster'.
12 See Terry, *Condemned To Repeat?*. This issue is also taken up in Luttwak, 'Give War a Chance'.
13 Maley, *The Foreign Policy of the Taliban*, p. 24. For further perspectives on these dilemmas, see also Newberg, *Politics at the Heart*; and Donini, 'Principles, Politics, and Pragmatism in the International Response to the Afghan Crisis'.
14 See Groom & Taylor, 'The United Nations System and the Kosovo Crisis', pp. 300–2.
15 See Dallaire, *Shake Hands with the Devil*.
16 See Maley, 'A New Tower of Babel?'.
17 See Sipress, 'Peacekeepers Won't Go beyond Kabul, Cheney says'.

[18] See Rubin et al., *Through the Fog of Peace Building*; and *Afghanistan Aid Flows as of November 2003*.

[19] Daalder & Lindsay, *America Unbound*, p. 114.

[20] United Nations, *A More Secure World*.

[21] International Commission on Intervention and State Sovereignty, *The Responsibility To Protect*.

[22] United Nations, *A More Secure World*, paras 207, 252–53, 257.

[23] Keating, 'An Insider's Account', p. 509.

[24] Rieff, *A Bed for the Night*, p. 330.

BIBLIOGRAPHY

Abiew, F., *The Evolution of the Doctrine and Practice of Humanitarian Intervention*, Kluwer Law International, The Hague, 1999.

Acharya, A., 'Collective Identity and Conflict Management in Southeast Asia', in Adler and Barnett, *Security Communities*, pp. 198–227.

Adeniji, O., 'Mechanisms for Conflict Prevention in West Africa: Politics of Harmonisation', *African Centre for the Constructive Resolution of Disputes (ACCORD) Occasional Papers*, 1997.

Adler, E. & M. Barnett (eds), *Security Communities*, Cambridge University Press, Cambridge, 1998.

Agence France-Presse, 'UN Mission Headquarters in Ivory Coast Besieged by Pro-Gbagbo Youth Rally', 15 May 2004.

Agreement for Self-Government in KOSMET, Serbian Counter-Proposal, 19 March 1999, <http://www.serbia-info.com/news/1999-03/19/9864.html>.

Allison, G., *Essence of Decision: Explaining the Cuban Missile Crisis*, Little, Brown, Boston, 1971.

Altman D., 'HIV And Security', *International Relations*, vol. 17, no. 4, 2003, pp. 417–27.

Altvater, E. & Von der Währungskonkurrenz zum Währungskrieg, 'Was passiert, wenn der Ölpreis nicht mehr in US-Dollar fakturiert wird?', in ÖSFK (Hg.), *Schurkenstaat und Staatsterrorismus. Die Konturen einer militärischen Globalisierung*, Agenda, Münster, 2004.

Arend, A. & R. Beck, *International Law and the Use of Force: Beyond the UN Charter Paradigm*, Routledge, London, 1993.

AusAID, *HIV/AIDS in Papua New Guinea: Fact Sheet*, AusAID, Canberra, 2003.

—— *Papua New Guinea and the Pacific: A Development Perspective*, AusAID, Canberra, 2003.

Australian Government, *Transnational Terrorism: The Threat to Australia*, Canberra, 2004.

Australian Strategic Policy Institute (ASPI), *Beyond Bali: ASPI's Strategic Assessment 2002*, ASPI, Canberra, 2002.

Ayad, C., V. Gomez & T. Hofnung, 'La vitrine fêlée de la France en Afrique' (The cracked shop window of France in Africa), *Libération*, 15 January 2003.

Ayad, C. & T. Hofnung, 'Les représentants des rebelles et des partis politiques se réunissent dans l'Essonne pour neuf jours' (The representatives of the rebels and the political parties meet in the Essonne for nine days), *Libération*, 15 January 2003.

Ayad, C. & M. Jean-Dominique, 'L'opération Lucerne s'enferre dans ses contradictions' (Operation 'Lucerne' becomes entangled in its own contradictions), *Libération*, 3 January 2003.

Ball, D., *Strategic Culture in the Asia–Pacific Region: With Some Implications for Regional Security Cooperation*, Working Paper no. 270, Strategic and Defence Studies Centre, Australian National University, Canberra, 1993.

Barnett, M., 'Partners in Peace? The UN, Regional Organisations, and Peace-keeping', *Review of International Studies*, vol. 21, 1995, pp. 441–33.

Barnett, M., *Eyewitness to a Genocide: The United Nations and Rwanda*, Cornell University Press, Ithaca NY, 2002.

Barnett, T. P., 'The Pentagon's New Map', *Esquire*, March 2003, pp. 174–81.

Baroness Symons of Vernham Dean, Statement to the United Kingdom Parliament Outlining the Government's Legal Justification for the NATO Intervention in the FRY, *Written Answers*, UK Parliament, London, 16 November 1998, WA 140.

Beazley, K., 'If You Have To Fight, You Might As Well Win: Australia's Defence Minister Talks to IDR', *International Defense Review*, vol. 20, no. 10, 1987.

—— 'Self-Reliance: Labor's National Defence Strategy', Ryan Memorial Lecture, 13 October 1989.

Benjamin, B., 'Unilateral Humanitarian Intervention: Legalising the Use of Force To Prevent Human Rights Atrocities', *Fordham International Law Journal*, vol. 16, 1992–93, pp. 120–58.

Berger, L., 'State Practice Evidence of the Humanitarian Intervention Doctrine: The ECOWAS Intervention in Sierra Leone', *Indiana International and Comparative Law Review*, vol. 11, 2001, pp. 605–32.

Blainey, G., *The Tyranny of Distance: How Distance Shaped Australia's History*, Macmillan, Sydney, 1983.

Boot, M., 'The New American Way of War', *Foreign Affairs*, July/August 2003, pp. 41–73.

Boutros-Ghali, B., *An Agenda for Peace: Preventive Diplomacy, Peacemaking, and Peacekeeping*, United Nations, New York, 1992.

—— 'An Agenda for Peace: One Year Later', *Orbis*, vol. 37, no. 3, 1993, pp. 323–32.

—— 'Interview mit dem früheren Generalsekretär', *Der Spiegel*, Nr. 2, 11 January 1999.

Bowker, R., *Palestinian Refugees: Mythology, Identity, and the Search for Peace*, Lynne Rienner, Boulder CO, 2003.

Brenchley, F., 'The Howard Defence Doctrine', *Bulletin*, 28 September 1999, pp. 22–4.

Brownlie, I., *International Law and the Use of Force by States*, Clarendon Press, Oxford, 1963.

—— *Principles of Public International Law*, 5th edn, Clarendon Press, Oxford, 1998.

Bunzl, J., 'Krisenherde im Nahen Osten', in *Die Zukunft Südosteuropas. Friedensbericht 1997*.

Bush, G. W., 'Graduation Speech at West Point', New York, 1 June 2002.

—— 'The National Security Strategy of the United States of America', Washington DC, September 2002.

Butler, R., *Saddam Defiant*, Phoenix, London, 2000.

Cadiou, Y. L., *French Foreign Legion: 1940 to the Present*, Arms and Armour, London, 1986.

Caldwell, J., 'It's Everyone's Problem: HIV/AIDS and Development in Asia and the Pacific', AusAID Special Seminar, AusAID, Canberra, 2000.

Caplan, R., *A New Trusteeship? The International Administration of War-torn Territories*, Adelphi Paper no. 341, Oxford University Press, Oxford, 2002.

Carment, D., 'Assessing State Failure: Implications for Theory and Policy', *Third World Quarterly*, vol. 24, no. 3, pp. 407–27.

Cassese, A., '*Ex iniuria ius oritur*: Are We Moving towards International Legitimation of Forcible Countermeasures in the World Community?', *European Journal of International Law*, vol. 10, no. 1., <www.ejil.org/journal>.

Centre for Defence Studies, *The Strategic Defence Review: How Strategic? How Much of a Review?*, Brassey's, London, 1998.

Centre for International Economics, *Potential Economic Impacts of an HIV/ AIDS Epidemic in Papua New Guinea*, CIE, Canberra, 2002.

Chalk, P., *Non-military Security and the Global Order: The Impact of Extremism, Violence and Chaos on National and International Security*, Macmillan, London, 2000.

Charlesworth, H., 'What's Law Got To Do with the War?', in R. Gaita (ed.), *Why the War Was Wrong*, Text Publishing, Melbourne, 2003, pp. 35–60.

Cheeseman, G., 'Australia: The White Experience of Fear and Dependence', in K. Booth & R. Trood (eds), *Strategic Cultures in the Asia-Pacific Region*, pp. 273–98.

Clausewitz, C. von, *On War* (ed. and trans. M. Howard & P. Paret), Princeton University Press, Princeton, 1976.

Coady, C. A. J., *The Ethics of Armed Humanitarian Intervention*, Peaceworks Report no. 45, United States Institute of Peace, Washington DC, 2002.

—— 'Hobbes and the Beautiful Axiom', *Philosophy*, vol. 65, 1990, pp. 5–17.

—— 'The Meaning of Moralism', *Journal of Applied Philosophy*, forthcoming 2005.

—— 'War for Humanity: A Critique', in D. K. Chatterjee & D. E. Scheid (eds), *Ethics and Foreign Intervention*, Cambridge University Press, Cambridge, 2003, pp. 274–95.

Codner, M. *Aircraft Carriers: The Next Generation?*, ISIS Briefing no. 70, London, 1998.

Collett, M., 'Influence but not Interference: France and the Côte d'Ivoire Civil War of 2002–03', Honours thesis, University of Wollongong, 2003.

Commager, H. S., 'Ethics, Virtue, and Foreign Policy', in K. W. Thompson (ed.), *Ethics and International Relations*, vol. 2, Transaction Books, New Brunswick, 1985, pp. 127–37.

Conetta, C., *Strange Victory: A Critical Appraisal of Operation Enduring Freedom and the Afghanistan War*, Research Monograph no. 6, Commonwealth Institute, Project on Defense Alternatives, Cambridge MA, 30 January 2002, <http://www.comw.org/pda/0201strangevic.html>.

—— *The Wages of War: Iraqi Combatant and Non-Combatant Fatalities in the 2003 Conflict*, Monograph no. 8, Project on Defense Alternatives, Commonwealth Institute, Cambridge MA, 2003.

Conetta, C. & C. Knight, 'A UN Legion for the New Era', in V. Kroning & G. Verheugen (eds), *Defensive und Intervention: Die Zukunft Vertrauensbildender Verteidigung*, Temmen, Bremen, 1998.

—— *Vital Force: A Proposal for the Overhaul of the UN Peace Operations System and for the Creation of a UN Legion*, Monograph no. 4, Project on Defense Alternatives, Commonwealth Institute, Cambridge MA, 1995.

Cook, G., 'France's Chirac Begins US Visit', *Agence France-Presse*, 18 February 1999, <Westlaw.com>.

Cooper, A., R. Higgott & K. Nossal, *Relocating Middle Powers: Australia and Canada in a Changing World Order*, Melbourne University Press, Melbourne, 1993.

Cooper, D., 'Collective Responsibility', *Philosophy*, vol. xliii, July 1968, pp. 258–68.

Corbett, E. M., *The French Presence in Black Africa*, Black Orpheus Press, Washington DC, 1972.

Cour, J.-M. & S. Snrech (eds), *Preparing for the Future: A Vision of West Africa in the Year 2020*, Organisation for Economic Co-operation and Development, Paris, 1998.

Crocker, C., 'Engaging Failing States', *Foreign Affairs*, vol. 82, no. 5, 2003, pp. 32–44.

Cuny, F. cited in C. Off, *Carol Goes Off: Writer and Journalist Carol Off Speaks Out about Genocide, War, and the United Nations*, 2000, <http://varsity.utoronto.ca:16080/archives/121/nov20/review/carol.html>.

Daalder, I. H. & J. M. Lindsay, *America Unbound: The Bush Revolution in Foreign Policy*, Brookings Institution Press, Washington DC, 2003.

Dallaire, R., *Shake Hands with the Devil: The Failure of Humanity in Rwanda*, Random House, Toronto, 2003.

Department of Defence, *The Defence of Australia 1987*, Australian Government Publishing Service, Canberra, 1987.

—— *Defence 2000: Our Future Defence Force*, Commonwealth of Australia, Canberra, 2000.

—— *Defence Report 1991–92*, Australian Government Publishing Service, Canberra, 1992.

—— *Force Structure Review*, Australian Government Publishing Service, Canberra, 1991.

—— *Strategic Review 1993*, Australian Government Publishing Service, Canberra, 1993.

Department of Foreign Affairs and Trade, *Australia's Regional Security*, Australian Government Publishing Service, Canberra, 1989.

—— *Solomon Islands: Rebuilding an Island Economy*, Canberra, 2004.

Diehl, P. F., 'Institutional Alternatives to Traditional UN Peacekeeping: An Assessment of Regional and Multinational Options', *Armed Forces and Society*, vol. 29, no. 2, 1993, pp. 209–30.

Dinnen, S., *Law and Order in a Weak State: Crime and Politics in Papua New Guinea*, University of Hawai'i Press, Honolulu, 2001.

Dinstein, Y., *War, Aggression and Self-Defence*, Grotius Publications, Cambridge, 1994.

Donini, A., 'Principles, Politics, and Pragmatism in the International Response to the Afghan Crisis', in A. Donini, N. Niland & K. Wermester (eds), *Nation-building Unraveled? Aid, Peace and Justice in Afghanistan*, Kumarian Press, Bloomfield, 2004, pp. 117–42.

Downer, A., 'Security in an Unstable World', National Press Club address, Canberra, 26 June 2003.

—— 'Solomon Islands: Rebuilding an Island Economy', speech, Brisbane, 20 July 2004.

Doyle, M. W., 'Kant, Liberal Legacies, and Foreign Affairs (Parts I and II)', *Philosophy and Public Affairs*, vol. 12, nos. 3–4, 1983, pp. 205–54, 323–53.

Dutton, D., 'A British Outpost Facing North', in D. Goldsworthy (ed.), *Facing North: A Century of Australian Engagement with Asia*, vol. 1, 1901 to the 1970s, Department of Foreign Affairs and Trade & Melbourne University Press, Melbourne, 2001, pp. 21–60.

Eberstadt, N., 'The Future of Aids', *Foreign Affairs*, vol. 81, no. 6, pp. 22–45.

Economic Community of West African States, 'Treaty of ECOWAS', 1975.

Emmett, D., *The Role of the Unrealisable: A Study in Regulative Ideals*, St Martin's Press, New York, 1994.

European Security and Finnish Defence, *Report by the Council of State to Parliament on 17 March 1997*, Oy Edita Ab, Helsinki, 1997.

Evans, G., 'Australia's Regional Security Environment', in D. Ball & D. Horner (eds), *Strategic Studies in a Changing World: Global, Regional and Australian Perspectives*, Canberra Papers on Strategy and Defence no. 89, Strategic and Defence Studies Centre, Australian National University, Canberra, 1992, pp. 373–85.

Evans, G. & B. Grant, *Australia's Foreign Relations: In the World of the 1990s*, 2nd edn, Melbourne University Press, Melbourne, 1995.

Fearon, J. & D. Laitin, 'Neotrusteeship and the Problem of Weak States', *International Security*, vol. 28, no. 4, pp. 5–53.

Fickling, D., 'Australia Seen as America's Deputy Sheriff', *Guardian*, 10 September 2004, <http://www.guardian.co.uk/>.

Fieldhouse, D. K., *Colonialism 1870–1945: An Introduction*, Macmillan, London, 1976.

Finnegan, W., 'The Invisible War', *New Yorker*, 25 January 1999, pp. 50–73.

Fischer, M., 'Krisenprävention'. Modebegriff oder friedenspolitische Notwendigkeit?', in *Krisenprävention. Friedensbericht 1999*.

Fraenke, J., 'The Coming Anarchy in Oceania? A Critique of the "African-isation" of the South Pacific Thesis', *Commonwealth & Comparative Politics*, vol. 42, no. 1, March 2004, pp. 1–34.

Franck, T. & N. Rodley, 'After Bangladesh: The Law of Humanitarian Intervention by Military Force', *American Journal of International Law*, vol. 67, 1973, quoted in Abiew, *The Evolution of the Doctrine*.

Freedman, L., *Kennedy's Wars: Berlin, Cuba, Laos, and Vietnam*, Oxford University Press, Oxford, 2000.

French, H., 'Closing a Chapter', *Africa Report*, vol. 39, no. 2, 1994, pp. 19–22.

French, P., *Collective and Corporate Responsibility*, Columbia University Press, New York, 1984.

French Minister of Foreign Affairs, *Le Journal Du Dimanche*, Paris, 28 March 1999, <www.info-france.org>.

Fukuyama, F., *State Building: Governance and World Order in the 21st Century*, Cornell University Press, Ithaca NY, 2004.

Galtung, J., 'US Foreign Policy as Manifest Theology', in J. Chay (ed.), *Culture and International Relations*, Praeger, New York, 1990, pp. 119–40.

Garran, R., *True Believer: John Howard, George Bush and the American Alliance*, Allen & Unwin, Sydney, 2004.

Gaulme, F., *Intervenir en Afrique? Le dilemme franco-britannique* (Intervene in Africa? The French–British dilemma), vol. 34, *Les notes d'ifri*, Institut français des relations internationales, Paris, October 2001.

Gelber, H. G., *Sovereignty through Interdependence*, Kluwer Law International, London/The Hague/Boston, 1997.

General Accounting Office, *Operation Desert Storm: Operation Desert Storm Air War (Letter Report, PEMO-96-10)*, GAO, Washington, July 1996.

George, J., 'Australia's Global Perspectives in the 1990s: A Case of Old Wine in (Neo-liberal) Bottles', in R. Leaver & D. Cox (eds), *Middling, Meddling, Muddling: Issues in Australia's Foreign Policy*, Allen & Unwin, Sydney, 1997, pp. 12–43.

Global Policy Forum 2004, *US vs. Total Debt to the UN: 2004*, 2004, <http://www.globalpolicy.org/finance/tables/core/un-us-04.htm>.

Gomez, V., 'Un pays en mal d'identité' (A country with an identity crisis), *Libération*, 15 January 2003.

Governments of the United States, United Kingdom, the Soviet Union and China, *Declaration of Four Nations on General Security*, Moscow, 30 October 1943.

Grant, J., *The State of the World's Children 1993*, Oxford University Press, New York, 1993.

Grin, J., 'Krieg ohne überflüssiges Blutvergießen: Zur Legitimation von Militärinterventionen durch Technologie', in V. Kroning & G. Verheugen (eds), *Defensive und Intervention: Die Zukunft Vertrauensbildender Verteidigung*, Temmen, Bremen, 1998.

Groom, A. J. R. & P. Taylor, 'The United Nations System and the Kosovo Crisis', in A. Schnabel & R. Thakur (eds), *Kosovo and the Challenge of Humanitarian Intervention: Selective Indignation, Collective Action, and International Citizenship*, United Nations University Press, Tokyo, 2000, pp. 291–318.

Gubb, M., *The Australian Military Response to the Fiji Coup: An Assessment*, Working Paper no. 171, Strategic and Defence Studies Centre, Australian National University, Canberra, 1988.

Hankins, C. et al., 'Transmission and Prevention of HIV and Sexually Transmitted Infections in War Settings: Implications for Current and Future Conflicts', *AIDS*, vol. 16, no. 17, 2002, pp. 2245–52.

Harries, O., *Benign or Imperial?*, ABC, Sydney, 2004.

Harris, A. & P. Dombrowski, 'Military Collaboration with Humanitarian Organisations in Complex Emergencies', *Global Governance*, vol. 8, 2002, pp. 155–78.

Harris, D. J., *Cases and Materials on International Law*, 3rd edn, Sweet and Maxwell, London, 1983.

Harris, J. F. & R. Wright, 'Aid Grows amid Remarks about President's Absence', *Washington Post*, 29 December 2004.

Hauquitz, A., 'Looking down the Barrel of a Cannon: The Potential Economic Costs of HIV/AIDS in Papua New Guinea', paper presented at Australian Society for HIV Medicine Conference, Cairns, 23 October 2003.

Hayden, B., 'Don't Forget We Are on Our Own', *Australian*, 14 September 1999, p. 15.

Hayden, R., 'Humanitarian Hypocrisy', *Jurist: The Law Professors' Network*, <http://jurist.law.pitt.edu.kosovo.htm>.

Hayes, P., L. Zarsky & W. Bellow, *American Lake: Nuclear Peril in the Pacific*, Penguin, Melbourne, 1986.

Hehir, B., 'Intervention: From Theories to Cases', *Ethics and International Affairs*, vol. 9, 1995, pp. 1–13.

Helton, A. C., *The Price of Indifference: Refugees and Humanitarian Action in the New Century*, Oxford University Press, New York, 2002.

Hill, R., 'Defence Personnel to Come Home from Solomons', press release, Canberra, 28 October 2003.

—— Keynote address, Defence and Industry Conference, Canberra, 22 June 2004.

—— 'Military Drawdown as Progress Continues in Solomon Islands', press release, Canberra, 25 June 2004.

Hirsch, J. L., 'War in Sierra Leone', *Survival*, vol. 43, no. 3, 2001, pp. 145–62.

Hofnung, T., 'Côte d'Ivoire: un patriote peut cacher une femme', *Libération*, 13 February 2003.

Holzgrefe, J. & R. Keohane, *Humanitarian Intervention: Ethical, Legal, and Political Dilemmas*, Cambridge University Press, Cambridge, 2003.

Horner, D. (ed.), *Armies and Nation Building: Past Experience—Future Prospects*, Strategic and Defence Studies Centre, Australian National University, Canberra, 1995.

Howard, J., Transcript of the Prime Minister the Hon. John Howard MP Address at Informal Farewell Reception for the Troops and Police Heading to the Solomon Islands, RAAF Base, Townsville, 24 July 2003.

—— Transcript of the Prime Minister the Hon. John Howard MP Address at the Solomon Islands Taskforce Farewell, RAAF Base Townsville, 24 July 2003.

—— Transcript of the Prime Minister the Hon. John Howard MP Ministerial Statement to Parliament on Iraq, Canberra, 4 February 2004.

Hudson, Admiral M., *Australia's Defence in Review*, Institute of Public Affairs, Sydney, 1991.

Hughes, H., *Aid Has Failed the Pacific*, Discussion Paper no. 33, Centre for Independent Studies, Sydney, 2003.

Human Rights Watch, *Abuses against Serbs and Roma in the New Kosovo*, vol. 11, no. 10 (D), August 1999.

—— *Civilian Deaths in the NATO Air Campaign*, vol. 12, no. 1 (D), February 2000, <http://www.hrm.org/reports/2000/nato/index.htm>.

—— *Federal Republic of Yugoslavia: Humanitarian Law Violations in Kosovo*, vol. 10, no. 9 (D), October 1998.

Ignatieff, M., 'State Failure and Nation Building', in Holzgrefe and Keohane, *Humanitarian Intervention*, pp. 299–321.

Imobighe, T., 'ECOWAS Defence Pact and Regionalism in Africa', in Ralph I. Onwuka and Amadu Sesay (eds), *The Future of Regionalism in Africa*, Macmillan, Hong Kong, 1985, pp. 110–24.

Independent International Commission on Kosovo, *The Kosovo Report: Conflict, International Response, Lessons Learned*, Oxford University Press, Oxford, 2000.

Integrated Regional Information Networks, 'Côte d'Ivoire: UN Announces Wider Human Rights Probe', 17 May 2004.

Interim Agreement for Peace and Self-Government in Kosovo, Rambouillet, France, 18 March 1999, <http:jurist.law.ptt.edu.kosovo.htm#Rambouillet>.

International Commission on Intervention and State Sovereignty, *The Responsibility To Protect: Report of the International Commission on Intervention and State Sovereignty*, ICISS, Ottawa, 2001.

—— *Supplementary Volume to the Report 'The Responsibility To Protect'*, ICISS, Ottawa, 2001.

International Court of Justice (ICJ) website, <http://www.icj-cij.org>.

Jackson, R. & C. Rosberg, 'Why Africa's Weak States Persist: The Empirical and Juridical in Statehood', *World Politics*, vol. 35, no. 1, 1982, pp. 1–24.

Joint Committee on Foreign Affairs, Defence & Trade, *Australia's Relations with the South Pacific*, Australian Government Publishing Service, Canberra, 1989.

Joint Standing Committee on Foreign Affairs, Defence & Trade, *Papua New Guinea Update, Report on Proceedings of a Seminar 11 and 12 November 1996*, Australian Government Publishing Service, Canberra, 1997.

Journal Officiel, 'Accord de défense entre la France et la Côte d'Ivoire' (Defence agreement between France and Côte d'Ivoire), 1962, pp. 1261–5.

Kaldor, M., *New and Old Wars: Organised Violence in a Global Era*, Polity Press, Oxford, 1999.

Keane, F., *Season of Blood: A Rwandan Journey*, Viking Press, London, 1995.

Keating, C., 'An Insider's Account', in D. M. Malone (ed.), *The UN Security Council: From the Cold War to the 21st Century*, Lynne Rienner, Boulder CO, 2004, pp. 500–11.

Kelly, M., *Peace Operations: Tackling the Military, Legal and Policy Challenges*, Australian Government Publishing Service, Canberra, 1997.

Kelly, P., 'Punching above Our Weight', *Policy*, vol. 20, no. 2, Winter 2004, pp. 29–34.

Kennan, G., 'The Sources of Soviet Conduct', *Foreign Affairs*, vol. XXV, no. 4, July 1947, pp. 566–82, reprinted in G. Kennan, *American Diplomacy 1900–1950*, University of Chicago Press, Chicago, 1951.

King, P., 'Australia, Regional Threats and the Arms Race: Everyone Else out of Step?', in Graeme Cheeseman and St John Kettle (eds), *The New Australian Militarism: Undermining Our Future Security*, Pluto Press, Sydney, 1990, pp. 133–44.

Kiste, R. & R. Herr, *The Potential for Soviet Penetration of the South Pacific Islands: An Assessment*, US Department of State, Washington DC, December 1984.

Knight, C., L. Unterseher & C. Conetta, 'Military Research and Development after the Second Gulf War', in W. A. Smit, J. Grin & L. Voronkov, *Military Technological Innovation and Stability in a Changing World: Politically Assessing and Influencing Weapon Innovation and Military Research and Development*, VU University Press, Amsterdam, 1992. A revised version is available at: <http://www.comw.org/pda/0003refl.html>.

Krasner, S. D., *Sovereignty: Organised Hypocrisy*, Princeton University Press, Princeton, 1999.

Krisenprävention. Friedensbericht 1999, Rüegger, Chur/Zürich, 1999.

Kritsiotis, D., 'Reappraising Policy Objections to Humanitarian Intervention', *Michigan Journal of International Law*, vol. 19, pp. 1005–51.

Letter of NATO Secretary-General NATO of 10 June 1999, annexed to UN Secretary-General S/1999/663, <http://www.un.org/Docs/sc/letters/1999>.

Lewis, W. H., 'Peace Operations: Is a Standing Force Needed?', *Strategic Forum*, no. 27, National Defense University, Washington DC, 1995.

Leymarie, P., 'La Côte d'Ivoire à la dérive' (Côte d'Ivoire adrift), *Le Monde diplomatique*, 1 October 2002.

Libal, W., 'Kosovo nach dem Dayton-Abkommen', in *Die Zukunft Südosteuropas (Friedensbericht 1997)*, Rüegger, Zürich, 1997.

Libération, 'Les accords de Marcoussis' (The Marcoussis agreements), 8 February 2003.

—— 'Pari risqué' (Risky wager), 15 January 2003.

Lindenberg, M. & C. Bryant, *Going Global: Transforming Relief and Development NGOs*, Kumarian Press, Bloomfield CT, 2001.

Loescher, G., *The UNHCR and World Politics: A Perilous Path*, Oxford University Press, Oxford, 2001.

Loquai, H., 'Medien als Weichensteller zum Krieg', in Österreichisches Studienzentrum für Frieden und Konfliktlösung (ÖSFK) (ed.), *Schurkenstaat und Staatsterrorismus. Die Konturen einer militärischen Globalisierung*, Agenda, Münster, 2004.

Luban, D., 'Preventive War', *Philosophy and Public Affairs*, vol. 32, no. 3, July 2004, pp. 207–48.

Luttwak, E., 'Give War a Chance', *Foreign Affairs*, vol. 78, no. 4, July–August 1999, pp. 36–44.

Luxner, L. & T. Mbakwe, '"This is an Economic War": Pascal D. Kokora, Côte d'Ivoire's Ambassador in Washington, Blames France for His Country's Recent Woes', *New African*, March 2003, p. 26.

Lynch, C., 'US, France at Odds at UN: White House Seeks Smaller Ivory Coast Mission', *Washington Post*, 24 April 2003, p. A20.

MacFarlane, S., C. Theilking & T. Weiss, 'The Responsibility To Protect: Is Anyone Interested in Humanitarian Intervention?', *Third World Quarterly*, vol. 25, no. 5, 2004, pp. 977–92.

Macmillan, A., K. Booth & R. Trood, 'Strategic Culture', in K. Booth & R. Trood (eds), *Strategic Cultures in the Asia–Pacific Region*, Macmillan, Houndmills, 1999, pp. 3–28.

Malaquias, A., 'Peace Operations in Africa: Preserving the Brittle State (Regional Perspectives)', *Journal of International Affairs*, vol. 55, no. 2, 2002, pp. 415–43.

Maley, W., *The Afghanistan Wars*, Palgrave Macmillan, New York, 2002.

—— 'Bypassing UN Sets Dangerous Precedent', *Canberra Times*, 19 March 2003.

—— *The Foreign Policy of the Taliban*, Council on Foreign Relations, New York, February 2000.

—— 'The Humanitarian Imperative', in C. Reus-Smit, M. Hanson, H. Charlesworth & W. Maley, *The Challenge of United Nations Reform*, Keynotes no. 5, Department of International Relations, Research School of Pacific and Asian Studies, Australian National University, Canberra, 2004, pp. 18–25.

—— 'A New Tower of Babel? Reappraising the Architecture of Refugee Protection', in E. Newman & J. Van Selm (eds), *Refugees and Forced Displacement: International Security, Human Vulnerability, and the State*, United Nations University Press, Tokyo, 2003, pp. 306–29.

—— 'Twelve Theses on the Impact of Humanitarian Intervention', *Security Dialogue*, vol. 33, no. 3, September 2002, pp. 265–78.

—— 'The UN and East Timor', *Pacifica Review*, vol. 12, no. 1, November 2000, pp. 63–76.

Maley, W. (ed.), *Fundamentalism Reborn? Afghanistan and the Taliban*, New York University Press, 1998, 2001.

Maley, W. (co-ed.), *From Civil Strife to Civil Society: Civil and Military Responsibilities in Disrupted States*, United Nations University Press, Tokyo, 2003.

Mann, T., *The Rise of the Vulcans*, Viking, New York, 2004.

Masini, J., M. Ikonicoff, C. Jeliki & M. Lanzarotti, *Multinationals and Development in Black Africa: A Case Study in the Ivory Coast*, Saxon House, England, 1979.

Mearsheimer, J., *Conventional Deterrence*, Cornell University Press, Ithaca NY, 1983.

Memorandum of Understanding, 18 April 1991, 30 ILM 860 (1991).

Miller, S., 'Collective Responsibility, Armed Intervention and the Rwandan Genocide', *International Journal of Applied Philosophy*, vol. 12, no. 2, 1998.

—— *Social Action: A Teleological Account*, Cambridge University Press, New York, 2001.

Milliken, J. (ed.), *State Failure, Collapse and Reconstruction*, Blackwell, Malden MA, 2003.

Ministère de la Défense (Ministry of Defence), *Passation de commandement Licorne-ECOMICI* (Transfer of command from Licorne [Unicorn] to ECOMICI), 2003, <www.defense.gouv.fr> (cited 15 March 2003).

—— *The RECAMP Program (Reinforcement of African peace-keeping capabilities)*, Office of the Joint Chiefs of Staff, Paris, 2001.

Møller, B. & H. Wiberg (eds), *Non-Offensive Defence for the Twenty-First Century*, Westview Press, Boulder CO, 1994.

Morauta, M., 'Community Response to HIV/AIDS in Papua New Guinea', AusAID Seminar on HIV/AIDS in the Pacific, Canberra, 2000.

Morgenthau, H. J., *Politics among Nations: The Struggle for Power and Peace*, 6th edn, ed. K. W. Thompson, Alfred A Knopf, New York, 1979.

Morrison, L., 'The Global Epidemiology of HIV/AIDS', *British Medical Bulletin*, vol. 58, 2001, pp. 7–18.

Musah, A.-F., 'Privatisation of Security, Arms Proliferation and the Process of State Collapse in Africa', *Development and Change*, 2002, pp. 33–7.

Mutz, R., 'An den Verhandlungstisch gezwungen? Legenden über das Kriegsende in Jugoslawien', *Sicherheit und Frieden (S + F)*, vol. 14, no. 2, 1996.

Naumann, K., *Standortbestimmung, Informationen zur Sicherheitspolitik*, 35. Kommandeurstagung der Bundeswehr, Federal Ministry of Defence, Bonn, 1995.

Newberg, P. R., *Politics at the Heart: The Architecture of Humanitarian Assistance to Afghanistan*, Carnegie Endowment for International Peace, Washington DC, 1999.

Nkrumah, K., *Neo-Colonialism: The Last Stage of Imperialism*, International Publishers, New York, 1966.

Norton-Taylor, R., 'So Just What Was Achieved?', *Sunday Mail* (Queensland), 11 July 1999, p. 14.

Nwokedi, E., 'France, the New World Order and the Francophone West African States: Towards a Reconceptualisation of Privileged Relations', in C. Alden & J.-P. Daloz (eds), *Paris, Pretoria and the African Continent: The International Relations of States and Societies in Transition*, Macmillan, London, 1996, pp. 195–217.

O'Keefe, M. 'Enduring Tensions in the 2000 Defence White Paper', *Australian Journal of Politics and History*, vol. 49, no. 4, 2003, pp. 517–39.

Pelcovits, N., 'Peacekeeping: The African Experience', in H. Wiseman (ed.), *Peacekeeping: Appraisals & Proposals*, Pergamon Press, New York, 1983, pp. 256–97.

Pichler, R., 'Im Schatten von Dayton. Kosovo, Mazedonien, Albanien', in *Die Zukunft Südosteuropas (Friedensbericht 1997)*, Rüegger, Zürich, 1997.

Piot, P., 'UN Says Pacific Faces New Wave of HIV, with PNG on the Brink of an Epidemic', *AFP*, Sydney, 22 June 2004.

Pollack, K., *The Threatening Storm: The Case for Invading Iraq*, Random House, New York, 2002.

Power, S., *'A Problem from Hell': America and the Age of Genocide*, Basic Books, New York, 2002.

Putzel, J., *Institutionalising an Emergency Response: HIV/AIDS in Uganda and Senegal*, Crisis States Programme, London School of Economics, London, May 2003.

Reilly, B., 'The Africanisation of the South Pacific', *Australian Journal of International Affairs*, vol. 54, no. 3, 2000, pp. 261–8.

Reisman, M., 'Coercion and Self-Determination: Construing Charter Article 2(4)', *American Journal of International Law*, vol. 78, no. 3, 1984, pp. 642–5.

Republic of France, Ministry of Foreign Affairs website, <www.france.diplomatie.fr>.

Rieff, D., *A Bed for the Night: Humanitarianism in Crisis*, Simon & Schuster, New York, 2002.

Roberts, A., 'From San Francisco to Sarajevo: The UN and the Use of Force', *Survival*, vol. 37, no. 4, 1995–96, pp. 7–28.

—— 'NATO's "Humanitarian War" over Kosovo', in L. Minear, M. Sommers & T. van Baarda (eds), *NATO and Humanitarian Action in the Kosovo Crisis*, Occasional Paper 48, Thomas J. Watson Jr Institute of International Studies, Providence, 2000, pp. 121–50.

Rotberg, R., 'Failed States in a World of Terror', *Foreign Affairs*, vol. 81, no. 4, 2002, pp. 127–40.

Rotberg, R. (ed.), *State Failure and State Weakness in a Time of Terror*, Brookings Institution Press, Washington DC, 2003.

—— *When States Fail: Causes and Consequences*, Princeton University Press, Princeton, 2004.

Rubin, B. R., H. Hamidzada & A. Stoddard, *Afghanistan Aid Flows as of November 2003*, Center on International Co-operation, New York University, June 2003.

—— *Through the Fog of Peace Building: Evaluating the Reconstruction of Afghanistan*, Center on International Co-operation, New York University, June 2003.

Ruggie, J. G., 'What about the Log in Your Eye, Congress?', *International Herald Tribune*, 8 December 2004.

Sanger, D. E. & W. Hoge, 'U.S. Vows Big Rise in Aid for Victims of Asian Disaster', *New York Times*, 1 January 2005.

Schachter, O., 'In Defense of International Rules on the Use of Force', *University of Chicago Law Review*, vol. 53, Winter 1986, pp. 113–47.

—— 'The Legality of Pro-Democratic Invasion', cited in Simma, *The Charter of the United Nations*.

—— 'The Right of States To Use Armed Force', *Michigan Law Review*, vol. 82, nos. 5–6, April–May 1984, pp. 1620–45.

Schlesinger, A. Jnr, 'The Necessary Amorality of Foreign Affairs', *Harper's Magazine*, August 1971.

Senate Standing Committee on Foreign Affairs, Defence and Trade, *United Nations Peacekeeping and Australia*, Australian Government Publishing Service, Canberra, 1991.

Sengupta, S., 'Thousands Rally in Ivory Coast To Protest Peace Plan', *New York Times*, 2 February 2003, pp. 1–10.

Shaw, M. N., *International Law*, 4th edn, Cambridge University Press, Cambridge, 1997.

Shue, H., *Basic Rights: Subsistence, Affluence and US Foreign Policy*, Princeton University Press, Princeton, 1996.

—— 'Eroding Sovereignty: The Advance of Principle', in R. McKim and J. McMahan (eds), *The Morality of Nationalism*, Oxford University Press, Oxford, 1997.

Silber, L. & A. Little, *Yugoslavia: Death of a Nation*, Penguin, London, 1997.

Simma, B. (ed.), *The Charter of the United Nations: A Commentary*, Oxford University Press, Oxford, 1994.

Simma, B., 'NATO, the UN and the Use of Force: Legal Aspects', *European Journal of International Law*, vol. 10, no. 1, 1999.

Singer, P., *The President of Good & Evil*, Text Publishing, Melbourne, 2004.

Sipress, A., 'Peacekeepers Won't Go beyond Kabul, Cheney says', *Washington Post*, 20 March 2002.

Taylor, P., 'The United Nations and International Organisation', in J. Balis & S. Smith (eds), *The Globalisation of World Politics*, Oxford University Press, Oxford, 1997.

Terry, F., *Condemned To Repeat? The Paradox of Humanitarian Action*, Cornell University Press, Ithaca NY, 2002.

—— 'Reconstituting Whose Social Order? NGOs in Disrupted States', in W. Maley, C. Sampford & R. Thakur (eds), *From Civil Strife to Civil Society: Civil and Military Responsibilities in Disrupted States*, United Nations University Press, Tokyo, 2003, pp. 279–99.

Tesón, F., 'Collective Humanitarian Intervention', *Michigan Journal of International Law*, vol. 17, Winter 1996, pp. 323–71.

—— *Humanitarian Intervention: An Inquiry into Law and Morality*, Transnational Publishers, New York, 1988.

Thakur, R., 'Cheerleaders for War Round on the UN', *Canberra Times*, 14 December 2004.

Thomas, R., 'NATO and International Law', *Jurist: The Law Professors Network*, <http://jurist.law.pitt.edu.kosovo.htm>.

Thompson, A., *Australia's Strategic Defence Policy: A Drift towards Neo-Forward Defence*, Working Paper no. 29, Australian Defence Studies Centre, Australian Defence Force Academy, Canberra, 1994.

Time, 'Aftermath of Empire: Once a Ubiquitous African Presence, France Is Now Reducing Aid and Involvement in Its Former Colonies', 16 August 1999, p. 16.

Todorov, T., *Facing the Extreme: Moral Life in the Concentration Camps*, Metropolitan Books, New York, 1996.

Toungara, J. M., 'Francophone Africa in Flux: Ethnicity and Political Crisis in Côte d'Ivoire', *Journal of Democracy*, vol. 12, no. 3, 2001, pp. 63–77.

UN News Service, 'As UN Starts Peacekeeping Operation in Côte d'Ivoire, Annan Urges Reconciliation', 5 April 2004.

UNAIDS, *2004 Report on the Global AIDS Epidemic*, 4th Global Report, Geneva, June 2004.

United Kingdom, Defence Select Committee, *Lessons of Kosovo*, 14th Report, Session 1999–2000.

—— Foreign Office Policy Document No. 148 quoted in Harris, *Cases and Materials on International Law*.

—— Ministry of Defence website, <www.mod.uk/news/kosovo/legal.htm>.

—— *Statement in the UN Security Council by the Permanent Representative of the UK*, New York, 24 March 1999, <www.fco.gov.uk/news/archive.asp>.

United Nations, *A More Secure World: Our Shared Responsibility*, Report of High-level Panel on Threats, Challenges and Change, Department of Public Information, United Nations, New York, 2004.

United Nations, *Côte d'Ivoire—UNOCI—Facts and Figures*, 2004, <www.un.org>.

—— press release, SG/SM/6997, New York, 18 May 1999, <http://www.un.org>.

—— *Report of the Panel on United Nations Peace Operations*, A/55/305-S/2000/809, 2000.

United Nations Conference on the Law of Treaties, *Vienna Convention on the Law of Treaties*, Vienna, 1980.

United Nations Development Programme, *Human Development Report*, UN, New York, 2003.

United Nations General Assembly, *Declaration on the Granting of Independence to Colonial Countries and Peoples*, New York, 14 December 1960 (UN GA Res 1514 (XV).

—— *Declaration of Principles of International Law Friendly Relations and Co-operation among States in Accordance with the Charter of the United Nations*, New York, 1970.

—— *Resolution 2131(XX)*, New York, 21 December 1965, A/RES/2131 (XX).

—— *Resolution 2625 (XXV)*, New York, 24 October 1970, A/RES/2625 (XXV).

—— *Uniting for Peace Resolution*, New York, 3 November 1950, A/RES/377 (V) A.

United Nations Peacekeeping, *Meeting New Challenges*, 2004, <www.un.org>.

United Nations Security Council, *3988th Meeting*, S/PV.3988, New York, 24 March 1999.

—— *Report of the Secretary-General on Côte d'Ivoire*, S/2003/374.

—— *Report of the Secretary-General on the United Nations Mission in Côte d'Ivoire submitted pursuant to Security Council resolution 1514 (2003) of 13 November 2003*, New York, S/2004/3.

—— *Resolution 1162 (1998)*, New York, 17 April 1998, S/RES/1162 (1998).

—— *Resolution 1244 (1999)*, New York, 10 June 1999, S/RES/1244, 1999.

—— *Resolution 1441(2002)*, New York, November 2002.

—— *Resolution 1479 (2003)*, New York, S/RES/1479, 2003.

—— *Resolution 1528 (2004)*, New York, S/RES/1528, 2004.

—— *Secretary-General Appeals to Security Council for Financial Support to Sustain West African States' Côte d'Ivoire Peacekeeping Force*, New York, SC/7743, 2003.

—— *Statement by the President of the Security Council*, New York, S/PRST/2002/42.

United States Secretary of State, Statement, Press Conference at Lancaster House, Foreign and Commonwealth Office, London, 12 June 1998, <http://www.state.gov>.

Unterseher, L., 'Interventionism Reconsidered: Reconciling Military Action with Political Stability', Commonwealth Institute, Project on Defense Alternatives, Cambridge MA, September 1999, <http://www.comw.org/pda/9909interv.html>.

—— 'Krieg als beliebig einsetzbares Instrument: Fehlschlüsse und Illusionen', in Österreichisches Studienzentrum für Frieden und Konfliktlösung (ÖSFK) (ed.), *Pax Americana und Pax Europaea*, Agenda, Münster, 2004.

—— *Military Stability and European Security: Ten Years from Now*, Research Monograph no. 2, Project on Defence Alternatives, Commonwealth Institute, Cambridge MA, 1993.

Urquhart, B., 'For a UN Volunteer Military Force', *New York Review of Books*, no. 10, June 1993.

Van Evera, S. 'Offense, Defense, and the Causes of War', *International Security*, vol. 22, no. 4, Spring 1998, pp. 5–44.

Vaughn, B., 'Australia's Strategic Identity Post-September 11 in Context: Implications for the War against Terror in Southeast Asia', *Contemporary Southeast Asia*, vol. 26, no. 1, 2004, pp. 94–116.

Voon, T., 'Closing the Gap between Legitimacy and Legality of Humanitarian Intervention: Lessons from East Timor and Kosovo', *UCLA Journal of International and Foreign Affairs*, Spring/Summer 2002, pp. 31–97.

Wainwright, E., *Our Failing Neighbour: Australia and the Future of Solomon Islands*, Australian Strategic Policy Institute, Canberra, 2003.

Walzer, M., *Arguing about War*, Yale University Press, 2004.

—— *Just and Unjust Wars: A Moral Argument with Historical Illustrations*, Basic Books, New York, 1977 (3rd edn, 2000).

—— 'The Politics of Rescue', *Dissent*, vol. 42, 1995, pp. 35–41.

Watson, B. (trans.), *Basic Writings of MO TZU, HSUN TZU, and HAN FEI TZU*, Columbia University Press, New York, 1964.

Wax, E., 'Civil War Pushes Ivory Coast's Economy to the Brink', *Guardian Weekly*, 13–19 March 2003, p. 30.

Weiss, T. G., 'UN Responses in the Former Yugoslavia: Moral and Operational Choices', in J. H. Rosenthal (ed.), *Ethics and International Affairs: A Reader*, Georgetown University Press, Washington DC, 1995, pp. 213–35.

Welch, C. E., Jr, 'The Military Factor in West Africa: Leadership and Regional Development', in J. E. Okolo & S. Wright (eds), *West African Regional Cooperation and Development*, Westview Press, Boulder CO, 1990, pp. 157–83.

Weymouth, T. & S. Henig, *The Kosovo Crisis: The Last American War in Europe?*, Pearson Education, London, 2001.

White, H., 'Choosing War', *Res Publica*, vol. 12, no. 1, 2003, pp. 1–5.

White, N., *Keeping the Peace*, Redwood Books, Trowbridge, 1997.

White, N. & R. Cryer, 'Unilateral Enforcement of Resolution 687: A Threat Too Far?', *California Western International Law Journal*, vol. 29, Spring 1999, pp. 243–82.

Windybank, S., 'Papua New Guinea on the Brink', *Issue Analysis*, Centre for Independent Studies, Sydney, 2003.

Woodward, B., *Plan of Attack*, Simon & Schuster, New York, 2004.

World Bank, *Governance Matters III: Governance Indicators for 1996–2002*, Washington DC, 2003.

—— *World Development Indicators 2002*, Washington DC, 2002.

Zacklin, R., 'Beyond Kosovo: The United Nations and Humanitarian Intervention', *Virginia Journal of International Law*, vol. 41, Summer 2001, pp. 923–40.

Zartman, I. W., *Collapsed States: The Disintegration and Restoration of Legitimate Authority*, Lynne Reinner, Boulder CO, 1995.

Zumach, A., 'Dayton. Ein Friedensprozess' in Bosnien?', in *Die Zukunft Südosteuropas (Friedensbericht 1997)*, Rüegger, Zürich, 1997.

INDEX